THE ECONOMY OF THE GULF STATES

WORLD ECONOMIES

A series of concise modern economic histories of the world's most important national economies. Each book explains how a country's economy works, why it has the shape it has, and what distinct challenges it faces. Alongside discussion of familiar indicators of economic growth, the coverage extends to well-being, inequality and corruption, to provide a fresh and more rounded understanding of the wealth of nations.

PUBLISHED

Matthew Gray
THE ECONOMY OF THE GULF STATES

Vera Zamagni
THE ITALIAN ECONOMY

The Economy of the Gulf States

Matthew Gray

agenda
publishing

First edition published in 2019 by Agenda Publishing

Agenda Publishing Limited
The Core
Bath Lane
Newcastle Helix
Newcastle upon Tyne
NE4 5TF

www.agendapub.com

ISBN 978-1-78821-000-3 (hardcover)
ISBN 978-1-78821-001-0 (paperback)

British Library Cataloguing-in-Publication Data
A catalogue record for this book is available from the British Library

Typeset by Patty Rennie
Printed and bound in the UK by TJ International

Contents

Preface

The six Arab monarchies of the Persian Gulf – Bahrain, Kuwait, Qatar, Oman, Saudi Arabia and the United Arab Emirates (UAE) – are relatively small actors in the global economic system, but are of disproportionate importance because of their enormous reserves of oil and gas, and given the economic and strategic importance to the rest of the world of a stable supply of these commodities. These six states possess just under 30 per cent of the world's proven oil reserves, and account for about 24 per cent of the global oil trade. For the Gulf states, hydrocarbons are crucial for the state's ability to rule. Oil provides about half of the Gulf's gross domestic product (GDP), with the importance of natural gas considerably smaller but having markedly risen so far this century.

For net hydrocarbon exporting states such as these, however, this bequest from nature is both a blessing and a curse. While striking oil may seem like a country's equivalent of winning the lottery, and does create enormous windfalls that allow for rapid development, new infrastructure, and a greater economic power than otherwise, hydrocarbon revenues also have profound impacts on an economy. Rents impact exchange rates, or create inflationary pressure when exchange rates are fixed. Natural resources create highly-skilled, well-paying jobs, but relatively few of them, while also pushing up wages across the economy more widely. Oil demands large investments, which are diverted from elsewhere in the economy. And scholars have made a strong argument that oil-intensive economies are especially unlikely to democratize, and that rents may in fact create conditions for repression and, in some cases, internal or regional conflict. Historically, oil has attracted external attention and at times intervention in the region, which has rarely been welcomed and often has proven very disruptive. At the same time, the Gulf states have struggled to diversify their economies into new areas. The revenue from oil (and later, gas) has been simply too large, and the political bargains made among elites, and between state and society, would be imperilled by any reform that is excessively rapid or extensive. Given all this, it is perhaps not surprising that a former oil minister in Saudi Arabia, Sheikh Ahmad Yamani, is rumoured to have said "All in all, I wish we had discovered water instead".

This book is an attempt to explain the origins, trajectories, features and challenges of these six Arab Gulf economies. This is no simple matter, because while oil has dominated these economies, their economies, and the factors forming and shaping them, are numerous and in many cases fiercely contested. In some ways the Gulf states escape easy explanation because they have had unique historical experiences. None were colonial possessions or controlled by mandate in the same sense as most other Arab countries, and one (Oman) was at one time a colonial power in the Indian Ocean region, although that noted, the Gulf region has been profoundly affected by external intervention by virtue of its geographical location, good ports, trading roles and, later, its oil wealth. In recent decades and as a result above all else of oil wealth, the Gulf states have not fit with typical development pathways: while their development was relatively late, when it came, it was so rapid that these economies were able to largely bypass the usual industrialization phase of development. As a result, again at least in part of oil, they have also been able to build relatively large and efficacious government bodies and state-owned firms, giving them an economic structure that is arguably state capitalist, but quite uniquely so; it is a very dynamic form of state capitalism, with little of the populism and economic nationalism that characterized other postwar state capitalist models. At the same time, the Gulf states have struggled to build large, globally-competitive economic sectors beyond oil and gas. The harsh, predominantly desert environment rules out most agricultural activities, as well as making climate change an especial risk for these countries, while their late development means that they lack the industrial capacity or experience of more mixed economies such as Turkey, Iran, or Egypt. Some, most notably Dubai, have carved a range of niches in areas from aviation and tourism to education and as a regional hub and transit trade port, becoming virtually a household name around the world and setting an example that others have tried to replicate, if selectively. Its grand projects, from the world's tallest building to the development of gigantic offshore artificial island chains, attest to its outsized ambitions. Yet Dubai still faces some of the same constraints as the other Gulf states, plus a couple of unique ones too, and more importantly in a development sense, there is a limit to how many Dubai-style transformations are possible given the limits of the Gulf region's power within the global economy.

This book takes up all of these questions, and others, in the course of seeking to provide a brief yet comprehensive profile of these six Gulf states. It is predominantly a blend of political economy and modern history. By political economy is meant that it examines the economies from perspectives where the economic and the political overlap and influence each other; in a subregion such as the Gulf, it is essentially impossible to separate the political and the economic from each other anyway. Some points are specifically centred on economic dynamics and require little political context, but in the majority of the book's points of discussion, this is simply not possible. The Gulf states are fiercely contested political terrain, in which politics occurs among an array of societal actors and forces, between state and society, and between a particular Gulf state and other regional states or other international actors. At the same time as being a political economy, the book is a modern history insofar as its coverage and analysis is deeply embedded in historical context. There is a full chapter on the history of the Gulf – the longest chapter of the book – plus several other chapters include substantial amounts of modern history and other background and contextual detail. History continues to strongly ripple through the Gulf, and the subregion cannot be understood without a solid understanding of its past and of how this past continues to inform and shape the present.

The book is structured to make a key set of arguments about the nature of the six Gulf economies being examined. It seeks to strike a balance between depth and breadth of analysis. Its overarching theme, that any economic analysis of the region must include historical, political and societal analysis as well, and that the relationships between all these factors is more complex and subtle than typically presumed, is made across seven chapters. After an introduction, which also includes some elementary details about the subregion, Chapter 2 provides a historical survey of the subregion, primarily since the 1940s but with some discussion of its earlier history. It shows the immense importance of oil to the evolution of the region since the Second World War, while also cautioning against a focus on oil exclusively or overwhelmingly when seeking to understand contemporary economic dynamics. Chapter 3 provides some basic economic factual material on the six economies, covering their sizes, profiles, international linkages, and strengths and weaknesses. It contains the bulk of the straightforward economic descriptive material to be found here. Chapter 4 examines the form of the Gulf economies and is, in effect, the most fundamental *political* chapter of the book, although its discussions of the political do not stray far from their economic dimensions and impacts. It examines the roles of rulers, state institutions, state-owned firms, businesspeople and societal forces, among others. Chapter 5 examines the human resources side of these economies, looking at the demography of the Gulf, the dual labour market – relying so heavily, as it does, on foreign labour – as well as issues of education, training, gender, youth, corporate cultures, and workplace technological change. Many of these issues are typically examined in isolation, and have often been under-examined, by observers. Yet human factors have been central to many of the challenges faced by these economies, and will be crucial to the future success or failure of the Gulf's ambitious development and diversification strategies.

Chapter 6 provides insights on some of the less-common, or even unique, aspects of the Gulf's (political) economies, including the high degree of personalization in them, the importance of patron–client relationships, issues of geography and the environment, reform imperatives, and wider regional opportunities for and constraints on reform and change. This chapter seeks to highlight what is unique or unusual about the Gulf states, while also discussing factors that will be especially important to these political economies and societies in the future. Finally, Chapter 7, the conclusion, brings the themes and arguments of the book together, while also making some cautious predictions for the short- and medium-term future. It is focused on the energy sector and the international environment, both of which are in a period of profound change at present. The book's chapters vary in length and, to a lesser extent, in style, but each provides critical facts and analytical details that are essential to a comprehensive understanding and assessment of the Gulf. When taken in combination, these details paint an amalgamated but thorough picture of the pathways, dynamics and prospects for these six dynamic and important states.

The ideas in this book have been drawn from a range of works by others, duly cited (even though, for readability, I have tried to keep notes to a minimum). Crucial, too, are the innumerable conversations and debates I have had over many years. I would like to thank all the people – too numerous to name individually here – who have shared their insights, offered their analysis, or critiqued my assessments or assumptions. This includes interviewees over numerous visits to the Gulf since 1996, my students at the Australian National University over 2005–16 and at Waseda University since then, and the many colleagues with whom I share an interest in the Middle East in general, and especially the Gulf. More recently, I would like to thanks friends and colleagues in Tokyo who helped make my transition to life here so much easier than otherwise, and who have shown me so many aspects of this great city. At Waseda, I would like to thank the former Dean of the School of International Liberal Studies, Professor Adrian Pinnington, and Professor Keiko Sakurai, for bringing me in to Waseda and for helping make the move and the transition so smooth. Colleagues elsewhere in Tokyo have been very supportive; I particularly thank Professor Namie Tsujigami, now at Sophia University, for her support and advice. Among friends, I would like to particularly thank Mary and Woohyang (Chloe) for their advice about life in Japan and for the regular discussions and ideas that have supported my thinking, and Kazumi, whose personal and emotional support was so important, including for much of the period over which this book was developed and drafted.

I would like to thank Agenda Publishing for inviting me to write this book, and particularly Andrew Lockett, whose advice and encouragement as the commissioning editor was invaluable, and always clear and precise. Thanks also to Steven Gerrard, who so quickly and efficiently took the work through copy-editing and proofing, and on to publication. My gratitude also goes to the two anonymous reviewers of the first draft of the manuscript, who provided excellent feedback in the best spirit of peer reviewing: they were both strongly encouraging, while offering constructive advice on how to strengthen the manuscript, and locating more than one error which would have been embarrassing had it made it into print! This book is much stronger for the sharp advice and supportive ideas they both provided.

Finally, I thank my son Henry, who has been my greatest joy in life since the day he was born, and whose adventures in Australia, Japan, and occasionally the Middle East, have been so much fun for us both, as well as a constant reminder of the curiosity and wide-eyed wonder of children.

MATTHEW GRAY

Tokyo

Note on transliteration and terminology

There is no simple means of transliterating Arabic in English, since so many Arabic sounds lack a counterpart in English. The most scientific system, used by the *International Journal of Middle East Studies* and other major publications, adopts underdots, macrons and other symbols to try to present transliterations with precision. This, however, is arguably too specific for a book such as this one, targeting an audience that is presumed not to have had an exposure to the language. Whatever the shortcomings, I have adopted a fairly simple transliteration style here. For words that appear in English routinely, I have given them in their most common English format (thus, Emir, not 'Amīr; Qur'an not Qur'ān, etc.). This includes rendering some names in a way that is not exactly accurate: for example, the ruling dynasty in Saudi Arabia is usually given in English as "Al Saud", even though a scientific transliteration would be "Āl Suʿūd". I have used the former, however, for the lay-reader's ease and with apologies to those who do read Arabic and who would have preferred a more precise transliteration. The only exception is where it is crucial to distinguish a word from another or to make a meaning completely clear.

I have also avoided presenting full Arab names. Most people are known by a few names only, still running to four or five or more names, including their first name, then their father's first name, sometimes other indicators of lineage, and finally a dynastic or family name. This serves both to show their lineage and to distinguish them from other members of the extended family with the same first name. Full names, however, can be very lengthy, with considerably more detailed lineage. For example, the full name of the Saudi crown prince at the time of writing is Muhammad bin Salman bin Abdulaziz bin Abd al-Rahman bin Faisal bin Turki bin Abdullah bin Muhammad bin Saud. This is virtually never used in English, and rarely in Arabic, because of its length. More usual is to refer to him simply as Muhammad bin Salman, or Mohammed bin Salman (there's that transliteration variation again!), and many in the press and academia have even adopted the initials MbS, or MBS, instead. Here I have kept names as brief as necessary for clarity.

Finally, a small note on dynastic names and terms. The word "Al" is usually used to indicate a dynasty name; it means something like "of the line of" or "the family dynasty of". The ruling family of Saudi Arabia, for example, is usually referred to as the "Al Saud". This is not the same as "al-Saud": even though this is a common spelling, it is misleading, since "al-" is the usual transliteration of the Arabic definite article (which can appear in Arabic names sometimes, too).

Tables and Figures

TABLES

FIGURES

Map 1 The Middle East

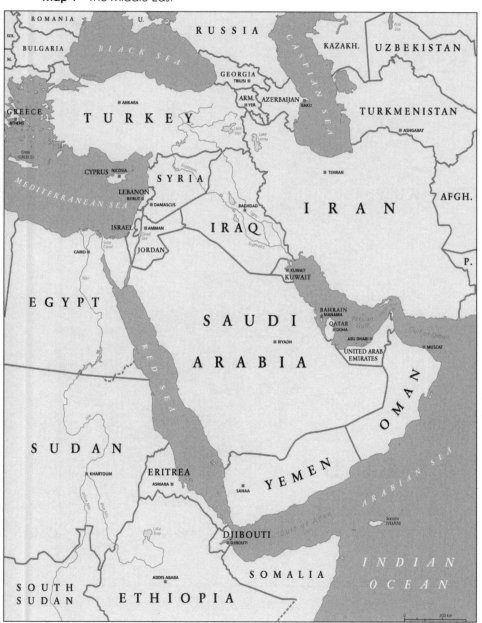

Map 2 The Persian Gulf

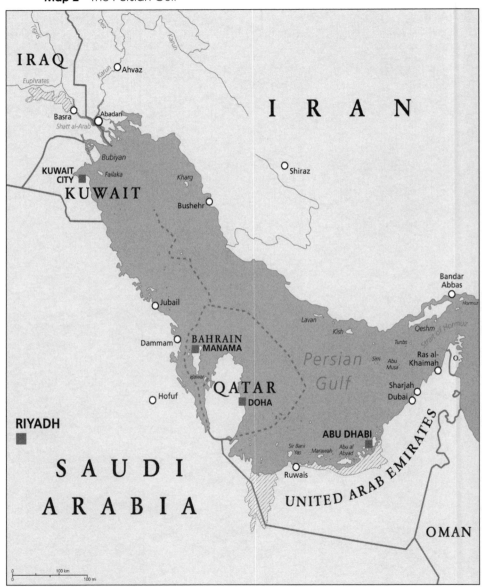

1

Introducing the Gulf economies

The Arab monarchies of the Gulf – Bahrain, Kuwait, Oman, Qatar, Saudi Arabia, and the United Arab Emirates (UAE) – seem to present something of a paradox. On the one hand, they have enjoyed enormous economic growth in the modern era, primarily thanks to their impressive hydrocarbon reserves. From small, modest cities as recently as the mid-twentieth century, Dubai, Abu Dhabi, Doha, Riyadh, and others have developed into global metropolises with their citizens enjoying standards of living comparable to those in North America and western Europe. Their economic transformation has been profound, bringing with it new technologies and industries, and accompanying improvements in people's lifestyles. On the other hand, this dramatic economic change has seemingly had little effect on politics. At first glance, Gulf societies seem conservative, hierarchical and reticent towards many forms of social change. Leaderships have faced occasional unrest, but with the arguable exception of Bahrain in 2011, have not confronted a genuine revolutionary impulse that risked bringing down the incumbent ruling family.

What this paradox in fact illustrates is that the political and economic systems of the Gulf are complex but relatively stable, shaped to a large extent by oil and its socio-political impacts, but not exclusively or overwhelmingly so. As elsewhere, political and social conditions in the Gulf are the result of a large and complex array of factors, not least of all economic

1

ones. Oil and gas revenues certainly play a prominent role in this, providing enormous injections of (albeit unpredictable) state income and reducing pressure on the state to tax its citizens, but at the same time introducing other dilemmas, including a need for economic diversification and the creation of productive jobs outside the energy sector. While the leaderships of these states can at a fundamental level be categorized as authoritarian, other actors have agency as well, including clerics, tribal figures, and members of the business community. Politics does not, therefore, operate on a simple formula, but rather is the product of various channels of communication and negotiation between and within states and societies.

Table 1.1 Gulf states' oil and gas reserves and production, 2016

Country	Oil reserves (billion bbls)	Average daily oil production (million bbls/day)	Gas reserves (trillion m³)	Annual gas production (billion m³)
Bahrain	NA	NA	0.2	15.5
Kuwait	101.5	3.2	1.8	17.1
Oman	5.4	1.0	0.7	35.4
Qatar	25.2	1.9	24.3	181.2
Saudi Arabia	266.5	12.3	8.4	109.4
UAE	97.8	4.1	6.1	61.9
Iran	158.4	4.6	33.5	202.4
Iraq	153.0	4.5	3.7	1.1
GLOBAL TOTAL	1,706.7	92.2	79.4	3,551.6

Source: Derived from data in the *BP Statistical Review of World Energy 2017*.

The Gulf states are of global strategic and economic importance, above all due to their oil and gas wealth, as shown in Table 1.1. The Middle East as a whole produced just under 32 million barrels per day (bbl/d) of oil, on average, in 2016.[1] Of this, Saudi Arabia, the UAE, Kuwait, Qatar, and

Oman accounted for over two-thirds, or an average of over 22.4 million bbl/d. A further 4.6 million bbl/d came from Iran, and over 4.4 million bbl/d from Iraq. The Middle East in 2016 contributed 46 per cent of global crude oil exports, and 17 per cent of refined hydrocarbon product exports, and was the source of all of the global increase in trade in these commodities. The majority of traded product, some 73 per cent, went to the rapidly-growing and energy-hungry economies of the Asia Pacific region, but with important exports to Europe and elsewhere. These figures were an increase of 5.7 per cent on 2015: a 3 per cent increase in Saudi production, and a more dramatic 18 per cent and 10.8 per cent increase from Iran and Iraq respectively. The region is also an important supplier of natural gas, producing 637 billion cubic metres (bcm) in 2016, of which the six Gulf states produced about two-thirds, or 420bcm. Iran's production, at 202bcm, was the largest in the Gulf. The region therefore matters greatly for global energy supply and for stability in the price of not just crude oil but also natural gas.

The Gulf matters to the global economy more broadly. Cities such as Dubai are becoming international trade and transport hubs; even a household name overseas, in Dubai's case. The Gulf's enormous energy rents are important sources of international investment. The region is also seeking a more activist role internationally, whether in hosting major events such as the 2022 FIFA World Cup in Qatar, in providing aid to regional states and others, or in global cultural and media roles. Not least of all, the Gulf matters to global geostrategic dynamics and international security. Iran's nuclear programme was a source of international concern, and a possible trigger for military conflict, after its extent became clearer in 2002; the 2015 Joint Comprehensive Plan of Action (JCPOA) agreement, if it survives and succeeds, may have resolved this issue. Even then, Iran and Saudi Arabia are also locked in a struggle for regional dominance, competing by proxy through conflicts in Syria, Yemen and elsewhere. Meanwhile, Iraq's stability – already precarious after the 1990–91 and 2003 wars and the civil strife following the latter of these conflicts – was worsened by the rise of the so-called Islamic State, or ISIS, after mid-2014. While seemingly

3

defeated, they may yet resurrect, whether in the same form or another. For all these reasons, the Gulf states cannot be ignored. They have the capacity to assist or undermine international security and economic stability, depending on the decisions they take and how they respond to events.

The long-term durability and stability of these systems depend on a number of factors. Not least – and perhaps the most commonly cited – is the end date for the oil era, either because reserves of oil (and eventually gas) will ultimately be exhausted, or because alternative sources of energy and the pressures of climate change will see the global demand for hydrocarbons decline strongly and irreversibly at some future point. At least one of these scenarios, most likely the latter, is indeed near-certain, although its timing remains a matter of conjecture. In the meantime, other challenges – overwhelmingly economic ones or ones with a strong economic element – will arise. These include the need to diversify the Gulf economies and create employment for rapidly-growing populations, the challenge from new technologies, the problem of low levels of innovation and entrepreneurship in these economies, the reliance on foreign workers, and regional security problems. Addressing all these, while maintaining economic performance and political stability, will be no small feat.

THE SCOPE AND THE FOCUS

Given the dynamics in the subregion and their economic power, the future of the Arab Gulf states' economies will, to a large extent, determine the future of the Gulf itself. The Gulf's political systems and societies, in turn, will shape their economic bearings and performance. It is the relationships among this array of actors, forces, and dynamics that are the focus of this book. While focused foremost on the economies of the Gulf, it is strongly *political* economy in flavour since the political and the economic are especially difficult to differentiate, much less separate, in such highly personalized, state-led systems as these. This work includes a notable amount of economic and political history, as context but also to highlight the continuity of many key features.

4

The book argues that states, and at the summit of states the incumbent ruling families, all have strong control over their political economies and that rulers seek to maintain their rule using four overlapping mechanisms, all economic in nature, and with further assistance from a fifth. These four mechanisms are rentierism, state capitalism, neopatrimonialism and economic statecraft. Rentierism involves the use by rulers of rents (externally-derived income from natural assets such as oil and gas) to both coopt and repress society. A proportion of rents are allocated to society, in the form of public sector employment, public services, subsidies, and even direct payments, in exchange for their political acquiescence, while rents also finance small but effective militaries, security apparatuses and elite relationships. The Gulf's new form of state capitalism gives the ruling elite control of economies through the state ownership of key firms and assets, and by their strict regulation of the economy, including control of where the private sector can operate and the careful use of economic favours. Neopatrimonialism is the framework in which elite relationships are handled, in which leaders use layers of patron–client networks to distribute favours and opportunities, in exchange for support, loyalty, and information from institutions and social groups. Economic statecraft gives leaderships the chance to manage their external relationships, and in turn to develop their economies and gain further support from society, by linking economic and diplomatic goals. The use of aid programmes, major events, tourism, media resources, and investment for public relations ends abroad are the main manifestations of economic statecraft, enhanced by strong and consistent national "branding" messages. In combination, these dynamics allow regimes to be "soft" in their authoritarianism – to privilege cooptation over repression – while also ensuring that their control of the political economy is extensive and that any concessions to non-state actors remain controlled by the state and its upper elite. For additional efficacy, Gulf rulers also articulate to society broad narratives of regime legitimacy, drawing on historical precedent, religion, security, or other factors to claim both a right and a capacity to hold power. These claims do not compete or supplant the other four mechanisms, but rather take the state beyond simple cooptation and repression to enhance their popular acceptance and legitimacy. When combined effectively, these factors are a very effective strategy for regime maintenance and durability.

To cover such a breadth of issues in a brief analysis, certain limitations have been placed on the book's scope. First, the time period covered in the discussion is mostly limited to the post-1945 period, which also coincides with changes to the international order around that time. The post-Cold War period after 1989 is given particular attention, as it coincides with the current era of transformation in the Gulf, which arguably has been even more dramatic than during the initial exploitation of oil or the first two oil booms over roughly 1973–83. The period since 1990 has seen the post-Cold War order emerge, the US-led war on terrorism, changes to the geostrategic setting of the Gulf, a selective globalization in the Gulf political economies, an oil bust, then boom, then bust again, and the emergence of key global cities such as Dubai and Doha. Chapter 2 provides the only earlier history of the region to be found in these pages.

Secondly, although an attempt has been made to include a breadth of topics in the following pages, some discrimination is necessary in terms of where to focus the analysis. As this work is designed to be an accessible one, there is little quantitative economic analysis included: readers looking for that angle are best consulting scholarly journals or specialized books. Rather, the analysis to be found here is grounded in the assumption that economic drivers and outcomes are both deeply embedded in the region's political, social, and strategic characteristics and imperatives. This arguably is the case anywhere, but is especially pronounced in the Middle East, and within that in the Gulf, where economic conditions and aspirations have regularly been frustrated by regional conflicts, problems of state formation, the weak political legitimacy of many leaders, rivalry from religious and other elites, and complex societal dynamics. The intricacy of these factors and their interconnections is such, however, that discussion of them is often brisk, although every effort is made to contextualize and explain them as fully as possible.

Perhaps the most important constraint is in the choice of countries that are included and excluded. The six Gulf monarchies of Bahrain, Kuwait, Oman, Qatar, Saudi Arabia, and the UAE have been placed together in part for analytical convenience. They share similar broad features as economies and societies, including their reliance on hydrocarbon income; their Arab and predominantly Sunni Muslim traditions; their historical, tribal, and political linkages and similarities; and, albeit as a generalization, their political cultures. While they are far from identical – in fact, as will become evident, they are far more different than is often recognized – they share enough resemblances and connections that it makes sense to examine them together, highlighting their broad similarities while showing where they contrast as well. They are deeply interlinked by their shared histories, similar concerns about Gulf stability, and the prospects for economic cooperation. While they have disagreements, including the "Qatar crisis" in 2017 between Saudi Arabia, the UAE and Bahrain on the one hand and Qatar on the other, they are also strongly bound together too. Approaching them individually, for the purposes of this series, would have been needlessly limiting and inefficient. They vary greatly in geographical, demographic and economic size, and while they are very important globally, for both economic and geostrategic reasons, they are not equally so. This variation adds to the case for examining them collectively, while their similarities would have made multiple volumes extremely repetitive.

Although both Iran and Iraq are also part of the Gulf subregion, having a littoral boundary on the Persian Gulf and also being embedded in the Gulf's economic and strategic dynamics, this book does not cover those two states. They are very different economies to the six examined here. Iran's is a populist, Shia clerical, quasi-democratic government running a diversified economy but one deeply damaged by its 1978–79 revolution, the eight-year 1980–88 war with Iraq, and a range of international sanctions. Iraq's political economy has likewise suffered near-continuous conflict since 1980, first with Iran, then against a US-led coalition in 1990–91 and 2003, with sanctions over 1990–2003 also eroding its economic capabilities. Iran and Iraq are, therefore, profoundly different political economies to those of the six Arab monarchies, making any comparison of all eight Gulf states a messy, complex, and ultimately imprudent approach.

Finally, it is worth including a note here on terminology, especially the sometimes-controversial term "the Persian Gulf". Historically, "Persian Gulf" was the most commonly-used term, and by most measures remains so to the present day. Since the 1960s and 1970s, there has been a fiercely contested argument over this terminology, with the countries on the southern shores commonly referring to it as the "Arabian Gulf". This arose at a time when these states were gaining their independence, and the period was also a high point for pan-Arabist ideologies, into which then-Egyptian leader Gamal Abdul Nasser and later some Gulf leaders were trying to tap by their use of the term "Arabian Gulf". At certain times it has been known by yet other names, including the Sea of Qatif and the Gulf of Basra. Ultimately it is a rather pointless argument, reflecting Iranian nationalism on one side, and Arabism and nation-building on the other. The term "the Persian Gulf" is used here simply because that has historically been the more commonly accepted term, and remains the preferred term of the United Nations and other key international bodies, although "the Gulf" also appears regularly as a shortened form of this.[2]

THE PLACE, THE PEOPLE, THE CULTURES

The term "the Gulf states" immediately betrays certain assumptions about Bahrain, Kuwait, Oman, Qatar, Saudi Arabia, and the UAE. There is the implication that they are fundamentally similar in cultural or other ways. This is, up to a point, true. However, they are conglomerated first and foremost because of their linked geography. They all have a coastline on the Persian Gulf, even though the length varies enormously, but as a result they are in geographic proximity to each other and share loosely similar climatic and other natural characteristics. As already noted, they are not the only states to possess a coastline along the Gulf. Iran actually possesses the single-longest stretch, at 1,176km, while Iraq, in contrast, has the shortest, at less than 58km, while of the six states that are the focus here, the UAE has the longest shoreline on the Gulf, at about 777km, followed by Saudi Arabia at 548km.[3] Saudi Arabia is also by far the largest of the six states being examined here. Oman has a very long coastline, but nearly all of it falls on the Indian Ocean coast: in the Gulf, it has only a small area on the southern side of the mouth, along the Strait of Hormuz, cut off from the rest of Oman by the UAE.

The Gulf itself is a semi-enclosed sea, extending from the Gulf of Oman at the northern end of the Indian Ocean. It is some 989km long and 251,000km^2 in surface area, with the Arabian peninsula to its west, Iran to its east, and the Shatt al-Arab waterway (the confluence of the Tigris and Euphrates rivers, part of which forms the current border between Iraq and Iran) emptying into the Gulf at the northern end. The Gulf is, geologically, a relatively new body of water, having formed as recently as 15,000 years ago, prior to which the area was likely a dry or swampy floodplain. It is, therefore, a very shallow body of water, 90 metres deep at its deepest point, but an average of only 50 metres deep, and with much of it unnavigable to large vessels. Its small mouth at the Strait of Hormuz, barely 38km at its narrowest point, means that water only circulates very slowly in and out of the Gulf; combined with its shallowness, this means that both the average temperature and the salinity of the water are higher than in the northern Indian Ocean (an area with already higher-than-average salinity compared to other oceans). The climate along the coast of the Gulf is dictated largely by the surrounding territories, as the Indian Ocean monsoon does not reach into the Gulf, only to the Indian Ocean coastline of Oman. The area has very hot and humid weather, with especially searing summers, although in winter its northern parts can be quite cool, and inland temperatures away from the coast can fall sharply at night. At times of temperature changes, say with a weather front, and where winds speed up above 25 knots, sandstorms and dust storms may occur; traditionally they are most common in autumn. In winter there can be morning fog, sometimes quite thick if usually brief, but otherwise the skies over the area tend to be fairly clear.

These conditions, however, are experienced somewhat differently in the various countries along the Gulf, given the geographic variations between them. Their sizes range from Saudi Arabia, which at 2,150,000km² occupies about four-fifths of the Arabian peninsula, to Bahrain, a set of small islands that add up to about 765km². Not surprisingly, the key challenge for settlements in the area has traditionally been to find a reliable supply of fresh water. There is very little rainfall, less than 100mm per year along much of the Gulf coastline, most of which falls in a handful of heavy downpours. The region thus has very little arable land: less than 1 per cent of Kuwait and Oman is arable land, some 1.6 per cent of Saudi Arabia, and the highest, Bahrain, is still only 4.3 per cent. Traditional primary industries included nomadic herding, which provided meat and milk, and fishing, with crops being limited to those suited to the climate such as dates. Iran and Iraq are better places for food production, since they have more varied climates and more lakes and rivers than do the Gulf monarchies.

Limited water supplies and hot climate conditions also historically dictated the patterns of human settlement. Iraq and Iran, with their great rivers and floodplains, provided the conditions for some of the earliest human empires to emerge. Down along the Gulf, and across much of Saudi Arabia, patterns of settlement were very different. The few small rivers and underground water sources along the Gulf attracted nomadic visitors, especially during the summer heat, and some permanent settlements. The coast was also attractive where trade was a priority, which it often was as a guarantee of food supplies and for the opportunities to trade pearls, the key natural resource in the area until modern times. Away from these areas, however, the desert could be especially brutal: there are parts of *al-Rub' al-Khali* (or "Empty Quarter"), an especially hot and harsh desert in south-eastern Saudi Arabia, for which there is no record of rainfall in modern times. Such areas could sustain, at best, small nomadic populations, and even then, these were seasonal, often moving out of the area in summer. Where larger towns and small cities arose in the region, it was usually where they had accrued wealth from trade or pilgrimage, and only when a reliable, permanent source of water was available. In Saudi Arabia, historically the western Hijaz area has seen the largest such urban settlements, as at Jedda, a trading port, and Mecca, a site of pilgrimage. In the smaller Gulf states, towns nearly always emerged on the coast, apart from a handful that grew up at large oases, usually along transport routes.

There are also cultural, linguistic and religious characteristics that are shared across much of the Gulf. The Arab parts of the Gulf historically were socially organized along extended family and tribal lines, with tribes often forming into larger confederations. For many people the tribe historically was the main or only source of justice, dispute resolution, emergency support and physical protection. People also held strong loyalty to their extended families, of course, but family networks were normally part of a larger tribal structure. In this sense, the Arabs of the Gulf shared broadly similar attitudes about family and social organization, which continues to the present day, even if the power and prominence of tribes has diminished as the role of the state has grown in modern times. Tribal links now vary, however, influenced by how long a family has been settled and how powerful tribes have traditionally been in that area. Somewhat in contrast, family is as important as ever in the region, and people will go to enormous lengths to protect the position, wealth and reputation of their families.

Other aspects of culture are also broadly shared, at least among the Arab populations of the Gulf. The tribal, migratory, and trading patterns of the past mean that the Arabic spoken in the Gulf is fairly similar. There are dialect differences; for example, Kuwaiti Arabic shares similarities with what is spoken in southern Iraq, and Omani Arabic has more noticeable differences to the other dialects. The coastal and Najdi (central-eastern Saudi Arabia) dialects are mutually comprehensible and very similar in many ways. Shared history and geography means that other cultural features such as foods and daily lifestyles are loosely similar in Arab Gulf societies; again, there are some variances, where more distant trade has influenced cultural practices, but as a generalization, there is not a lot to distinguish the traditional foods of, say, Qatar, Abu Dhabi, and Kuwait, especially compared to more distant Arab cuisines such as Lebanese or Egyptian. Clothing is another example. Men and women both wear loose fitting robes of some sort, women also covering their hair and often their face. The colour and style of these garments may vary, but they are broadly alike. Given their similarities and linked history, and their differences from other Arab peoples, there is an argument that the Arabs of the Gulf constitute a distinct sub-group, often referred to as *Khaliji* (translated loosely, "a Gulf person").[4] It is an emerging but quite persuasive idea.

In the religious sphere, Islam dominates the region, and is a powerful determinant of cultural practices and social values. The religion is deeply respected in the region, even among people who may not be genuinely pious. This respect is both a product and source of its cultural reach and historical importance. Nonetheless, there are sectarian and other variations in the subregion. The majority of the Gulf's Arabs – like the majority of the Muslim world – adheres to the orthodox Sunni sect of Islam, and within that the Maliki and Hanbali jurisprudential schools. However at more specific levels they vary. In the Najd heartland of Saudi Arabia, and along parts of the coast of Qatar and the UAE, the puritanical *Wahhabi* (sometimes called *Muwahhid*) doctrine dominates. It is named after Muhammad ibn Abd al-Wahhab, an eighteenth-century Islamic activist who believed that Islam had strayed too much from its core values and beliefs, and needed to revert to its original, core practices. Al-Wahhab's pact in 1744 with Muhammad bin Saud, the leader of the Al Saud clan that controlled parts of central Arabia at the time, is what cemented Wahhabism in the region: he offered bin Saud political allegiance in exchange for freedom to propagate his religious views. This pact has, in effect, survived since, through the fluctuations in the fortunes of the Al Saud dynasty, to remain a core political arrangement between the royal family and the Najdi clergy up to the present day.

Two other religious sects are worth noting as well. The first of these is the Shia, who are a majority in Iran (over 90% of the population), Bahrain (70–75%), and Iraq (about 65%), but a minority across the Gulf overall. They are an important minority in Saudi Arabia and Kuwait, where they constitute roughly 10–15 per cent and 35–40 per cent of the populations respectively. In Saudi Arabia, the Shia population has faced discrimination at various times, especially given the strong negative views held by the Wahhabi clerics towards Shi'ism, and the population has revolted against the Saudi government on several occasions, including in 1979–80 and again after the 2011 Arab uprisings. Sect is therefore a political identifier and mobilizing force not only at the national level, as say in the current Saudi–Iranian rivalry, but also at the sub-national level. In Bahrain especially, the Sunni monarchy faced a very real risk of being overthrown by protests in early 2011, which were dominated by Bahrain's majority-Shia population.

The second religious minority of note in the Gulf is the Ibadi sect, found almost exclusively in Oman. Ibadism is a very old movement, deriving from the now-defunct *Khawarij* (or "Kharajite") sect that rebelled against the Caliph, or ruler, of the Muslim world after the death of the Prophet Muhammad in 632 CE. Ibadism probably emerged from a moderate stream within the otherwise very conservative Kharijites – although Omanis object deeply to being referred or linked to the *Khawarij*. It is often argued that Ibadism promotes political quietism and that Ibadis are "tolerant puritans", possessing a strict set of doctrinal views, but in the modern world coexisting with other Islamic sects, and indeed other religions, very peacefully.

Cultural characteristics can be overstated, of course, and are almost always generalizations. This is true in the Gulf as well, and the features just discussed, and indeed the *Khaliji* concept, should not be exaggerated. Not all citizens fit the cultural, religious, or other frames laid out here. Moreover, it is important to recall that in most of the Arab Gulf states, the citizens are a minority of the population: they are outnumbered by large populations of foreign workers, who perform the bulk of unskilled jobs in the economy and expertise at higher levels where it is lacking among the native workforce. As shown in Table 1.2, in four of the six states citizens are a minority, sometimes a small one. Only in Saudi Arabia and Oman are they a majority, while still having large foreign populations.

Foreign workers are used extensively across the economy because they accept low-level, dangerous, or unpleasant jobs that many citizens

Table 1.2 Arab Gulf states' demographics

Country	Data date	Nationals	Non-Nationals	Total	% Nationals	% Non-Nationals
Bahrain	2016	664,707	759,019	1,423,726	46.7	53.3
Kuwait	2016	1,337,693	3,073,431	4,411,124	30.3	69.7
Oman	2017	2,488,755	2,110,296	4,599,051	54.1	45.9
Qatar	2010	243,073	1,456,362	1,699,435	14.3	85.7
Saudi Arabia	2016	20,064,970	11,677,338	31,742,308	63.2	36.8
UAE	2010	947,997	7,316,073	8,264,070	11.5	88.5

Source: Data derived from Gulf Research Center, "Gulf Labor Markets, Migration, and Population Programme".

simply do not want to do. The state, seeing this as a concession to society in exchange for their political acquiescence, has thus, in effect, outsourced the country's working class to foreign nationals. Citizens may take positions at more senior levels in the energy sector, although the oil and gas industries are not labour-intensive and so such positions are not copious; instead, citizens tend to dominate the public sector workforce and some state-owned firms. This practice has created economic inefficiencies, including redundant labour in the public sector, and the lack of highly-skilled citizens in the private sector arguably limits innovation as well. At the same time, this reliance on expatriates has brought some benefits, by controlling wages at the lower levels of the labour force and keeping inflation in check. It has also made the job of management easier, since foreign workers are prohibited from forming trade unions or other representative bodies, and of course cannot strike. Given such benefits, even though the Gulf states have policies in place to diversify their economies and create employment for nationals, the role of citizens in the workforce has not yet transformed in substantive ways. Only in Oman has there been a more forceful attempt to bring citizens into roles that have, in past decades, been dominated by foreign workers, and even then, this process has been tortuous. Any genuine attempt to compel or coerce Gulf citizens into lower-level jobs, however, would be both enormously politically risky and would bring shorter-term economic problems as well. The dual labour market is examined in greater detail in Chapter 5.

THE GULF ECONOMIES IN THE WORLD ECONOMY

The Gulf states' unique position in the global economic system conveys both benefits and disadvantages to them. The most obvious observation in this regard is the centrality of oil, and to some extent gas, in making the Gulf a globally-important region. The energy trade is in turn very important to the Middle East and especially to the oil-rich Gulf states: exports of these products accounts for between 20 and 40 per cent of the GDP of five of the six states (only Bahrain is lower, and even then it earns considerable money from associated industries and services). At times of high oil prices, energy is even more important, accounting for over 60 per cent of Kuwait's GDP, and almost 49 per cent of Saudi Arabia's, in 2011, when prices were last high by historical levels.

Yet the Middle Eastern share of world merchandise trade, including that of the Gulf, is modest, precisely because the region remains so reliant upon hydrocarbon exports. In 2015, the entire Middle East region accounted for only 5.3 per cent of total world merchandise trade and 5 per cent of world exports – much of it oil.[5] This figure fluctuates over time, in line with changes in oil prices. The region has been equally peripheral in services, despite having some areas of strength such as in air transportation and tourism. Were it not for oil and gas, however, the region would be in a highly marginalized position in the world trading system. It has few industries outside of energy where it enjoys an international comparative advantage. Yet because oil remains the world's most important strategic commodity, and the Gulf has such enormous, easily accessible, and quality reserves of it, the main Gulf hydrocarbon exporters have an outsized global importance and influence.

Added to this is the modest but growing importance of the Gulf as a source of international foreign direct investment (FDI). Here again the wealthy Gulf states dominate among Middle Eastern states in both inward and outward investment. In 2016, the Middle East as a whole had inward investment stock of about $696.5 billion, and outward stock of just under $355 billion – but this was only 2.6 per cent and less than 1.4 per cent of the respective global totals.[6] Moreover, the region's role in international investment is very uneven, with the UAE, Saudi Arabia, and Qatar dominating both inward and outward FDI flows. Beyond the Gulf, only Turkey is of similar importance. This is not unexpected, however, as the UAE and Qatar have economies that are wealthy and seeking to diversify through ambitious state-led strategies in which investment has figured prominently, while Saudi Arabia attracts investment, and raises funds to invest offshore as well, from its enormous oil sector. These states are also among the most ambitious with their sovereign wealth funds (SWFs),

Table 1.3 World regions' shares of world exports, 1953–2016

	1953	1963	1973	1983	1993	2003	2016
Value of total world exports ($ billion)	84	157	579	1,838	3,688	7,380	15,464
Share (%):							
North America	24.8	19.9	17.3	16.8	17.9	15.8	14.3
South and Central America	9.7	6.4	4.3	4.5	3.0	3.0	3.3
Europe	39.4	47.8	50.9	43.5	45.3	45.9	38.4
CIS/former USSR	—	—	—	—	1.7	2.6	2.7
Africa	6.5	5.7	4.8	4.5	2.5	2.4	2.2
Middle East	**2.7**	**3.2**	**4.1**	**6.7**	**3.5**	**4.1**	**5.0**
Asia	13.4	12.5	14.9	19.1	26.0	26.1	34.0

Source: World Trade Organization, *World Trade Statistical Review 2017*, p. 102 (Table A4).

investment bodies through which states seek to invest money long term, offsetting some of the negative economic impacts of energy rent flows, saving non-renewable income for the future, and in some cases funding economic diversification. While SWFs remain small in the global flow of investment funds, they are not insignificant, with just the largest of the Gulf monarchies' funds having assets worth almost $2.2 trillion in total in 2017.[7] The main funds include the Abu Dhabi Investment Authority ($828 billion); the Kuwait Investment Authority ($524 billion); the Saudi Arabian Monetary Agency's foreign holdings ($515.9 billion); and the Qatar Investment Authority ($320 billion).

The Gulf economies have changed profoundly since the 1990s, when long-term low oil prices created an impetus for economic diversification and reform, coming at the same time as many important new technological innovations and other drivers of globalization. The transformation of the Gulf led to the rise of key global cites, of which Dubai is the most widely recognized, but with Doha and others seeking to emulate parts of the Dubai experience. New industries have emerged, including the development of major media outlets (Al-Jazeera, Al-Arabiya, and many others); global transcontinental airlines (particularly Emirates, Etihad and Qatar Airways); and new manufacturing capabilities in aluminium smelting, plastics, cement and other specialized industries. Many of these remain niche capabilities, however, and alone are not a comprehensive reply to the imperatives of economic development and diversification, but the Gulf of the 2010s, compared to that of, say, the 1970s and 1980s, has transformed into a connected, globalized, activist area that few would have imagined a generation ago.

The pace and direction of economic reform has also been very deliberate on the part of Gulf leaderships. While every Gulf government – indeed, virtually every government anywhere – will claim that it wants to see the national economy diversify, innovate and sustainably develop, Gulf leaders have made a conscious decision not to pursue the full gamut of neoliberal economic reforms along the lines of what was done in, for example, Egypt and Tunisia. It is important, therefore, to distinguish between neoliberal reform and other types of economic reform. The Gulf states have taken only certain and modest steps towards the former: they have eschewed floating the currency, avoided substantive labour market reforms (especially for citizens), while controlling the sectors where foreign investment is to be permitted or encouraged. Yet they have nonetheless undertaken a range of reforms, aggressively trying to attract investment, boost trade, support innovation and entrepreneurship and generate new jobs. On most measures in the World Bank's annual *Doing Business* reports,[8] the Gulf states have sharply improved their rankings since the 1990s. They have reduced the cost and difficulty involved in establishing or closing a business, simplified bureaucratic procedures, improved access to credit, and other such reforms, along with creating free zones and improving state support for businesses and investors. These reforms are important, but they are not for the most part macroeconomic liberalization. Gulf rulers have chosen to be more selective in their reform programmes and to engage with globalization on their own terms, to the extent possible, rather than surrendering state economic sovereignty or control. This has been done partly to maintain the state capitalist structure of these political economies, in which the state's allocative, regulatory, and ownership role has long been, and remains, a key means of regime maintenance. State capitalism, in combination with rent allocations and economic statecraft, has sustained durable and stable political systems, while maintaining the rule of royal families and their key elite networks. This would have been a far more challenging prospect if these leaders had permitted a neoliberal-driven retreat of their states from their national economies.

This complex arrangement of rentierism, state capitalism, economic statecraft, and other legitimacy-building strategies did not simply emerge, but is the product of history. Ruling families often had to struggle for power against rival dynasties, in many cases forging alliances with societal or religious forces so as to gain and maintain power. Moreover, all the six Gulf monarchies have traditionally relied upon external support from a major power to underwrite their survival, even if the nature of such arrangements, and their relative importance, has varied. At the same time, economics has been central to all this. Economic resources have always been integral to Gulf politics, whether in the form of the oil and gas rents that dominate these political economies today, or trade or pilgrimage in the pre-oil era. The next chapter provides a modern history of the Gulf, with a particular focus on economic history, as a first step to explaining the trajectories of the Gulf political economies and their current profiles and dynamics.

2

The Gulf economic story

The recent history of the Gulf – the decades since the 1950s or so – has been written in large measure by oil. Oil, and later gas, was integral in funding the transformations of Gulf societies; transformations that in many respects have been nothing short of spectacular. Oil and gas rents deliver advantages to incumbent rulers and elites and have also defined the nature of these economies for both better and worse. The oil-rich Gulf states have world-class infrastructure, high quality of life indicators, and possess many of the trappings and luxuries of economic development, all paid for largely by hydrocarbon rents. Yet the same rentier dynamic has made these economies less competitive in non-energy areas, created large, even bloated, public sectors, enabled leaders to coopt society and helped them avoid substantive democratic reforms and accountability.

At the same time, there is much more to the Gulf than oil and gas. Even with the enormous cooptive and repressive means that regimes can purchase with rents, elites and societal forces still have agency. Oil and gas are global industries, and are susceptible to shocks and fluctuations. Earlier, the Gulf's pre-oil history set the stage for many of the political, economic and social structures and interactions that characterize these political economies today. The oil era is a continuation of some historical dynamics, such as the cooptive, personalized nature of politics and ruler–merchant relations, but in other ways oil has caused a divergence from the past, as with the dramatic development that rents have bought or the dual labour market that it has funded. As context for the dynamics that are the focus throughout the book, this chapter provides a historical survey of the Gulf. The aim is to highlight the key events and dynamics of both the pre-oil era and the oil era, with an emphasis on economic factors, showing the historical continuities, deviations and oscillations that have occurred and how they have shaped the Gulf's modern political economies.

THE HISTORICAL EVOLUTION OF THE REGION

According to archaeological evidence, the Arabian peninsula hosted animal herders at least 7,000–8,000 years ago, and pearl diving had been established by around 5,000 BCE. Earlier still, the seabed of what is now the Gulf may have been a lush floodplain, hosting a substantial population, but the evidence for this is only just starting to emerge. Yet this lengthy human settlement did not give birth to early great empires, as were seen further north in what is now Iraq and Iran, although there were important small cities and large towns along trading routes and near underground water sources. The more mountainous areas of the modern-day Yemen and the far southwest of Saudi Arabia hosted some substantial early settlements, while somewhere in what is now Bahrain or nearby was the site of the ancient civilization of Dilmun. Otherwise, historically the tribe was the most important social unit for people living in the Arabian peninsula. Even in the present day, when the majority of most Gulf populations have settled in urban centres, traditional tribal affiliations and values remain strong.

The pre-Islamic historical record on the Gulf is very thin compared to what is available on the major empires in other parts of the region.[1] There are records of Assyrian contact with some areas on the Gulf in the sixth and seventh centuries BCE, some ancient sea trade around the area, and exploration by parties sent by Alexander the Great after 325 BCE. The Sasanian empire (224–651 CE) saw the Persians seek dominance on the Gulf's coast, and their ambitious merchants, with political support, boosted the commercial importance of the area. In 622 CE, Islam formally emerged when the Prophet Muhammad fled from Mecca to Medina and established at the latter the first Muslim society. The historical record after this time is far more extensive. Mecca and Medina were established trading and political cities at that time, albeit modest compared to imperial capitals and trading centres elsewhere, and a few places such as nearby Taif, Qatif on the Gulf coast, and some settlements in what is now Yemen, were also of note.

The first Islamic caliphate (meaning an Islamic polity controlled by a recognized successor to the Prophet Muhammad) was the Rashidun caliphate (632–61), based in Medina for most of its brief existence. Islam rapidly spread during and after this time, even though it was also a time of political contest and disagreement. The schism which split the Muslim world into Sunni and Shia brought the Rashidun era to an end. The Sunni, the majority of the world's Muslims, consider themselves as the main or orthodox sect; the word "Sunni" derives from *ahl al-sunna*, or "people of the tradition", meaning the traditions of the Prophet Muhammad. The Shia are named from the *shi'at ali*, or "followers of Ali" movement from which they emerged, believing that Ali, the Prophet's cousin and son-in-law, was his rightful successor as leader of the Muslim community, and Ali's sons after him. Ali became the fourth caliph during the Rashidun period, but after a five-year reign and nasty civil conflict, he was assassinated in 661, leading to the Sunni–Shia schism.

The subsequent Sunni empires were based not in the peninsula but further north, in more fertile areas that could sustain larger imperial armies and bureaucracies.[2] The first was the Umayyad caliphate (661–750), based at Damascus and then briefly Harran, followed by the greatest Muslim empire in history, the Abbasid caliphate, based for its first half a millennium in Baghdad (750–1258). The Gulf and the Arabian peninsula were part of all these empires, although their reach was usually most effective along coastlines, in key cities and towns, and along major trading and pilgrimage routes. Away from these areas, empires have always struggled to maintain much control, especially given the strength of tribal loyalties. The caliphates led to the necessary creation of a new administrative and military structure, which had some impacts further into the Arabian peninsula. Many officials and military personnel came from urban families, but over time an increasing number were supplied by the main tribal families of western Arabia and beyond. These were integral to the expansion and consolidation of Islam, conquering new territories and then usually ruling the area from a nearby camp or sometimes by establishing a new city. Yet for the bulk of the Arabian peninsula, change was less dramatic. The new rules and cultural practices that came with Islam took some time to become accepted and adopted, while tribal allegiances and authority remained strong. For the most part, economic activities barely changed, with agricultural processes, trade and taxation all remaining similar to just before the arrival of Islam. Changes to social and family life began to occur where Islamic law was implemented.

Over time, trade grew strongly as merchants travelled more widely, along with explorers, scholars and pilgrims. The earliest important settlement in the Gulf in the early Islamic era was at Basra, in what is now southern Iraq. It was founded in the early years of the Rashidun caliphate, as an important producer of textiles and ceramics and a port through which other goods flowed between the Tigris-Euphrates valley and the Gulf coast. The southern and Gulf coast areas of Persia also quickly grew as trading posts; in later centuries Hormuz would become an especially important and prosperous trading city.[3] In the Hijaz, there had long been trade along the Red Sea, which grew further after the arrival of Islam when the *Hajj*, or pilgrimage to Mecca, was established as one of the five pillars of the religion. The more remote parts of the peninsula, however, remained peripheral, their geography and climate deterring the creation of grand cities.

By early in the second millennium CE, the Abbasid empire began its gradual decline. In the mid-900s what is now Iran, Iraq and Oman fell under the control of the Buyids in Iran, who pacified and revivified the trade routes around the Gulf. When Buyid power declined, the central Asian Saljuks gained control of much of these areas, although an Arab tribal revolt led to a largely independent dynasty being formed in Bahrain and Hasa, lasting a century. Beginning in the 900s but especially during the thirteenth century, Hormuz grew into a regional power. Hormuz, located on the Persian side of the Gulf near its mouth, included a substantial city and nearby island, supported by Qeshm island. Its location at the entrance to the Gulf allowed it to become a major trading hub between the Middle East and India and East Africa for many centuries, until the arrivals of the European powers.

Prior to the arrival of Europeans, the Indian Ocean and Middle Eastern trading system was extensive, consisting of a network of land and sea routes, ports, and supporting industries and services, laying broadly under Arab control. It dated back to the rise of Islam, after which time the spread of Islam helped to unify the Indian Ocean into an interconnected commercial web. This period was, as one observer notes with little exaggeration, "the era of Sindbad, of mariners scouring the Indian Ocean".[4] It was a remarkable system, linking the Middle East with the far reaches of the Indian Ocean and even to China – a two-year return voyage. The Gulf was a critical component of this network, possessing new ports such as Basra, Muscat, and then Hormuz that lay between the well-established overland trade routes in the Middle East and the wider world.

This all changed in the 1500s, after Vasco de Gama's circumnavigation of the Cape of Good Hope in 1498 and the arrival of the first European power, the Portuguese, followed later by the Dutch, British and French. Over the sixteenth century, the Portuguese took Muscat, Hormuz, and then Bahrain, effectively gaining control of the sea routes of the Gulf and northern Indian Ocean. Regional politics were changing, too, which challenged and eventually removed the Portuguese. The resurgence of Persian power under the Safavids saw Shah Abbas seize Bahrain in 1602 and later, with British help, Hormuz, while the rise of the Ottoman Empire had already put a stop to Portuguese expansion into the Red Sea after the Ottomans defeated them at Jedda in 1517. Finally, once Oman was released from Portuguese domination by local tribal forces in 1660, Muscat returned to its previous position as a powerful commercial centre, becoming in the nineteenth century a maritime empire in the northern Indian Ocean and East African coast.

25

The Turkish Ottomans dated back to the mid-1300s, but their power increased sharply after their seizure of Constantinople (now Istanbul) in 1453, which brought the Byzantine empire to an end.[5] In the early 1500s, the Ottoman ruler Selim I (r. 1512–20) conquered Egypt, the Levant, and the Hijaz and Tihama (the Red Sea coast of Yemen). The eastern shore of the Red Sea thus came under Ottoman control, and let Selim I claim guardianship over the pilgrimage routes to Mecca and Medina, even though the area remained somewhat autonomous and under the control of Meccan elites for some time. Under Selim's successor, Suleiman the Magnificent (r. 1520–66), Ottoman power reached its peak. Suleiman is most famous perhaps for his 1529 siege of Vienna, which nearly brought central Europe under Ottoman control, but for the Gulf the period was important for his conquest of Baghdad and his extension of Ottoman reach about mid-way into the Arab coast of the Persian Gulf, to Hasa, which accepted Ottoman rule in 1550. Although the Ottomans claimed all of the Arabian peninsula, their control of it varied: the climate and terrain were harsh, and local leaders retained enormous loyalty from their populations. The Ottomans were, at any rate, more interested in checking Portuguese and Safavid power than in gaining territorial possession per se. By the seventeenth century, the Ottomans were suffering internal problems and began their lengthy decline, and the more remote areas of the Arabian peninsula avoided Ottoman conquest. In the Najd, this independence was critical to the survival of the Al Saud dynasty and its conquest of much of the peninsula after the 1740s. Ottoman decline also saw tribal leaders in Hasa reassert their independence in 1670. It was the latter part of the 1800s before the Ottomans again, and only in the final decades of their empire, controlled Hasa and the Gulf coast.

THE ORIGINS OF THE CONTEMPORARY GULF STATES

In the eighteenth century, the power of the Persians, Ottomans and Portuguese all waned and the French struggled to have any real reach into the area, leaving the British the dominant power in the Indian Ocean and the Gulf. This, especially their links to key local leaders, created or solidified a political order in the Gulf that, succeeded by independent states, largely determined the borders and political structures of today.[6] In Najd and central Arabia, the 1744 pact between Muhammad ibn Saud and al-Wahhab led to the formation of the first of three Saudi emirates (sometimes called Saudi states): the first over 1744–1818; the second, 1824–91; and the third, the current state, pronounced in 1932 but beginning in effect after Ibn Saud's return from exile in 1902.[7] Its borders were very similar to those of modern Saudi Arabia, with the Saudi forces coming out of Diri'iyya, near the current capital of Riyadh, and seizing the centre, north, Gulf coast, and other areas, plus finally the Hijaz in the early 1800s. The second emirate, over 1824–91, was smaller, dominating the centre and east of the peninsula, and weakened by dynastic divisions. Despite its problems, the survival of the Saudi dynasty was an impressive feat, given the Ottoman, Egyptian, and European challenges they confronted and the difficulties of ruling such a large, diverse territory. The Saudi emirates are also noteworthy because, although some parts fell briefly under outside control, the bulk of what is now Saudi Arabia, including the core Najd region, was never colonized by a foreign power.

In the seventeenth and eighteenth centuries along the southern coast of the Gulf, a series of migrations into coastal areas by the central Arabian Utub tribal group led to the establishment of the dynasties that now rule Bahrain, Kuwait and Qatar.[8] The ruling Al Sabah family in Kuwait traces its rule back to the 1750s, after which it quickly came to compete with Basra as a trading port. In 1766, part of this same tribe ruling Kuwait also settled in Qatar, which had previously only hosted nomadic and seasonal populations. The permanent settlement in Qatar created new trade links with Kuwait and elsewhere. In the late 1700s, the rulers in Qatar expanded into Bahrain. Initially they were attacked by forces based in Persia, which controlled Bahrain at the time, but they repelled the attack and went on to take control of Bahrain in 1783. Bahrain's Al Khalifa dynasty faced a number of subsequent threats, and on several occasions made brief opportunistic alliances with other local powers, but they were able to avoid becoming a dependency of the Saudis.

Further down the coast, several other ruling families emerged around this time.[9] The Bu Said emerged as the ruling family in Oman in 1749, after foreign interventions and a generation-long civil war, although it took until the 1790s for the family rivalries to be ironed out and for the dynasty to stabilize. Oman grew into a regional power in the 1780s and 1790s, for two reasons. The first was its strong economic base and sound trade policies. By 1790, Muscat was a major commercial port city, with about half of all trade between India and the Gulf passing through it, and it also grew influential in the Yemeni coffee trade. It had clear and predictable tariffs, at a time when other ports such as Basra were unstable and risky for traders. Second, Oman entered into a treaty with the British in 1798; a pragmatic move probably designed to improve its access to Indian ports and avoid conflict with the British. This was the first treaty among several, through which the British eventually gained effective control of the Gulf. Also at this time, in the area that is now the UAE, some of the key dynasties of the emirates were emerging. The Qasimi dynasty had established itself at Ras al-Khaimah in the early eighteenth century and then at Sharjah mid-century, while the Bani Yas dynasty in Abu Dhabi consolidated their position, and military forces, in the mid-eighteenth century as well, founding Abu Dhabi around 1761 and within 30 years or so building it into an important fort and local hub.[10]

The 100 or so years that followed this – roughly from 1820 until the First World War – was a period of British dominance in the Indian Ocean, and in the Gulf it was a time of relative stability. The era also marked a shift in economic importance to the Arab side of the Gulf, with Basra and the Iranian ports declining in influence, while settlements along the southern coastline grew, enhancing the trading power of ports such as Muscat, Sharjah, Bahrain and others. The British, motivated above all by economic concerns and ambitions, and focused on their prize colonial possession of India, sought treaty arrangements with Gulf (and other) rulers that would exclude other European powers from the area and support the Royal Navy's operations. The General Maritime Treaty of 1820, which London signed with the rulers of Abu Dhabi, Sharjah, Umm al-Quwain, and Ajman, and the year after with Bahrain, outlawed piracy and slavery, and in effect gave the British administrative purview over maritime matters in the Gulf. There were maritime clashes in the Gulf, as in 1835 when the sheikhs of the lower Gulf intervened in an Omani civil conflict. Naval warfare had not been outlawed by the Treaty, and so the British stepped in and arranged a truce, later codified in an 1853 permanent peace. This trucial system was a very different method of control from what external powers, including the British, had usually adopted elsewhere. In holding local leaders to treaty obligations and making regular port visits, while also avoiding intervention in local politics and underwriting the autonomy of local leaders, the trucial arrangements were an attractive structure to most local leaders, in contrast to the resentment created by conquest and other forms of direct domination.

Still, the Gulf sheikhdoms suffered from instability and in-fighting from time to time, as well as rivalries between rulers. Abu Dhabi's leaders and the Qasimi clashed over control of territory, and there was an on-going dispute over control of the large and strategically important Buraimi oasis. The Omani Bu Said dynasty's ambitions of expanding its territory further into the Gulf were checked by the British; instead, Oman expanded its power in the Indian Ocean over the second quarter of the nineteenth century. It developed the economy of its possession Zanzibar, but Muscat's declining importance in Gulf trade, and internal divisions, sent it into decline from the mid-1850s onward. The British expanded their role there to the point of domination by the late-nineteenth century, a brief French foray notwithstanding, although the intrigue and internal rivalries within the Bu Said meant that the British did have to intervene in political disputes occasionally and more emphatically than in other areas of the Gulf. The other source of instability through much of the nineteenth century was the territorial ambitions of the second Saudi emirate. While the Saudis did not dare confront the British directly in the Gulf, they seized inland areas, including Hasa and Buraimi, exacting tribute from local sheikhs. The second Saudi emirate eventually collapsed due to internal divisions, but only late in the century after intervention by the Rashidi dynasty to the north.

The nineteenth century also saw the Ottomans reassert themselves in the Gulf after a long period of near-absence. Although going through a transformation of its own during the *Tanzimat* ("Reform") era of 1839–76, the Ottomans also imposed a modernization on Baghdad and central Iraq after 1869. As the second Saudi emirate was crumbling, the Ottomans retook their old possession of Hasa. This did not create direct conflict with London, but was clearly designed to check British expansion from the Gulf inland. From Hasa, the Ottomans also reasserted control over Qatar, making it in effect a vassal under the (Ottoman-appointed) governor of Hasa. The British at the time were turning their attention to Iran, where the Qajars had failed to deliver reform, eventually leading to the 1905–06 constitutional revolution, when strikes by merchants and popular demonstrations forced the Shah (king) to adopt a constitution and form a legislature. The weakness brought about by these events saw the British invade Iran in the south, followed by the Russians invading in the north. These two foreign powers had previously agreed on such spheres of influence, with a buffer between them as they fought the so-called "Great Game" for domination of Central and South Asia. Russia's presence in Iran would last until the 1917 Bolshevik revolution. The British, who had made the Gulf's first oil discovery in western Persia in 1908, and knowing the economic and military value of it, took a 51 per cent stake in the Anglo-Persian Oil Company (APOC) in May 1914. They would continue to dominate Iran and its oil industry into the middle of the twentieth century, including through political intervention that remains an Iranian grievance to the present day.

The First World War had a range of impacts on the Gulf. It contributed to the Russian revolution and their withdrawal from northern Persia, as noted, but more importantly, it showed the centrality of oil to military capability, which made the Middle East pivotal in major power politics during the interwar years, the Second World War and then the Cold War.

It also brought the Ottoman empire to an end, leading to the creation of new states across the Arab world, the majority of them under the control of Britain and France through mandates from the League of Nations. The mandates were intended to provide external support in preparation for independence, but typically these territories were treated more like possessions. In some cases, such as Iraq, local opposition to foreign rule, and the creation of a client monarchy, led to an end to the mandate and to Iraq declaring independence in 1932. In other cases, things were messier still: the British mandate in Palestine was especially badly-handled by the British and contributed to the Arab–Jewish violence there in the interwar period. The French did little better by the region.

Britain retained its dominance in the Gulf after the First World War, not through mandates but by its military and economic power, its role as adviser to friendly leaders, and on a few occasions by intervention, especially in Persia. The leaders in the smaller sheikhdoms at the time were still engaging in basic nation-building and in developing their capacity to rule. They also faced formidable economic challenges, especially the disastrous impact on the pearl industry of the Japanese development of cultured pearls, which saw a collapse in the price of natural pearls. This came in the early-1930s, at the same time as the impacts of the Great Depression were at their worst. Although some oil began to flow in this period, and the region contained important ports, this helped only in a few places and did not come close to compensating for the loss of the pearl industry or deeper global economic problems.[11]

The 1920s, and especially the 1930s and 1940s, were a challenging time for both the rulers and populations of the Gulf. In Bahrain, the ruling Al Khalifa faced both Shia opposition and tension with the British.[12] The Shia had long complained of unfair and at times violent treatment by the Al Khalifa, and this was the source of a 1922 Shia uprising that demanded substantive administrative and tax reforms. Although Sheikh Isa yielded on some of these demands, the situation was serious enough for the British to push him out of power in 1923. His son Hamad tried even more significant economic and judicial reforms, which sharply raised Sunni–

Shia tensions. For a time, at least, the early exploitation of oil helped offset these problems. Bahrain was the first Arab Gulf sheikhdom to discover oil, in 1932, and to begin exporting it, in 1934. This offset some of the impacts of the Great Depression and the collapse of the pearl trade – certainly much more than in neighbouring sheikhdoms, where oil exports only commenced later – and also brought Sunni and Shia communities closer together, both as workers in this new and lucrative industry, and because of the social spending that followed the arrival of rents.

In Kuwait, the merchants tried to gain a greater political role in the 1930s, culminating in the 1938 Majlis Movement, when key opposition forces demanded political reforms from the ruling Al Sabah family, including the creation of a *majlis*, or parliament.[13] The ruler, Sheikh Ahmad, agreed to the creation of such a body, on British advice, to placate his opponents, but the *majlis* had a very precarious and brief life. It was twice dissolved, in late 1938 and again in early 1939; on the second occasion the reformist movement was also suppressed. This episode upset what had until then been a peaceable cohabitation between the merchants and the political elite, but occurred at a time of economic transformation. The worst effects of the Great Depression had passed by 1938, which was also the year that oil was discovered in Kuwait. By the time Sheikh Ahmad died in 1950, oil production was high enough that the ruling family no longer needed the merchants for loans and customs taxes, and at the same time had tremendous cooptive capacity from the influx of oil rents.

In Qatar, although there was not the sectarian or ruler–merchant conflict seen in Bahrain and Kuwait, there was strife within the ruling Al Thani dynasty, which consisted of a collection of cadet branches that had long challenged the ruler or demanded resources from him.[14] To make matters worse, Qatar was especially badly hit by the pearl industry collapse, and did not begin exporting oil until after the Second World War. In the trucial states, meanwhile, both inter-family and intra-family conflict was the dominant political problem. The Al Nahayan dynasty in Abu Dhabi saw, between 1912 and 1928, three rulers murdered and succeeded by their own brothers. During some of these disputes, desert tribes were often brought in as allies of one side or the other. This was a problem in itself for political stability, especially when some tribes sought protection from the Saudis in nearby Hasa in the 1920s. This could have led to Saudi territorial claims on Abu Dhabi, had the British not undertaken to pro-tect the Al Nahayan and not engaged in substantial diplomacy with the tribes to restore Abu Dhabi's control. Yet Abu Dhabi's economy remained hobbled by Sheikh Shakhbut's frugality and fear of modernization, which remained a problem into the 1960s, well after the exploitation of oil had begun, when Abu Dhabi still lacked the infrastructure, commercial opportunities, and social services of the rest of the Gulf.[15] Sharjah wit-nessed elite squabbling similar to Abu Dhabi's, which led to the secession of Ras al-Khaimah into a separate sheikhdom in 1921. Only Dubai and Ajman were fairly peaceful in the interwar period.

In Oman in the early twentieth century, the Sultan enjoyed authority only in the main ports and coastal areas, while tribal elements controlled inland areas. At times the latter had been strong enough to threaten some of Oman's ports. As a result, trade stagnated and official revenues plum-meted, forcing Sultan Taimur to accept British advisers in exchange for a loan in 1918. Things improved after this time, first when the British helped negotiate the 1920 Seeb Agreement, which ended the conflict between the Sultan and the inland tribes. Around this time, moreover, the search for oil – while initially unsuccessful – provided an excuse for the Sultan to increase his physical and cooptive reach further into the interior. In 1932, Sultan Said took power, and was more interested in the daily intricacies of ruling, and much keener on modernizing government and its finances. It was the 1950s, however, before he could attempt to bring the interior under his control.

In what is now Saudi Arabia, Ibn Saud came out of exile in Kuwait in 1902 and began seeking to re-establish a third Saudi state across the bulk of the peninsula.[16] Initially the north was under Rashidi control, the Hijaz under Sharifan control (and briefly, was independent as the Hashe-mite Kingdom of Hijaz). Other areas were ruled by various local leaders. Ibn Saud gained control of Najd and Hasa during the 1910s, and then quickly defeated the Rashidis, taking Ha'il in 1921. He turned to Hijaz, taking Mecca from the Hashemites in 1924 and then Jedda. As in earlier Saudi emirates, Ibn Saud used the backing of the Wahhabi clerics to legitimize and consolidate his power, and in his military activities drew on an informal group of supportive, mostly tribal, warriors, the *ikhwan* ("the Brethren"). The *ikhwan* were effective and fervent, and wanted to continue on to conquer Iraq and Transjordan (as Jordan was then known). However, this would have brought Ibn Saud into direct conflict with the British, who had mandates over those territories. Knowing he would be defeated against the British, and probably lose power, he instead cracked down on the *ikhwan*, who had begun rebelling against what they now viewed as an overly-cautious ruler. In 1929, the *ikhwan* were decisively defeated in the Battle of Sibila, and by early the following year, the remaining *ikhwan*, with most of their leaders dead or having fled, surrendered. With the borders of his territorial control now virtually those of the contemporary state, Ibn Saud proclaimed the Kingdom of Saudi Arabia in 1932. Nation-building was a much more complicated challenge. Among his dozens of marriages, he took wives from key tribes such as the Banu Khalid, Shammar, and Ajman, and from notable families such as the Al Shaykh and Al Sudairi – with both groups essential to elite support for his rule – although the political utility of his polygamy has been questioned.[17] Less debated is the patronage he dispersed through traditional elites, and the loyalty he constructed by appointing loyal members of his family to key posts. Although oil exports did not flow in any volume until after the Second World War, that quickly became an additional tool – and quickly, the *key* tool – through which Ibn Saud and his successors maintained and consolidated their power and legitimacy.[18]

Although oil wealth had begun to flow to some Middle Eastern leaders before the Second World War, the industry was predominantly foreign-owned and -controlled, and usually backed by the oil companies' home governments. The share of the oil income that flowed on to local leaders was modest. The British dominated Iranian oil from its earliest days in effect, and then formally as of 1914, when London took a

51 per cent stake in APOC. The Shah tried to seize APOC's assets in 1932, but eventually agreed to a new agreement and higher royalties from the British instead. In Iraq, the government granted a concession to the Turkish Petroleum Company (soon thereafter the Iraq Petroleum Company, or IPC), which gave the British dominance there, too, with a share to the French and Americans as well. The lack of Iraqi state ownership or input into the oil industry caused enduring resentment among many Iraqis, yet the Iraqi agreement was also to be "both the parent and the prototype for other joint ventures in the Middle East".[19] In Bahrain, although under British control, London was not interested in the concession, which went instead to an American firm, Socal, which more crucially also gained the first Saudi oil concession too. In Kuwait, the British and American governments discreetly competed, with the British eventually gaining the concession there for British Petroleum (BP). This pattern repeated across many other states, due to the foreign penetration of the region at the time and the lack of oil expertise within these states. The rise of Middle Eastern oil was an important element of both the expansion and consolidation of the giant, integrated companies, commonly referred to as "the Seven Sisters", which dominated the global oil industry in the second and third quarters of the twentieth century.[20]

THE COMING OF THE OIL AGE, 1945–72

By the mid-1940s, the Gulf states had begun to take the geographic and political shape that they possess today, and in terms of economics and trade, oil had either started to flow or was being aggressively searched out. The borders of the smaller states were mostly still not set, but it was the ports and towns that mattered most for political and economic power, and by the Second World War these were, generally, in uncontested hands. While the Gulf was a peripheral area in the Second World War, it was affected by the outcomes of the conflict. Most obviously, the British role as a world power went into inexorable decline, while the United States rose as a superpower, along with the Soviet Union. The subsequent Cold War rivalry dominated international relations for almost half a century after. In the Middle East, the postwar political environment was characterized by the rise of nationalism, independence movements against European powers, and state-led economic policy approaches. The Gulf did not escape this. The postwar period was one of significant political, economic and social development.

Figure 2.1 Gulf oil production, 1906–50 ('000 bbls/day)

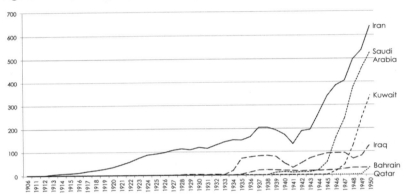

Source: From statistics originally collated in Etemad, *et al.*, *World Energy Production, 1800–1985*, in Anon., "Historical Energy Production Statistics".

As already mentioned, and evident from Figure 2.1, the discovery of oil in the Gulf occurred at very different times. The first was in Persia in 1908, followed by Iraq in 1927. The discovery of commercial quantities of oil in Bahrain in 1932 sparked a broader search around the Gulf for more such fields, leading to discoveries in Saudi Arabia and Kuwait in 1938 and Qatar in 1939. Yet the Gulf did not develop an oil export industry until later: Qatar did not export oil in commercial quantities until the 1950s, Abu Dhabi until the early 1960s, or Oman and Dubai until the 1960s. At any rate, the oil age really only commenced after the Second World War. US entry into the war in late 1941 generated new interest in the Middle East. Yergin notes how Washington recognized the absolute strategic necessity of oil, as the commodity that would win or lose the war for the

Allies.[21] However during the conflict, the US supplied most of the Allies' oil. Middle Eastern exports came almost to a stop, given the diversion of resources at the time and the challenges of securely supplying oil from the region.

The US courted Saudi Arabia with desperately-needed aid during the war, encouraged by the Saudi-American Oil Company (Aramco), the US company that had won the first concession in Saudi Arabia in 1933 and which came to monopolize its oil and gas industry. The postwar US–Saudi relationship was cemented by a meeting near the end of the war between US President Franklin Roosevelt and Saudi King Abdel Aziz. They met on 14 February 1945 on the cruiser USS *Quincy*, on Egypt's Great Bitter Lake, during Roosevelt's return from the Yalta conference. At the meeting, the Saudis agreed to US port visits and the construction of a US airfield, while reaffirming the Aramco oil concession and agreeing to the construction of the trans-Arabian oil pipeline across the north of the Kingdom.[22] The meeting on the *Quincy* established the loose symbiotic agreement of US oil supply security from the Saudis in exchange for a US security guarantee in return, which was the backbone of their relationship after the war and, in effect, through to the current day.

In the other Arab Gulf states, British influence continued for longer. The British retained influence in the Gulf sheikhdoms until its withdrawal from the region in 1971, and to a diminished extent after that time, although the imperatives of the Cold War meant that the US established a naval base in Bahrain as early as 1949. However, Washington evolved into the security guarantor for all six Arab Gulf states as British global power declined, and given the importance of oil to the geoeconomic position and military capability of the United States. US interest in the Gulf was also a by-product of the postwar economy in the developed world. Postwar reconstruction, a growing western consumer power, and the mass production of new technologies such as the motor vehicle placed hydrocarbons at the centre of the world's wealthier economies, and created an explosion in demand, with the unsurprising result that ensuring secure and reliable access to oil supplies became a central pillar of US and western foreign policies.[23] In 1948, as the Cold War was unfolding, the US became a net importer of oil,[24] making it reliant on foreign suppliers for the lifeblood of its economy and the main sustenance of its military power. From that time onward, the sheer size and quality of the Middle East's reserves meant that the region could probably never have avoided becoming entangled in international politics as it did during and after the Cold War.

A key point of contention in the early Cold War era, however, was over the ownership and effective control of oil, including access to its profits. Even after Iran's oil concession was renegotiated in 1932, resentment remained, and in 1953 Prime Minister Mohammed Mossadeq tried to nationalize the Anglo-Iranian Oil Company (AIOC), as APOC had then become. However his declining support base, and logistical and coordination support from the US and the UK, led to his popular overthrow in August 1953 and the return of the Shah from a brief exile.[25] This played a role in the control of oil shifting from the international companies to Middle Eastern states, as did the 1956 Suez Crisis and the rise of pan-Arabism. It had begun in 1943, when Venezuela demanded a 50:50 split of profits between the international oil firms and the state. The 50:50 arrangement quickly spread to the Middle East, first to Saudi Arabia, which negotiated new 50:50 terms with Aramco in 1950, and then to Kuwait and Iraq. Nevertheless, a number of other states retained older agreements under which they were paid very little; there was, in effect, two classes of oil agreement in the region (and globally) in the 1950s.

Even as the oil states gained better financial terms from international oil companies, they sought a still-greater share of the profits and sovereignty over the resources that lay underneath their territory, even though the international firms still largely controlled the oil price. This, especially the sheer concentration of production and consumption power in the US, prompted the creation of the Organization of the Petroleum Exporting Countries (OPEC) in 1960. Driven by Venezuela initially, and then Saudi Arabia and Iraq, OPEC was formed out of the Baghdad conference of 10–14 September 1960, with these three states plus Iran and Kuwait as founding members. OPEC was intended as an international cartel of producing states, serving as a venue for agreement on production quotas and stable, but fair, oil prices. OPEC's immediate impact was limited to making international firms much more cautious about acting unilaterally or cutting prices and at first was hampered by a glut in world oil supply and disagreements and rivalries among member states. However it grew in size and power over the 1960s to become a much more influential actor in the 1970s, with 15 members at its peak. A regional body, the Organization of Arab Petroleum Exporting Countries (OAPEC), was set up in 1968, initially to coordinate regional oil policy among the conservative Arab states, but in the 1970s its membership and power expanded greatly, especially after it decided on the oil embargo against the US during the 1973 Yom Kippur/October/Ramadan War.[26]

Figure 2.2   Gulf oil production, 1951–72 ('000 bbls/day)

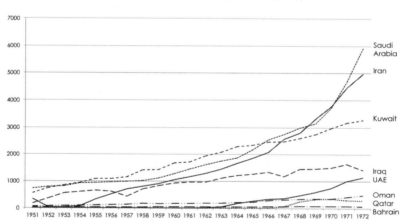

Source: From statistics originally collated in Etemad, *et al.*, *World Energy Production, 1800–1985*, in Anon., "Historical Energy Production Statistics".

OPEC's creation also coincided with new oil discoveries and new export sources, which sustained low prices throughout the 1960s and early 1970s, but large rents nonetheless flowed into the Middle East and especially to the main Gulf producer states. This contributed to a rapid development of these economies, starting in Iran, Iraq, and Kuwait in the 1950s, where the first commercial exports had begun, and by the 1960s including Saudi Arabia, the UAE, and others. Oil-driven development was accelerated, even if from a modest base, by increased production and the adoption by some states of 50:50 profit sharing. In Iraq, for instance, oil revenue rose some 511 per cent between 1951 and 1958, from 13.7 million dinars to 83.8 million (roughly $36.4 million to $234.6 million).[27] As shown in Table 2.1, in the Gulf's Arab monarchies, the increase was similarly dramatic over the 1950s, and still enormous throughout the 1960s too (if a little slower since it was starting from a higher base).

Table 2.1 Gulf states' petroleum revenues ($ millions): 1950, 1960, 1970

Country	1950	1960	1970	% Increase 1950–60	% Increase 1960–70
Bahrain	3.3	15.0	35.0	355	133
Kuwait	11.0	465.0	895.0	4,127	92
Qatar	1.0	54.0	122.4	5,300	127
Saudi Arabia	57.0	355.0	1,200.0	523	238
UAE	—	3.0	233.0	—	7,700

Source: Petroleum revenue figures from al-Naqeeb, *Society and State in the Gulf and Arab Peninsula*, 81 (Table 5.4); percentage calculations are the author's.

These rapid rises in income led to the emergence of the *rentier* state. Rentierism refers to income that is externally-derived and largely unproductively-earned: where international firms were doing the searching and drilling for oil, virtually all the profits received by states was "unproductively" earned in the sense that the income is gained from an inherent natural feature of the territory, and not from the activities and innovations of productive sectors of the economy. Even when oil companies were nationalized and thus a state-owned firm was taking on more productive aspects of the industry, this productive component still only covered a small minority of the revenues received. That oil revenues came through the state allowed governments to rely on the distribution of some of this income rather than having to tax and redistribute national wealth. Rulers used this income, not surprisingly, to buy the support, or at least the tolerance, of society, and to purchase a repressive capability as needed. The changes to the Gulf's political economies were rapid and dramatic: bureaucracies expanded, as rulers used the public sector to create employment for citizens; transfer payments from the state boomed; health and education was expanded, usually at no cost to citizens; and foreign workers began arriving in the Gulf to do work that was too dangerous or unpleasant for native workers. All this made the state very autonomous from society and allowed it to avoid making democratic bargains.

In the original rentier state theory (RST) of the 1980s that sought to explain these dynamics, states were categorized by Giacomo Luciani, an early rentier theorist, as either "allocation" (rentier) states or "production" (taxing and redistributive) states.[28] The extension of the rentier argument typically is that, in the Gulf monarchies, oil has therefore reinforced traditional patterns of wealth, power and privilege, allowing ruling families to consolidate power over the state and society by virtue of their incumbency – which gave them control of the oil wealth used in this process. The Gulf's rulers were allocative and cooptive long before oil, but the enormous wealth that hydrocarbons brought gave them immense new powers, enhanced by the institutions of modern states. This rentier pattern, albeit in increasingly nuanced and sophisticated ways and with new pressures at times threatening to undermine it, remains a feature of state–society relations in the Arab Gulf states.[29] The distributive mechanisms may change and develop, but the underlying tactics of the state, and the elite structures that control it, remain largely unchanged.

Concomitant with the development of the rentier dynamic, oil wealth also has reinforced two other basic features of the Gulf political economies: neopatrimonialism and state capitalism. Neopatrimonialism refers to a system of interpersonal mechanisms, with a leader who creates and manages a web of elites around himself, also allowing or encouraging those elites to form their own patron–client networks out into the institutions of the state and the economy. As a result, politics is highly personalized, with the leader at its core and (usually) unchallenged, and with resources and opportunities distributed by the leader largely through these patronage networks. In return, the leader's elites, and the elites' sub-elites in turn, send loyalty and information back through these webs to the leader. Provided that a little rivalry or mistrust is maintained between key elites, so that they cannot combine forces against the leader or exert inescapable pressure on him, this is a very effective political mechanism, allowing a ruler and a small group of loyal elites to control an extensive political system, even that of a large, modern nation-state.

State capitalism – specifically, the current "new" variety of it that is a characteristic of the Gulf monarchies (and elsewhere) – is a third pillar of control in the Gulf political economies. It is based on the much older concept of "state capitalism", in which the state is a disproportionate owner of the means of production in an economy and is highly regulatory and paternalistic towards the private sector. It often allows market forces to set prices and, while privileging state-owned firms, allows a sizeable private sector to exist, especially at the small and medium-sized firm levels. The idea of a "new" form of state capitalism emerged in the early 2000s, conceptually established by Ian Bremmer in 2010 and then developed further by others.[30] It refers to a state capitalist system, but one in which the state is long term in its thinking, and even "entrepreneurial" in its ambitions.[31] The state is not strongly driven by distributive justice or ideological concerns, as in most previous state capitalist systems, but instead seeks to expand its resources and economic reach so as to enhance its legitimacy and control. The Gulf states are "new" state capitalist, it can be convincingly argued, because they are state capitalist in terms of their ownership and regulatory roles, while also, when it comes to state-owned firms, being tolerant of commercial risk, open to fostering new industries, and in most cases concerned with efficiency and profitability. They may have only transitioned into new state capitalism systems in recent decades, especially after 1991, but the seeds of it were sown in the early oil decades, when state capitalism was established in these political economies.

These concepts are introduced here because they are *all* related strongly with oil. That noted, they have their origins in the pre-oil era. Rentierism is consistent with the allocative behaviour of Gulf rulers over centuries. Neopatrimonialism stems from the traditional patron–client mechanisms that have characterized political leaders, tribes and families in the Arab world since the earliest of times,[32] and even state capitalism, while newer, probably would have emerged with or without oil. Yet oil is absolutely critical to all three, especially in accounting for their durability and their strengthening of each other. Oil wealth provides the funds for rentierism, but also for the investment needed for new state capitalism. Neopatrimonialism is a useful mechanism for rent allocation, and provides strong elite networks that often substitute for strong institutions, and is funded by rents and supported by state capitalist structures. (New) state capitalism helps compensate for weaknesses in rentier systems, by providing mechanisms to coopt elites and by smoothing out economic performance as rents fluctuate. By the 1970s, neopatrimonialism was embedded in the Gulf systems, rentier mechanisms were in place, and state capitalism was a feature, even if its "new" variety was yet to emerge.

These have been the main features of the Gulf states' political economies, dating back before independence. Saudi Arabia, formed in 1932 and having never been colonized, is unique among the six for becoming an independent state before the commercial exploitation of oil commenced. Among the five smaller states, Kuwait was the first to gain independence, in 1961. The royal family had used oil income to invest heavily in economic and social programmes, perhaps out of political necessity, given the demands for representation they had faced. Such demands remained, however, and a Constituent Assembly was formed in 1962. The parliament was most likely also a product of the unique and real security threat faced by Kuwait: at the time of independence, in June 1961, Iraq, having long claimed Kuwait, seemed poised to invade it.[33] That the Kuwaiti royals relied on British help to deter this threat was probably a reason why they had to make the concessions they did to demands for consultative rule. Iraq's later invasion of Kuwait in 1990 demonstrated how real this threat indeed was.

In the other Gulf states in the late-1960s, given their small size, there was some brief discussion about combining the Trucial states, Bahrain and Qatar into a single state.[34] This did not eventuate, however, due mostly to a Bahraini desire for independence, which it declared in August 1971, followed by Qatar, which had a small population but substantial oil income, in September. The formation of the UAE took a little longer, but was driven by the fact that the tiniest of the sheikhdoms (Ajman, Fujaira, Ras al-Khaimah, Sharjah and Umm al Qawain) had no oil and were not viable as independent states, while Abu Dhabi and Dubai, although possessing oil, wanted the security of a federation. The UAE was declared an independent state in December 1971, with Ras al-Khaimah initially opting out of the federation but then joining in early 1972. There were issues with the federation, especially an historical rivalry between Abu Dhabi's ruling Nahayan family and Dubai's Al Maktoum, but a balance of sorts between them was found and a strong centralistic constitution agreed.[35]

Oman was a little different. On the one hand, it was viable on its own, and thus was never a contender to join a federation. On the other hand, it faced internal divisions, including a rebellion in the southern Dhofar region over 1964–76, in which the British were strongly involved in support of the Bu Said ruling family. In 1970 Qaboos ibn Said Al Said overthrew his repressive, exceptionally conservative, and increasingly unpopular father Said ibn Taimur and began modernizing the country. Qaboos' declaration of the Sultanate of Oman in 1971 is typically treated as its independence, even if it had nominal independence earlier and yet also relied on British support after.

The broad patterns of regime maintenance and consolidation after independence continued from the preceding decades. Oil was crucial in forming rentier-based state–society relationships and in developing neopatrimonial politics and state capitalist structures. Leaders relied on more than just oil for survival, however, legitimizing their rule by draw-ing on claims of historical precedent, family experience, magnanimity, or elite consensus. As the oil wealth flowed into these economies, rulers focused on spending at least some of it in ways that would strengthen their "eudaemonic"[36] legitimacy: free education was expanded and improved, state services were boosted, and public works projects were inaugurated. Eudaemonic legitimacy relies on economic capacity, and while economic capacity is not the *only* factor in determining state legitimacy and durabil-ity, in the case of the Gulf states it has been absolutely central.

OIL BOOMS AND BUSTS, 1973–89

The first quarter-century or so of the postwar years were relatively stable ones for oil supply and prices, at least compared to what came later, begin-ning in 1973 with an oil embargo and dramatic price rise, and followed by a decade of further instability and price increases. This had a severe effect on the major developed economies, which were oil importers and the growth of which had long been sustained by relatively cheap oil. Only in the mid-1980s did the crude oil price decline, falling so sharply that it created a new economic crisis – this time for the oil exporting states, including those of the Gulf.

By the early 1970s OPEC was an increasingly powerful body. Oil demand had risen and spare production capacity had fallen, the US dol-lar had begun weakening, and US output had peaked, even as demand remained strong. OPEC (and OAPEC) suddenly had far greater power over oil supply and prices, and member states were also starting to nationalize their oil sectors.[37] The international oil companies (and importing states) had little choice but to go along with this. Some of the Arab oil exporters had tried to use oil supply as a "weapon" in 1967, during the Arab-Israeli Six Day War of that year, to deter western governments from supporting Israel, but the states were lukewarm about the embargo and, at that time, lacked the strength and solidarity needed for an embargo to work. It was a marked contrast to what happened as a result of the 1973 war.

The 1973 oil embargo was the product of the 1973 Arab-Israeli war. The war began when Egypt and Syria attacked Israel on 6 October, hoping to reverse the Arab losses of the 1967 war. The Arab militaries initially made strong gains, but once Israel fully mobilized its forces, it began pushing its enemies back, albeit it with large losses of equipment and ammunition. On 9 October, the Nixon administration agreed to resupply Israel to replace material losses, and likely provided important intelligence support as well. On 19 October, angered by US support for Israel, OPEC placed an oil export embargo on the US, with OAPEC also embargoing other states seen as supportive of Israel, including Canada, the Netherlands, Britain and Japan. Adding to this were production cuts, which given the tight supply at the time added upward pressure to prices. Although the war ended with a UN-brokered ceasefire soon after, on 25 October, the embargo remained until March 1974. By then, the posted oil price had roughly quadrupled, from $2.90/bbl in the middle of 1973, to $5.12 in mid-October 1973, to $11.65 at the end of 1973.[38]

Figure 2.3 Average annual oil prices, 1945–2016 (US$/bbl)

Source: BP Statistical Review of World Energy 2017.

Just how dramatic this was, compared to the stable, low prices of previous decades, is evident in Figure 2.3. The economic impacts on the United States and many other western economies were severe, because of the "stagflationary" effects of a sharp rise in oil prices.[39] Since oil is both a final product and an input into production, an increase in its price has an inflationary impact, pushing up not just gasoline prices, but the price of any goods and services that are reliant upon oil (transport, some agriculture/foods, products with plastics or certain chemicals, and the like). At the same time, unemployment rises because higher oil prices weaken the economy, as consumers divert spending to cover the higher costs of fuels and oil-reliant products. The effect was more varied across other western economies, however, due to the differing policy positions that they took towards Israel and the 1973 war; indeed, the diplomatic divisions that the embargo caused among oil-importing countries was another notable impact of it.

Table 2.2 Gulf states' petroleum revenues ($ millions), 1970–83

Country	1970	1974	1977	1980	1983
Bahrain	35	169.8	226.5	253.6	NA
Kuwait	895	4,765	8,819	17,246	9,900
Qatar	122.4	1,979	1,975	5,587	3,000
Saudi Arabia	1,200	31,163	41,114	102,372	46,100
UAE	233	6,306	9,237	19,456	12,800

Source: al-Naqeeb, *Society and State in the Gulf and Arab Peninsula*, 81 (Table 5.4).

Concurrently, the higher prices created a windfall for oil exporters. The quadrupling of oil prices in 1973–4, and the approximate doubling of that again in 1979–80, when the 1978–9 Iranian revolution and the start of the 1980–88 Iran–Iraq War reduced supply and added new uncertainty to oil security, pushed the oil price to a record level in 1980 of $36.83 per barrel ($107.27 in 2016 dollars) – a price that would not be seen again,

THE ECONOMY OF THE GULF STATES

in inflation-adjusted terms, until 2008. Table 2.2 shows the oil revenues received by the Gulf oil exporters, which increased by even larger multiples. This was the result not just of the higher per barrel price, but of higher output as well: the largest producers – Saudi Arabia, Iran, Iraq, and the UAE – all increased their oil output greatly over the 1970s. Many also gained a far larger share of the barrel price since, by 1980, they had nationalized their oil industries and often invested in new midstream or downstream activities too.

The effects of this influx of wealth were both positive and negative, and occurred rapidly across the three main categories of rentier state expenditure: capital outlays, public transfers and public consumption.[40] Among the positive or mostly positive impacts was a massive expansion in state spending on new infrastructure and other development projects. Awash with enormous funds, the main oil exporters of the Middle East (the Gulf states, plus Iraq, Libya and Algeria) in the latter half of the 1970s "allocated nearly $275 billion to domestic investments, more than four times that of all the other Arab states combined", and by 1980 held "a roughly equivalent sum in net foreign assets".[41] Saudi Arabia, by virtue of its size and massive oil income, dominated this spending and investing, but all the main oil states contributed to it. State spending focused on the expansion of socioeconomic infrastructure, roads and other transport systems, major assets such as hospitals and schools, and new investment in public works and utilities. There is no denying that this spending developed the Gulf economies: most economic and socioeconomic conditions in the Gulf states increased strongly in the 1970s and 1980s.

Yet the oil boom was not universally positive in its impacts. A great deal of rent money was lost to corruption and inefficiency, and of course the rentier structure of these political economies was solidified by such expenditure. Not only are public works one of the ways in which rents find their way to society, but more specifically, they boost the wealth of the private sector through government contracts, yet also make these businesses more reliant on the state for long-term survival and growth. Such spending also increases the public sector payroll, across both the bureaucracy and state-owned firms, thus transferring rents to the public through wages. The rise in consumer spending and public consumption in this period spurred large rises in imports, often stretching facilities such as ports, transport networks, and retail systems to their limits and necessitating new spending on those, too.

The oil boom also deepened the Gulf's rentier structure. As rents increased and government services became more extensive and better quality, the rentier "bargain" between state and society expanded. A greater range of rent transfers were introduced, and societies, generally speaking, embraced the deal, such that little or no taxation and extensive, high quality state services soon became seen by societies as an entitlement. In most cases the indigenous private sector, rather than contributing to non-oil economic growth, ended up as compradors to the state, coopted by the opulent contracts that states were awarding for construction, infrastructure development, and new state services.[42] Furthermore, ostensibly in the course of diversifying their economies, Gulf states began investing in new state-owned firms, which strengthened their state capitalism structures. Many of the larger state-owned firms were established at this time, including many in downstream oil and gas (such as in petrochemicals). Given state fears of becoming over-reliant on oil, however, they also invested in other sectors of the economy. In Saudi Arabia, economic diversification is mentioned as early as in their first five-year plan, which ran 1970–75, although the second and later plans give it more attention.[43] In Bahrain, where oil reserves were more modest, a plan to diversify, as part of a strategy to become a regional economic and commercial hub, dates to the mid-1970s, when the outbreak of civil war in Lebanon in 1975 saw Bahrain try to succeed Beirut as the region's banking, tourism, transport and business services hub.

Yet such diversification strategies had very limited success. The oil boom demonstrated the risks of rapid influxes of wealth, and later the problem that rentier arrangements are extremely difficult to reverse. The oil boom led to a sharp increase in the numbers of foreign workers in the Gulf (see Table 2.3), including a remarkable explosion in the number of expatriates in Saudi Arabia and the UAE. This hunger for foreign workers attracted unskilled and semi-skilled workers looking for better wages than they could otherwise obtain and willing to do dangerous or dirty work in construction, industry and services. It also included skilled workers and professionals, who were invited to fill gaps in the labour market. Typically, however, skilled workers did not (or for various reasons, could not) pass on their skills to citizens of the oil economies, despite this usually being a justification for the importation of such skilled and expensive labour. Most often, citizens mostly sought out government positions, which offered better conditions and more prestige than most private sector roles, while foreign workers dominated in the private sector. There was little structural incentive for the Gulf's citizens to seek out employment in the private sector, nor to be innovative or entrepreneurial, even if a few did establish businesses. Generally, however, oil dampened the private sector's stomach for risk and made it more reliant upon the state for business opportunities – something that, in the long run, is not good for economic development or for economic diversification.

Table 2.3 Foreign workers in the Gulf: expatriates as percentage of total population, 1970–90

Country	1970	1975	1980	1985	1990	1995	2000
Bahrain	17.3	22.1	29.8	33.1	35.1	37.5	37.8
Kuwait	62.3	65.7	69.6	71.1	72.4	58.7	62.2
Oman	5.4	8.2	15.2	21.4	24.5	26.3	24.8
Qatar	61.4	69.6	72.2	78.2	79.1	77.2	76.0
Saudi Arabia	6.2	12.8	20.0	26.4	29.6	24.7	23.9
UAE	29.3	58.9	70.8	71.5	71.2	70.5	70.4

Source: Data from Shamsi, "Evaluation of Labor Immigration Policies in the GCC: Lessons for the Future", cited in United Nations, *International Migration and Development in the ESCWA Region*, 24 (Table 3).

Oil had a powerful set of other effects on Gulf economies, many of them negative ones often referred to as "the oil curse". While the oil curse is a contested concept, the Gulf of the latter 1970s and 1980s showed some of its features, including high inflation, a level of prosperity out of line with the productive capacity of the economy, and, given the high wages that oil encourages, a rise in imports and decline in total factor productivity.[44] Also part of the "oil curse" according to many accounts, the oil boom led the region to spend much more on defence and to begin importing far greater volumes of military equipment. While such spending was perhaps less of a luxury after the price rises of the 1970s, such spending was nonetheless ineffective. In the absence of any (sub)regional multilateral security architecture, such as a security bloc that comprises all of the states in the region, arms purchases prompted other regional actors to follow suit, and there was nothing to stop this cycle evolving into an arms race. Over the 1970s, an arms race is exactly what happened, as the Shah's Iran, Saudi Arabia, and Iraq struggled for dominance. The Middle East was, by the 1980s, the most militarized region in the world, with the oil economies accounting for the large majority of total spending and arms imports.[45] At the time, the Shah aspired for Iran to become a global power, and increased his military spending accordingly, while Saudi Arabia and Iraq, also awash with oil rents, sought to keep up with Iran. The smaller Gulf states invested in their armed forces even though they lacked the ability to protect themselves from large regional powers. This remains a basic security feature of the Gulf to the present day. Some sources even blame this rise in spending *directly* for the conflicts that the region witnessed in the 1980s and 1990s.[46] Just as important was the boost in spending on internal security, in effect in enhancing regime security. The power and reach of internal security agencies and intelligence services increased along with oil prices, despite the economic inefficiency of such spending.

The two large oil price rises, in 1973–4 and 1979–80, generated tremendous wealth for the Gulf, but the spending that it supported seemed predicated on the assumption that such prices would be permanent. In fact, the 1970s ushered in a new era of considerable volatility in oil prices.

The oil boom decade from 1973 ended with a sharp drop in prices in the early/mid-1980s, then a sustained period of low prices until the early 2000s, when a third oil boom began, followed by another collapse in prices in 2014. Put bluntly, "the Middle East's economic fortunes collapsed with the price of oil"[47] in the 1980s. Per capita GDP fell sharply, as shown in Figure 2.4, and the share of oil and other extractive industries, as a percentage of GDP, fell markedly. Not only did GDP fall in nominal value, therefore, but other areas of the economy had been weakened by the oil boom and could not step in to help offset the fall in oil prices.

Figure 2.4 Gulf GDP per capita, 1980–89 (current $)

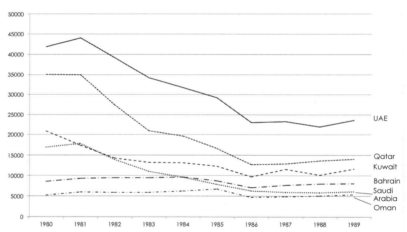

Source: Author's calculations, using data from *World Bank Open Data*, https://data.worldbank.org/country (accessed 18 October 2018).

Given the centrality of rents to state income, the capacity of states to continue to provide for society – to maintain the rentier "bargain" – was suddenly in peril. When faced with the prospect of reform in exchange for less state largesse, or borrowing to sustain rentier commitments, the Gulf states chose the latter. Those with smaller populations and larger oil production rates faced less of a problem, but all these states sought to reduce state expenditure at this time, cancelling or delaying new projects, reducing foreign worker numbers where possible, and as necessary, borrowing to sustain most existing commitments.[48] Where they investigated or even introduced reform, this was *economic*, not political, reform, with a focus on economic diversification, the development of citizens' skills, improving the investment climate, and integrating further along the energy sector, especially downstream.[49] Such reform was more easily discussed than implemented, however, and as discussed later, many of these same goals reappeared in the 1990s and again in the 2010s when economic diversification and reform were again needed. In the 1980s, diversification and industrialization were constrained by the modest returns on capital in non-oil sectors, the low cost of competing imports, and by problems in the supply and quality of local labour.

This period coincided with a more challenging political and security environment in the region, which had further economic impacts as well. One was the changing role of Iran, perceived by the Gulf monarchies as a more activist and threatening one. The 1978–79 Iranian revolution, while fundamentally an anti-Shah uprising at first, saw Iran's clerics gain control out of the revolutionary chaos. The leading clerical figure, Ayatollah Ruhollah Khomeini, was able to implement his vision of an Islamic system, a cleric-controlled, quasi-theocratic political system, with populist economic policies. The new Iranian regime's revolutionary rhetoric, the creation of potentially threatening institutions such as the Revolutionary Guards, and a new foreign policy orientation all made the Arab Gulf ruler fearful. While Iran had been a major military and economic power before the revolution, it was now more radical, with new strategic, sectarian, and economic implications, even though the revolution had a negative impact on Iran's economy as populist and statist economic policies were introduced, often opaquely and chaotically.[50]

Economic confidence and stability were further undermined by the brutal eight-year war between Iran and Iraq from 1980 to 1988. The war's origins lay in, among other things, a combination of regional power rivalry, ethno-nationalist and sectarian tensions, and territorial disputes (especially along the Shatt al-Arab waterway, which formed part of their shared border).[51] The conflict was the longest conventional war of the twentieth century, costing around 680,000 lives, wounding a further 1.8 million, and with a financial toll of around $1.1 trillion (in 1988 dollars).[52] Yet there was no clear victor.

The war affected the Arab Gulf monarchies in a number of ways.[53] An outright victory would have strengthened the regional influence of the winner, undermining Saudi Arabia's claim to subregional power status. It therefore perhaps suited the non-combatant Gulf states to have the war drag on as it did, although there were risks attached to this, including that the conflict might spill into other parts of the region. Moreover, the supply of oil to international markets was made vulnerable by the conflict, and indeed was disrupted at times. The Gulf monarchies therefore varied, both between themselves and over time, in their positions on the conflict.

By the late 1980s, the perspectives of both elites and the broader populations in the Arab Gulf monarchies had markedly changed from what had been common in the 1970s. The future of the Gulf and of its economies was more uncertain. They had not used oil wealth very wisely in the first two booms, with large sums lost to inefficiencies, corruption, poor investments and credit bubbles, or had seeped out as imports, often of unnecessary goods, or as repatriated funds sent home by foreign workers.[54] While they were superficially far wealthier than they had been less than two decades earlier, the Gulf states had not used their oil wealth to build diverse, productive economies beyond oil. The 1990s would prove to be just as uncertain and difficult as the 1980s.

FROM THE GULF WAR TO THE IRAQ WAR, 1990–2003

The early 1990s were a period of transformation globally, including in the Middle East. Regionally, the decade began on a troubling note, when on 2 August 1990 Iraq invaded Kuwait. Outlining a range of grievances and implementing a long-standing Iraqi claim to sovereignty over its small neighbour, Iraq immediately annexed Kuwait and declared it the nineteenth province of Iraq. This was the first and, to date, only case in the

Arab world of one sovereign state invading another with the intent of permanently incorporating it into their territory. With the Soviet Union in the process of collapse, Cold War dynamics did not dictate international reaction to the crisis, as Iraqi President Saddam Hussein may have assumed. Instead, the United States was able to gather together an international coalition, pass United Nations (UN) Security Council resolutions imposing sanctions on Iraq and demanding that it withdraw unconditionally. When diplomatic efforts and sanctions failed, the coalition launched a military campaign in early 1991 to forcibly evict Iraqi forces from Kuwait, authorized in November 1990 by UN Security Council Resolution 678. The US-led coalition began an air campaign on 17 January 1991, followed by a brief ground conflict over 24–28 February. Iraq crumbled quickly, its mostly-conscript military outmanoeuvred and easily defeated by superior coalition forces. A formal ceasefire was signed on 3 March, but the UN sanctions remained in place, as did Saddam and his inner elite.

The 1990–91 Gulf War had important impacts on the Gulf states, including from the paradoxical nature of the war. On the one hand, it was one of the quickest and most unevenly-matched military conflicts in modern history, and so was seen in the United States, at least initially, as a resounding military success, although in fact the outcome of the war was far less clear. The decision to leave Saddam in power was a complex and contested one,[55] but his survival allowed him to continue to play a role in the Gulf throughout the 1990s and until the 2003 Iraq War, which finally removed him. Leaving Saddam and sanctions in place meant that the strategic and economic outcomes of the war remained opaque. It kept Iraq's economy weak, which gave greater relative influence in the Gulf to Saudi Arabia, but also to Iran, while also allowing Saddam to remain a hindrance to regional stability and a persistent (if greatly diminished) regional security threat. The US and the Gulf's leaders handled Saddam's survival poorly, seeking to constrain his ability to act and threaten the neighbourhood, while also frustrating Iran but not slowing its regional ambitions. Nothing was done to create better security architecture in the Gulf.[56]

The Iraqi invasion of Kuwait was a reminder to the leaderships of the small Gulf states that, no matter their wealth or allocative capacity, their ability to defend their countries against threats from major regional powers was limited, even after all their military spending and promises of security for their populations. Iraq's quick conquest of Kuwait highlighted this limitation in the rentier arrangement. This prompted the Gulf states to move closer to the United States and, in particular, to seek a strategic relationship with the US that would underwrite their security. This had been a core element of the US–Saudi relationship since 1945, but the on-going US military presence in the Gulf after 1991 was arguably something supported, and even discreetly sought, by Gulf regimes. It also explains why security structures such as the Gulf Cooperation Council (GCC) were not significantly enhanced at the time: for the small states, Saudi dominance of the GCC was unappealing, while the US was more capable of protecting these states. A strong US role undermined the need and urgency to augment subregional security structures.[57] Yet this US presence was a mixed blessing, perhaps offering greater protection for Gulf regimes, but also reminding citizens of their leaders' inability to guarantee security. It also created anger and new opposition in some quarters, including from groups such as al-Qaʿeda, which soon became a security threat to Gulf regimes.

At the same time, the 1990s were the start of a new era of globalization and economic development, mostly due to the global economic and technological transformations that were unfolding. The process of globalization can be conceptually difficult to pin down, but usually is treated as a process of "internationalization", increasing "interdependence and exchanges across borders" and normally having a liberalizing effect that reduces the reach or control of states.[58] It presented Gulf leaders with the urgent decision of how to respond. This is often treated as a binary decision – to either accept globalization or to reject it – but in fact the Gulf rulers, quite deftly, came around to something in between, accepting the technological and some economic aspects of it, while doing so on their own terms, seeking to limit its social, cultural and above all political impacts. The economic case for globalization was perhaps the simplest and easiest to make; after all, the Gulf's leaders had been trying for some time to diversify their economies, and globalization promised to increase trade and investment, open new markets, and reduce transaction costs.[59] Other impacts of globalization were more concerning to rulers, if not their subjects, especially deterritorialization, new media, and the spread of cultural ideas and practices. Their fears were that this would usher in challenges to their legitimacy and new demands for political reform. There were also concerns, whether from religious elites or political ones, that Islam, Arab culture, and other features at the core of local identity would be undermined by globalization.

While the Gulf states did face some new pressures in the 1990s, these were not primarily from globalization. In fact, an argument can be made that globalization has, on balance, been positive for both the elites of the Gulf and for broader populations. Economically, the Gulf oil economies were already linking more deeply to international trade and finance as early as the 1970s oil boom,[60] and so were well-placed to open their economies, carefully and selectively, in the 1990s. Oil had improved state capacity, allowing rulers to dictate trade and investment terms, while the more industrialized, state-led, and poorer economies in the Arab world had the more difficult task of liberalizing their economies without provoking a popular backlash.[61] The selective and specific ways in which the Gulf states opened their economies at the time highlight this contrast. The Gulf states promoted new investment and trade, and encouraged the private sector into certain parts of the economy. They simplified government processes, made business activity easier, improved access to finance and established free trade and investment zones. However the Gulf states also eschewed the more dramatic neoliberal economic reforms seen in Egypt, Tunisia, and elsewhere, and instead kept the state in control of the higher reaches of the economy. While liberalization elsewhere widened wealth and income gaps within society, and weakened the control of the state, in the Gulf this was not the case. Initiatives such as exchange rate liberalization, substantial labour market reforms, finance sector liberalization, and extensive privatizations were largely absent.

The sustained low oil prices of the 1990s meant that attention to the economy was nonetheless important, and all six of the Arab Gulf monarchies undertook economic initiatives at this time, driven by the budgetary pressures they faced, as well as continuing to pursue economic diversification. They all made foreign direct investment into their economies easier, if in different ways, seeking to attract foreign investors while keeping key sectors off-limits, such as the energy sector and typically telecommunications, defence, aviation and security. Other less strategic or sensitive sectors such as agribusiness, retail, education and tourism, however, were opened to foreign or domestic investors, sometimes very broadly. Investment laws, processes, and approval procedures were simplified, and sometimes taxes reduced too, as in Kuwait, Oman, Qatar and Saudi Arabia. This was also a period of stock market development and (limited) liberalization.

Among other reforms were attempts to reduce state expenditure. These were simple enough if they required simply shelving or delaying projects, but were more politically sensitive if they involved cuts to public sector staffing or conditions, or crackdowns on inefficiencies or underperformance, which occurred in a few cases.[62] A slower but, in the longer-term, important reform was the creation of sovereign wealth funds (SWFs). These are state-owned funds in which oil income is invested, to be used for compensating future generations, paying for future development initiatives, and to help offset fluctuations in rent income.[63] While a few of these funds date back several decades, most were created in the 1990s and 2000s. Finally, the 1990s in particular were a time when, in the pursuit of new trade and investment, the Gulf states looked to join the World Trade Organization (WTO), the main multilateral body that determines the rules and regulations of international trade. Bahrain and Kuwait acceded in 1995, the UAE and Qatar in 1996, and Oman in 2000. Saudi Arabia announced its intention to accede in the late 1990s, and did so in 2005. This not only marked their growing trade ambitions, but also brought them more closely into the international trade and investment system, including in new and emerging areas such as the trade in services and copyright protection.[64]

While notable, these reforms were not comprehensive. Over the 1990s and 2000s, all six GCC states promised labour market reforms and reforms to state-owned firms, but only very limited changes were actually implemented. Both remained too politically sensitive. Labour market reforms, if they affected citizens' employment prospects or conditions, had the potential to directly impact the rentier bargain. Privatizations, if extensive, would have reduced the state's non-oil assets and eroded its state capitalist structure. In fact, "new" state capitalism accelerated in the early 2000s, with ambitious development, diversification, and commercially-driven "branding" strategies implemented in Dubai, Qatar, Abu Dhabi, and to a lesser extent other economies.

Thus the 1990s marked the beginning of a substantive and important shift in the political economies of the Gulf. The strategy essentially was, and remains, three-pronged: a transformation from simpler rentier bargains to a "late-stage" form of rentierism;[65] the development and enhancement of the "new" state capitalism that was emerging at the time; and the start of national "branding" efforts, which in turn were linked to economic statecraft and to commercially-driven foreign and security policies. Late rentierism is, in effect, a more nuanced form of the simpler, earlier rentier dynamic. The cooptive bargain between state and society remains fundamentally in place, but is refined, with the state responding to societal views (while remaining undemocratic), opening selectively to globalization and investment, becoming more sophisticated in its commercial and development policies, and planning towards a post-oil future. Meanwhile "new", or entrepreneurial, state capitalism is also a feature of these systems and of late rentierism, as already discussed, and the two are mutually reinforcing. New state capitalism sees the state retain its disproportionate control over the means of production and continue to play a strong regulatory role, but doing so not for the industrialization, import-substitution, and class-driven political goals typical of the earlier state capitalism in the Arab republics, such as Egypt, Syria, Iraq and Algeria, but rather as a means of supporting selective globalization, protecting the economic sovereignty of the state, to buy the support of elites, and to counter some of the negative features of rentierism while preparing for life after oil. Finally, the 1990s and 2000s saw the expansion of economic statecraft strategies, in which states sought to manage their external relationships, and in turn to develop their economies and gain further support from society, by making economic goals central to their foreign relations, security strategies and statecraft. They have used aid programmes, public relations spending and national "branding" strategies to raise international awareness of their countries among potential investors, traders and tourists. These efforts were largely funded by rents, but as with new state capitalism and other development strategies, sought to shift economies on to more solid non-energy bases, while also enhancing the security of the country and the regime.

A critic might charge that, given all this, the Gulf political economies changed less profoundly than might be assumed. Indeed, is late rentierism not just a more nuanced form of rentierism? Is new state capitalism just a more conservative version of old state capitalism? This is the case only at a superficial level of investigation, and such arguments mask tremendous changes that have taken place. Late rentierism is a much more profound rearrangement of state–society relations than simply cosmetic alterations to previous arrangements. By the 1990s, population growth, the demands of younger generations and the power of online communications made simple rentier tactics outdated. The Gulf rulers had to undertake reform, but wanted to avoid ceding much political or economic power to society. The combination of these three approaches, and the ways in which all three support, benefit, and reinforce each other, mark the attempt to do just that.

This shift continued into the new millennium. The Gulf was impacted by two major events in the early 2000s: the 11 September 2001 terrorist attacks in the United States and the associated war on terrorism, and then the 2003 Iraq War. The September 11 attacks created a deep rift in US–Saudi relations.[66] Fifteen of the 19 hijackers that day were Saudis, and two more Emiratis. This alone created anger in the US towards Saudi Arabia. Saudi Arabia's strict and austere Wahhabi form of Sunni Islam added to the suspicion that Saudi sympathies tended towards Islamic radicalism, as did a history of individuals in Saudi Arabia providing funds to al-Qaeda and other extremists. Meanwhile, the US war on terrorism was disruptive, creating new security issues and economic uncertainty for the Gulf states.[67]

For the small Gulf states, the war on terrorism offered the chance to deepen and consolidate relations with the US. This suited both their security goals of closer ties to the US, and linked to the international economic and branding strategies of Qatar and the UAE in particular. The US–Saudi relationship was largely repaired over the couple of years following the attacks. The military-economic symbiosis between the two was strong, and Saudi Arabia was also targeted by extremists at this time, letting it claim common cause with Washington. The relationship was ultimately one based on mutual convenience, not on deeper bases such as shared values or identity, but the forces drawing them together were strong.

The region was also impacted by the 2003 Iraq War. Saddam's survival after his 1991 military defeat was not to the liking of Gulf rulers, but popular opinion opposed a second US-led war against Iraq. The United States felt emboldened to go to war after the September 11 attacks, even though Iraq played no role in them. The war was argued on the claim that Iraq possessed weapons of mass destruction, found after the war to be a faulty claim, when the justification changed to a mix of democratization, regional stabilization, and anti-terrorism. The US and a small number of key allies proceeded with the war, primarily fought from 20 March to 9 April 2003 (but technically until 1 May). As in 1991, in a military sense the war was a straightforward victory for the US. Unlike the first war, however, the victors removed Saddam from power and then subsequently occupied Iraq. The removal of Saddam and various errors made during and after the war destabilized Iraq and created new problems, not just in Iraq but in the sub-region. For the GCC states, the war had been an unwanted risk to regional stability and a source of popular anger. Kuwait and Qatar openly supported it, hosting US forces and allowing the US to launch operations from their territory. The others attempted more of a balancing act, trying to provide some discreet assistance to the US while not openly supporting the war.

THE THIRD OIL BOOM, 2004–14

Challenging as September 11 and the 2003 Iraq War were for the Gulf's leaderships, it came at a time when a third oil boom was about to commence. This third oil boom provided an enormous injection of wealth into the subregion, but in contrast with the earlier booms, this time much more care was taken to avoid some of the mistakes made previously. As this period is the focus of this book, only a broad sketch is provided here.

The exact sources of the third oil boom and their relative importance remain a matter of debate. As Yergin has noted, they lie in both supply and demand.[68] OPEC's pricing strategy shifted after 2000, from protecting a minimum price to targeting a higher price range, which may have played some role. OPEC then agreed production cuts in 2004 that pushed up prices significantly. At the time, demand for oil was growing, and the economies demanding it were diversifying. The traditional industrialized economies became less important customers, and new markets, especially China, emerged.[69] At the same time, there was an underlying shortage of supply. In many developed economies, there were problems with the supply chain, especially in shipping, refining, and distribution, which had been cut back during the 1990s when prices were low. Investment in new wells and infrastructure had also been cut back in the exporting states.

The oil boom was also a product of speculation and concerns about long-term supply. The growth of futures and options as investment tools, and their speculative short-term trading, amplified price movements. When the oil price peaked at $147.27 in July 2008, even producer states became worried, fearing that it could spark an international recession. This prompted the Saudis to criticize speculators and increase production in mid-2008.[70] Prices soon fell, due to the unfolding global economic crisis rather than the additional Saudi production. By the end of 2008, the oil price had plummeted below $45 per barrel; its lowest point that year, on 23 December, was a mere $30.28. Beyond speculators, concern about the long-term supply of oil had also pushed up the price, especially concerns about "peak oil". This concept argues that, since oil is a finite resource, if extraction rates peak without demand then fall, prices will be pushed extremely high by the shortfall of supply.[71] The emergence of viable unconventional oil extraction soon pushed any peak oil concerns into the distant future, but in the mid-2000s, things looked less certain.

The third oil boom's impacts were mixed. There were positive elements to it, including the injection of enormous funds into the region, primarily the Gulf, spurring new infrastructure development and the retirement of debt from the era of low oil prices. After the waste of previous oil booms, this time Gulf leaders had learned to save some of the wealth for the future. The rate of oil revenue that was saved more than doubled during the boom (although revenues more than tripled).[72] The Gulf states became important global investors at the time, while attracting new inward foreign investment too. It seemed that the region was becoming more globally integrated and more economically sophisticated. Yet the boom brought downsides and risks as well. Some were a repeat of the past, such as negative macroeconomic impacts from large, sudden injections of wealth. With fixed exchange rates, inflation soared, reaching double-digit rates in Kuwait, Oman, Qatar and the UAE in 2008. The boom also let states pay less attention to long-term goals such as economic diversification and reductions in the size of expatriate labour forces. The Gulf economies were not immune from the oil curse, or at least some elements of it.

PATHS TAKEN AND NOT TAKEN

Any report card on the Gulf governments' management of their economies over the past half century must be mixed in its assessment. By almost any measure, the Gulf states became more mature and long term in their approach to economic and socioeconomic policy. They increased their economies' international engagement, especially since the 1990s, formulated more sophisticated and ambitious development strategies, and created SWFs or other long-term investments. At the same time, their overall reliance on oil and gas did not substantially change. By most measures they were just as reliant on oil and gas in the 2010s as they were in the 1970s, allowing for price fluctuations. Therefore, measures of rent reliance, such as public sector employees as a share of the economically-active adult population, have improved only slightly from the 1980s to the 2010s.[73] The public–private balance in these economies has not altered much, especially once population rises are taken into account. Spending remains high, with the oil price required to balance state budgets increasing markedly during the third oil boom, its 2000–11 average having more than doubled by 2014.[74]

All the GCC states now speak about wanting to diversify their economies, and have strategies in place that are ambitiously pursuing this goal. It will be a challenge to achieve. Dubai provides one of the few cases of successful diversification, having become since the mid-1980s a regional commercial and transport hub, a banking and investment centre, and a successful transhipment port, achieved based on some generic features, such as investment-friendliness and rapid state decision-making, and more specific ones, especially its "first-mover advantage".[75] However it is doubtful whether this sort of success can be replicated in other Gulf cities. This leaves the question of what alternative options the Gulf states have in pursuit of development. History has set the subregion on specific political and economic paths. They are now well-off, even very wealthy, and yet are confronting important and potentially serious future development challenges. The chapters that follow examine these political economies from various angles, covering their economic structures, performance, and how political and economic dynamics impact and shape each other today. These factors will all play a part in determining the future of the Gulf.

3

Measuring the Gulf economies

The Arab Gulf economies share broad features and characteristics, but each have some unique features, too. They are all heavily reliant upon oil or gas revenue, or both, and increasingly on downstream and associated activity as well. They all have broadly similar positive and negative attributes that stem from this reliance on hydrocarbons. They all are seeking to diversify their economies, to move away from being so vulnerable to energy price shocks and to expand other economic sectors where a greater range of employment opportunities and diverse workforce skills are required – and they are all struggling, in broadly similar ways, to make progress in this regard. Yet individual features vary economy by economy. The importance of rents is not the same across all six. While they are all relatively affluent, falling near the top on lists of the Middle East's GDP per capita or on measures of socioeconomic development, the sizes of these economies vary enormously. So too does the income per capita: the Gulf economies are a mix of upper-middle- and high-income economies. Beyond energy, they have built competitive businesses in some of the same sectors, but most have also developed some unique commercial strengths. Finally, the trading and commercial history of the Gulf's ports and cities differ, which has created different sized commercial classes in the region, formed contrasting business–government relationships across the region, and even influenced their political and social structures.

AN OVERVIEW OF THE SIX GCC ECONOMIES

All six Gulf states are relatively well-developed, middle-upper and upper-income economies. While they have been important to the global economy since the mid-twentieth century, due to their oil exports, in the past two decades or so they have more actively sought to integrate more deeply into it. Important as they are, the Gulf states' economies constitute only a small share of the world economy. In 2015, the total GDP of the six GCC states added up to just under $1,392 billion, or less than 1.9 per cent of the global total of $74.5 trillion.[1] Arguably, had 2015 not been a period of such low energy prices, the figure would have been higher, but only a little. While small and dominated by energy exports, the Gulf economies are increasingly well-integrated into the international trade and economic system. As an example of their extensive links to the world economy, in 2015, the value of their trade as a percentage of their GDP varied from a low of 72.1 per cent in Saudi Arabia to a high of 196.4 per cent in the UAE; for all but Saudi Arabia, the figure was close to or over 100 per cent. These figures are significant because the world average was far lower, at 58 per cent.

Table 3.1 shows the variations and fluctuations in GDP across all six of the Arab Gulf states for the years 1975, 1985, 1995, 2005 and 2015. It shows the development of these economies, while the dates also coincide with various international dynamics: 1975 was during the first oil boom; 1985 and 1995 were during a sustained period of low oil prices, but with greater openness and new investment reflected in the 1995 figures; while the boom of the 2000s is evident in the 2005 figures but also, to some extent, in the 2015 ones. These figures are a reminder, however, of how tightly linked these economies are to oil and gas prices, with any sharp jump or drop in prices reflected, within a year or so, in GDP figures. The per capita GDP figures are also a reminder of the impact of rapid population growth rates: even when nominal GDP figures across a particular ten-year period evidence solid growth, this is far less impressive on a per person basis when population growth rates are high. Saudi Arabia's GDP per capita figures demonstrate this, showing how lower oil prices from the

Table 3.1 Gulf states' GDP performance and indicators, 1975–2015

Country	1975			1985			1995			2005			2015		
	GDP*	GDP growth†	GDP per capita‡	GDP*	GDP growth†	GDP per capita‡	GDP*	GDP growth†	GDP per capita‡	GDP*	GDP growth†	GDP per capita‡	GDP*	GDP growth†	GDP per capita‡
Bahrain	N/A	N/A	N/A	7,099.4	-4.8	17,291	12,350.8	3.9	21,910	19,620.4	6.8	22,066	30,779.2	2.9	22,436
Kuwait	12,024.1	-8.0	11,732	21,442.6	-4.3	12,330	27,191.7	4.9	16,882	80,797.9	10.1	35,490	114041.2	1.8	28,975
Oman	8,816.5	24.4	9,996	23,184.9	14.0	15,473	35,920.4	5.0	16,296	44,278.5	2.5	17,632	71,694.8	5.7	17,071
Qatar	2,512.8	4.2	15,283	6,153.3	-8.2	16,582	8,137.9	10.4	15,849	44,530.5	7.5	51,488	164641.5	3.6	66,347
Saudi Arabia	251,539	-8.9	33,860	207,527	-9.8	15,735	349,402	0.2	18,649	349,402	0.2	18,745	461,601	5.6	19,309
UAE	56,806.7	16.5	102,479	110,504	-3.6	79,439	151,381	6.7	61,818	257,366	4.9	56,199	367,632	3.8	40,160

* In constant 2010 $ millions, rounded to one decimal place (i.e. to the nearest half-million 2010 dollars); figures for Kuwait and Qatar are in current $.

† Percentage (%) rounded to one decimal place; Qatar figures for 1975, 1985 and 1995, and the UAE for 1975, are the author's calculations.

‡ In constant 2010 $, rounded to the dollar; figures for Kuwait and Qatar are in current $.

Source: Based on data from the World Bank's *World Development Indicators* database: https://data.worldbank.org/country (accessed 26 October 2017).

Table 3.2 Gulf states' basic socioeconomic indicators, 2016 or latest

Country	GDP/ capita ($)[a]	Oil reserves (bn bbls)	Size (km²)	Total population (million)[b]	Citizen population (million)[c]	Life expectancy	Education spending (% GDP)	Health spending (% GDP)	HDI rank	Freedom House ranking[d]	Ease of Business ranking[e]
Bahrain	50,700	minimal	760	1.4	0.73	79.0	2.6	5.0	47	12	63
Kuwait	71,900	101.5	17,818	4.4	1.50	78.2	4.0[f]	3.0	51	36	102
Oman	46,100	5.4	309,500	3.2	1.92	75.7	5.0	3.6	52	25	66
Qatar	125,100	25.2	11,586	2.3	0.32	78.9	3.5	2.2	33	26	83
Saudi Arabia	55,300	266.5	2,149,690	28.6	18.0	75.5	5.1	4.7	38	10	94
UAE	68,100	97.8	83,600	9.2	1.45	77.7	2.0[f]	3.6	42	20	26

[a] Purchasing power parity (PPP) figure for 2016.; [b] Population figures are typically not published or are contestable, and should be treated with caution; [c] Author's estimates; [d] 2017 aggregate score; on the aggregate score, 0 is the least free and 100 the most free; [e] From 0 (easiest, or most business-friendly) to 190 (hardest, or most business-unfriendly); [f] Author's estimate.

Source: Derived from numerous sources including; data available from the *BP Statistical Review of World Energy 2017*; Central Intelligence Agency; *CIA World Factbook*, various country profiles; Freedom House, *Freedom in the World 2017* report and data, https://freedomhouse.org/report/fiw-2017-table-country-scores (accessed 10 January 2018); data from the World Bank's *World Development Indicators* database, https://data.worldbank.org/country (accessed 26 October 2017); and World Bank, Doing Business 2017, especially the "Country Tables". Author's estimates were made by comparing the data and methodology of two or more sources.

early 1980s to the early 2000s, and a near-doubling of its population over the same time, meant that its GDP per person peaked in the 1970s.

Physically, economically and demographically, Saudi Arabia is dominant among the six states. Its size has also given it a very diverse population, the result of its foundation as a modern state through Ibn Saud's conquests in the early part of the twentieth century, which incorporated various tribal areas, the more cosmopolitan Hijaz region, the Shia-dominated northeast, and other areas. It is not the most diverse country in terms of sect, however: Bahrain's Sunni monarchy rules over a population that is majority Shia, Kuwait's Shia are a very large minority, and Oman has both a Sunni and Ibadi tradition, modest though their differences often seem today.

Table 3.2 lays out some of the basic geographical, economic, and social indicators for the six Arab Gulf states, most of which highlight this Saudi dominance. A couple of important caveats are required. First, some of the figures on these states are unpublished and thus are estimates, or are likely to be inaccurate. Population figures are an example, for which Saudi Arabia publishes its total *resident* population; the proportions who are citizens and non-citizens needs to be extracted from this. Oil reserves are another example, with the Gulf states preferring to publish total reserve figures, with scant detail available on individual fields. These figures therefore need to be treated with caution, especially as they seem to have changed arbitrarily in the past. There are particular reasons for this issue with statistical detail: population is seen by states such as Saudi Arabia as a security concern, since Iran and Iraq have larger populations, and oil reserves are held tightly so that extraction costs, future production rates, and the timing of any peak in production cannot easily be determined by competitors and rivals.

Second, while Saudi Arabia dominates the Gulf in terms of size and total economic power, it is not the wealthiest economy per person. As shown in Table 3.1, that honour goes to Qatar, which had a GDP *per resident* of over $66,000 per annum in 2015, having approached some $90,000 per person when energy prices were high back in 2012 and 2013. Since only about one-eighth of Qatar's population are citizens, and the remainder are residents, the net wealth per citizen is dramatically higher than the per resident figure. Table 3.1 also shows that Saudi Arabia, while very well off in the 1970s, has subsequently become an upper-middle income country, with Qatar, the UAE, and Kuwait well ahead in GDP per person. This is a driver of its ambitious economic reform and development strategy, the Saudi *Vision 2030* strategy, more on which later. It must also be noted, however, that GDP and other such measures have been criticized as simplistic, showing almost nothing about the distribution of wealth and disparities or inequalities within an economy. These criticisms of GDP have particular strength in oil and gas economies, where GDP figures are often skewed by simple fluctuations in hydrocarbon prices, regardless of the progress or regression made in production, productivity and the utilization of capital stocks.[2]

Finally, these figures help little in assessing the potential for political stability or instability in any particular state. In fact, political risk finds its sources most often in dynamics that are not easily quantified, such as the degree of state legitimacy, the specifics of the state–society relationship, the social origins of the ruling family, the sectarian balance, and the popular perception of the state's performance. Arguably, Saudi Arabia faces greater security and stability challenges than do the smaller states with higher per capita wealth, with the exception of Bahrain, which faces considerable risk of instability given the 2011 protests, which drew on both sectarian grievances and a broad perception that King Hamad had failed to deliver promised political reforms.

Despite the above, there is also no denying that oil and gas wealth has brought tremendous benefits to people in the Gulf, including marked improvements in the basic socioeconomic indicators in all six states. Almost every such measure has shown consistent growth and improvement since the 1960s, whether in schooling, life expectancy, infant mortality rates, or any number of other measures, from the prevalence of certain diseases to higher education completion rates. Moreover, oil wealth has meant that the Gulf states have been able to outspend most of the less resource-rich economies, most of the time, both in absolute terms and even as a percentage of GDP.[3]

The Human Development Index (HDI) seeks to quantify socioeconomic development, and despite some flaws in its scope and methodology it provides a reasonable approximation of the general state and direction of human development in various countries. It provides a composite figure for each country that goes beyond simpler or more specific measures such as GDP, to conglomerate income, life expectancy, education, and other socioeconomic measures into the single figure. On the HDI measure the Gulf states show strong improvement as well, all of them rising, for the most part consistently, over the period from 1990 to 2015. In 2015, the Gulf states ranked at between 33rd and 52nd globally, out of 188 countries. The six Gulf monarchies take six of the top seven places on the HDI for the Middle East, with only Israel outperforming them (ranking 19th in the world in 2015 and again in 2016).

Table 3.3 Gulf states' Human Development Index (HDI), 1990–2015

Country	1990	1995	2000	2005	2010	2015	Global Rank (2015)
Bahrain	0.745	0.775	0.794	0.81	0.812	0.824	47
Kuwait	0.713	0.747	0.786	0.787	0.792	0.8	51
Oman	n.d.	n.d.	0.705	0.748	0.797	0.796	52
Qatar	0.754	0.783	0.809	0.835	0.827	0.856	33
Saudi Arabia	0.698	0.722	0.742	0.767	0.804	0.847	38
UAE	0.726	0.764	0.798	0.823	0.824	0.84	42

Source: United Nations Development Programme (UNDP), *Human Development Reports: Human Development Data (1990–2015)*: http://hdr.undp.org/en/data# (accessed 27 December 2017).

Like GDP, the HDI has also been criticized, including for providing data at a national level (below which development often varies) and for using flawed or weak data in its calculations. Yet a cursory glance at the physical environment of the Gulf, especially the infrastructure and the signs of wealth in its major cities and urban centres, suggests that such measures are broadly accurate. This does not stop major disruptive events from altering the course of a political economy in the future, much as the 1978–79 revolution disrupted and undermined Iran's, or the 1990 Iraqi invasion of Kuwait, and the subsequent 1991 Gulf War, brought Iraq's development to a grinding halt and then caused it to sharply regress. Such events are rare, however, and while there remains political uncertainty in the region, its economies are now all well-developed, and almost-certainly far better off than they would have been without oil. Still, the Gulf's economies are not as secure as the more mixed, diverse, and taxation-based ones of, say, Europe, North America and Japan. An examination of their sectoral profiles highlights the problems that stem from their continued reliance on hydrocarbons.

BASIC SECTORAL STRUCTURES

The centrality of oil and gas to the Gulf economies should be obvious from the previous two chapters, however some additional features are important to note. First, while oil is absolutely central to the GDP and state revenues of the six Gulf states, both the volume of their oil reserves and reserves per capita vary enormously. Table 1.1 in the Introduction showed the enormous variations in oil (and gas) reserves. Figure 3.1, below, shows the oil and gas reserves per capita, making the relative wealth across the subregion clearer. Saudi Arabia has by far the largest total reserves, but this is less impressive when per capita reserves are considered. Qatar's incredible wealth is evident in its gas reserves per capita. But in all six states, oil or gas matters. Even in Bahrain, where oil production is small and dwindling, Saudi oil shipments pass through and are refined there. Second, natural gas is also important to the Gulf, and increasingly so. Qatar in particular has developed its gas sector, as international demand for gas has grown in the twenty-first century. However (and again as Table 1.1 showed), gas reserves are far less evenly distributed across the Gulf than are those of oil. Within the GCC, Qatar has far and away the largest reserves – *over fifteen times* those of the UAE, which comes a distant second – due to the massive field it shares with Iran under the Gulf seabed; the Qataris refer to this as the North Dome, and Iranians as South Pars.[4] Iran's gas reserves are even larger than Qatar's, but its population is far greater (over 300 times larger), giving it less gas reserves per citizen than Qatar.

Figure 3.1   Gulf states' oil and gas reserves per citizen, 2016

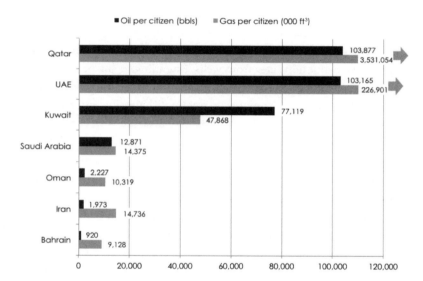

Source: Author's calculations and estimates, drawing on *BP Statistical Review of World Energy 2017*; population data from the Gulf Research Center, *Gulf Labour Markets, Migrations, and Population Programme*; and cross-checked with various media sources.

A final point on hydrocarbons is that the reserves figures are only esti-mates, and need to be treated with caution. Total reserves are the sum of estimates for the various oil fields in the country, with these usually being based on the 50 per cent probability of a defined amount of oil being extracted given a defined set of conditions in the field and sometimes externally. Total reserve figures are variable: since the scenario conditions include factors such as extraction costs, for example, reserves may fall if the price falls under the cost of production. The degree of confidence attached to particular fields may vary too. Moreover, the oil reserve figures are quite malleable, and are widely assumed to include "political" reserves; that is, that reserve figures have sometimes been arbitrarily increased for the political purpose of making other states believe that a country possesses more oil than it does. Over 1985 to 1990, for example, much of OPEC suddenly increased their reserve figures, with the lack of new discoveries strongly suggesting that these increases were politically or economically motivated.[5] That said, over the longer-term reserves will not fall exactly in line with production, because technological developments improve the extraction rates from wells, extending its life or output from what initial estimates had specified. Further blurring the reserve figures is the fact that some governments do not publish detailed information on fields, and even when they do, analysts may disagree with each other on the accuracy of their reserves estimates.[6]

Figures 3.2 and 3.3 illustrate a couple of other points about Gulf oil and gas. Figure 3.2 shows the length of time remaining for oil and gas production in each of the GCC states, assuming current production rates remain and that there are no further improvements in extraction (even though there almost-certainly will be). It illustrates just how different the long-term prognosis for energy production is across the GCC. The pressures on Bahrain and Oman to diversify their economies and plan for life after oil are clear, with only 14–15 years of oil production remaining in Oman and pressure on Bahrain too. In contrast, Qatar has 130 years or more of gas remaining at current production rates. While diversification is important for the creation of new, skilled jobs in non-energy sectors and to avoid the problems associated with rent fluctuations, assuming that global demand for hydrocarbons does not collapse, states like Qatar can count on a stable flow of gas rents for several more generations. Figure 3.3 places the Gulf's oil sector into an international context, showing how total GCC reserves have changed over time, including having been abruptly raised more than once, but also showing a small but unmistak-able decline as a share of the global total. This is even more pronounced when unconventional reserves are included as well,[7] although the Gulf's oil will remain attractive for the foreseeable future given its good quality and low extraction cost.

Figure 3.2 Gulf states' oil and gas reserves-to-production (R/P) ratios, 2016 (at current reserves levels and production rates)

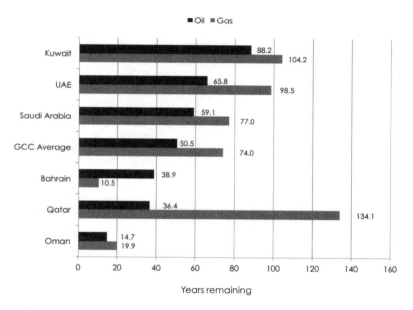

Source: Author's calculations, combining data from *BP Statistical Review of World Energy 2017*.

The Gulf economies consist of more than just hydrocarbons, dominant though they are. Figure 3.4 shows the contributions of various economic activities to GDP across the six states. Oil, gas, and other extractive activity falls under "Mining & manufacturing", which explains why this category is so large. Moreover, given their rentier political economies, the Gulf states have high levels of government spending, and as a result, some of the activities covered by "Other activities" are funded by oil or gas, flow-ing through and from the state, which distinguishes these economies from wealthy but non-energy-centred economies.

Figure 3.3   GCC oil reserves as a share of the global total

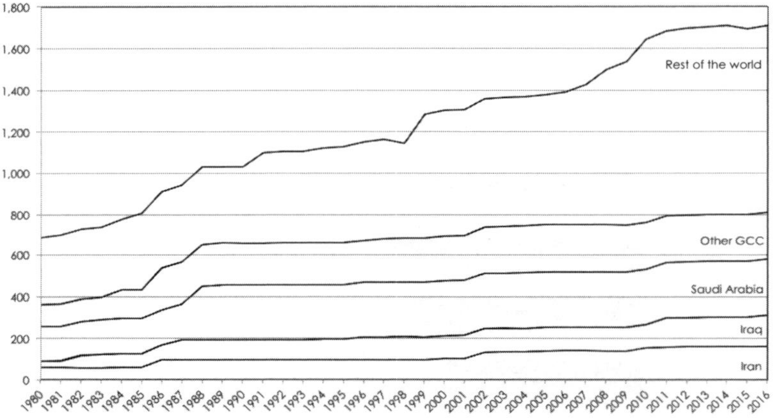

Source: *BP Statistical Review of World Energy 2017*.

These economies are diverse beyond just their energy sectors, as Figure 3.4 also shows. By virtue of their geography and climate, their primary industries are very small, accounting for at most 2.3 per cent of GDP in 2015 (in Saudi Arabia), and only a fraction of 1 per cent in Bahrain, Kuwait, Qatar, and the UAE. The figure is a little higher in Saudi Arabia in part because of its more diverse geography, but mostly because of the state-sponsored agricultural programmes from the 1970s to the early 2000s, where the state subsidized the development of agriculture in an ultimately-unsustainable attempt at economic diversification.[8] Some related agribusiness activity remains, however, such as in food process-ing, while a small number of firms are noteworthy for their success, such as Almarai and Al Safi Danone in the dairy industry and companies in food packaging, seafood and other areas. These firms benefit from prefer-ence in government contracts and the need for foreign firms to have local

Figure 3.4 GCC states: composition of GDP, 2015 (%)

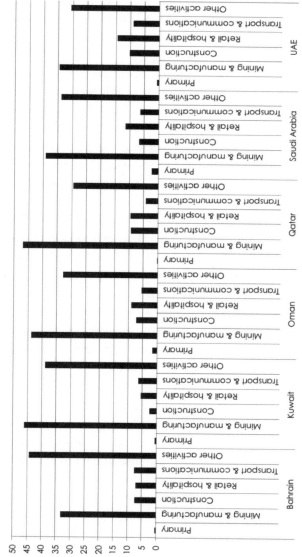

Source: Author's representation, drawing on data from the United Nations' Statistics Division, *National Accounts Main Aggregates Database*, https://unstats.un.org/unsd/snaama/dnlList.asp (accessed 26 October 2017).

Note: On definitions/coverage in each column: *Primary* (sector) refers to agriculture, hunting, forestry and fishing; *Mining & manufacturing* includes utilities; *Retail & hospitality* covers wholesale, retail, restaurants and hotels; *Transport & communications* includes storage and other parts of the supply chain; and *Other activities* covers an array of services and government spending, including some financial services, real estate, business services, public administration, defence, (compulsory) social security, education, health, social work, other community and social services, and economic activity in private homes.

partners, but they have also been very effective at adopting new practices and technologies and in vertically integrating their operations. Some other Gulf states followed the Saudi example, while others, such as Oman, already had a stronger agricultural sector. The Gulf states all have successful firms in areas related to agribusiness and food, especially in food packaging, storage, distribution and retailing.

In a somewhat similar pattern, industry has a significant economic role, but is at least in part sustained by oil wealth and state policies of economic diversification. The Gulf has successful firms involved in downstream oil and gas, especially petrochemicals and industries that are energy-intensive such as minerals and metals processing.[9] However these are typically state-owned, especially the petrochemicals industry, or are very highly regulated. They often benefit from receiving highly-subsidized oil or gas, or subsidized electricity generated by hydrocarbons: in the case of Saudi Arabia, for example, the *Vision 2030* strategy aims to reduce these, which industrial firms claim will be significant enough to have a notable impact on their profits. Not all industry is this reliant upon the state or on oil wealth, however. Again, taking the case of Saudi Arabia, industries including clothing, textiles, machinery, paper, and others have been successful, are not (usually) state-owned, and their growth has outpaced that of the hydrocarbon sector. The challenge for the industrial sector, now and into the future, is to ensure its global competitiveness and its viability in the absence of state support or protection.

One area where the private sector has played a prominent and autonomous role is in the services sector. This is the result in part of history. All of the Gulf states possessed powerful merchant families, dating back well into the pre-oil era, who had their own economic bases of power, and who regularly were influential enough that ruling families were forced to consult, even negotiate, with them. Many of these survived into the oil era without losing their autonomy to the increasingly powerful state, although as oil wealth grew, many from the younger generations began to choose state employment over continuing the family business. Second, in most cases the state has not shown the same interest in owning the assets of services firms, nor the same propensity to regulate or manage it compared to, say, the energy sector or other "strategic" areas of the economy. The businesspeople engaged in services are rarely seen as much of a political threat to rulers, and increasingly they are instead viewed as positive for the economy, and in turn for state legitimacy, given the employment they often generate. Only in certain services – finance, telecommunications, air transport – has the state retained a dominant role, and even then, has allowed an increasing role for the private sector. Banking, for example, was partially opened and competition introduced during the oil boom of 2004–08,[10] even though new entrants had trouble pushing aside the dominant state-owned banks. And while the Gulf's main airlines are either state-owned (Emirates, Etihad) or owned by political elites (Qatar Airways), greater competition has been introduced into the industry, and plans are underway for the privatization of some airlines, such as Saudia.

Finally, services have been at the forefront of economic diversification strategies, both in the current wave of development plans as well as in older diversification strategies. Since the sector is very diverse, and in many cases its firms were a side interest of citizens who also held salaried jobs, it was an obvious candidate for such strategies. Moreover, simpler services firms such as those in hospitality, distribution and retailing can usually be established with limited capital and, in some cases, with the owner possessing little experience. The development strategies of the Gulf states have therefore prioritized some services such as in tourism, hospitality and retailing. Where more complex services are encouraged – say, in higher education, construction, information technology and professional services – foreign direct investment (FDI) is usually encouraged, with the aim of enhancing the competitiveness and profitability in these areas of the economy by the inward transfer of technology, skills and business practices.

Whatever achievements might have been made in economic diversification by the Gulf economies, however, they remain focused on energy. Even in Bahrain and Oman, where hydrocarbons are approaching exhaustion, they remain at the core of the economy. The Gulf states all rely on rents for a majority – in most cases, a *large* majority – of state revenues,[11] which dictates the profile of these economies and hampers their prospects beyond the energy sector. Yet that noted, the Gulf states' macroeconomic settings and policies are also important, if also influenced by the dominance of hydrocarbons in these economies.

MACROECONOMIC SETTINGS AND CONDITIONS

Economists continue to debate the relative importance of various underlying sources of economic growth in any economy, whether in the Gulf or elsewhere. However, focus is typically put on four main drivers: the stock of capital (in effect, investment); human capital; total factor productivity; and institutional and regulatory effectiveness. These areas all require attention from Gulf governments if their ambitious plans for economic development and diversification are to be realized.

The Gulf's levels of investment and capital formation were fairly high in the 1990s and 2000s. This was the result of the maturing of the oil sector, which did not require the same levels of investment as when it was expanding in earlier decades, and because of the diversion of state resources towards economic diversification. It was also a period when major economic diversification was occurring in Dubai, and to a lesser extent elsewhere such as in Abu Dhabi and Qatar. As a share of non-oil GDP, the Gulf's stock of capital expanded faster than the average for developed economies; over 1990 to 2009, by one estimate, it increased by roughly 200 per cent, although this total masks enormous variations between states. Traditionally savings invested abroad were a problem for the region's capital stock, but this is being addressed as states construct sovereign wealth funds (SWFs) and encourage new investment by state-owned firms.

Human capital is somewhat similar in principle. It refers to the stock of appropriately-qualified people in the labour force, and how well this matches the current and projected demands of the economy. Human capital has been a particular focus for Gulf governments, which as a development tactic have long sought to expand and improve secondary

80

and tertiary education. Measured purely by the number of years of average schooling they appear to have had some success, but lurking behind such indicators is the problem of whether this investment has been as appropriate and effective as it could have been and the formidable future challenges confronting these economies.[12] For example, while the expansion of university education in earlier decades was crucial for development, there remains a heavy emphasis on it, leading many people to pursue degrees in fields that are already well-supplied with graduates, such as in the humanities, social sciences, and religious studies, while other important professions face a shortage of skilled workers.[13] There is also a preference among young people to attend university, at the expense of supposedly less-prestigious trades and technical jobs, even though employers' demands for many of these trades and technical skills is high.

In other respects human capital remains in need of further reform. The reliance on foreign workers to perform not just menial roles but also many highly-skilled ones remains a problem. It is partly the result of the rentier arrangement in these economies, in which the state provides free education and then well-paid employment to people, often with insufficient regard to the labour demands of the public sector and with too little emphasis on measuring and addressing performance. Yet many of the areas of the Gulf's economies likely to see the greatest growth in coming years are those that require workers in less prestigious roles, and which to date have been disproportionately performed by foreign workers. Convincing citizens to accept jobs in less prestigious fields is a difficult and politically-risky thing, whatever the merits of the economic case for it.

The third basis for economic growth is total factor productivity (TFP). This is a somewhat contested concept, because it is attempting to capture an array of opaque and qualitative factors that might contribute towards productivity and competitiveness. Broadly, it covers the elements of productivity that are not explained by the traditional, measurable inputs into production (that is, capital and labour).[14] It includes things like the use of technology to improve productivity, improvement in workers' skills, greater trade openness, the quality of political and economic institutions, the impacts of a good legal system, and even the advantages of geography and history. This means that two identical investments, in two different economies, will differ in their impact as a result of variations in TFP. The problem when examining the Gulf economies, however, is the limited potential to quantify the components of TFP: there are known shortcomings in workers' skills or in institutional effectiveness, for example, but the relative importance of these and other factors is impossible to unequivocally discern. Furthermore, there is not a clear pattern between TFP in the Gulf states and their investment in new technologies or work processes, suggesting that it is not just the components of TFP that matter, but their interactions with and influences on each other too. Therefore, gaining a sophisticated understanding of the various elements of TFP in the Gulf is, for the moment, beyond reach, for reasons of quantifiability. Nonetheless, there is little doubt that many of the components of TFP are extremely important for economic growth in the Gulf states.

Finally, institutional and regulatory effectiveness, while typically included as an aspect of TFP, is important. It goes beyond TFP, however, when it refers to non-economic dynamics.[15] At the simplest level, there are likely to be some correlations between political freedoms, transparent processes and the quality of political-legal institutions. The exact correlation between these dynamics and economic growth is far less clear, however. By some measurements, there is little correlation. Disappointing as this may be to proponents of democratization, the links between economic growth and other, more technical aspects of institutional and regulatory effectiveness – property rights, bureaucratic processes, anti-corruption protections – is much stronger. This suggests that, in terms of economic performance and growth, what matters more for the Gulf states is the type of reform that they have focused on over the past couple of decades – not democratization but reforms that improve economic rights, enhance business confidence, protect investments, increase institutional transparency, and lower transaction costs.

Having noted these foundational aspects of economic growth, what are equally important are the policies and actions of governments, above all the macroeconomic settings they adopt. These include fiscal policies such as state spending, subsidies and policies on investment; monetary policy, including interest rate settings, exchange rate policies, and approaches to handling inflation; and policies on labour markets, including on wages and the regulations related to expatriate workers. Important too is international trade policy and other government policies that affect economic openness and investment, which is taken up in the subsequent section.

Fiscal policy – the means by which governments raise money and how they then spend these funds – is important in every economy because of the size of the state as an economic actor and its regulatory power. It is even more important in the Gulf because of the size of rents, defined here as income from natural resources or by virtue of geography or history, in excess of the costs of bringing such resources into economic production, and (in the case of the Gulf's oil and gas income) mostly received from foreign sources. Rents dominate any assessment of the Gulf economies because of their tremendous size, the deep impact they have on nearly all corners of the economy, and of course because they mostly accrue to the state, or state-owned and state-controlled institutions, rather than to the private sector or societal actors and forces.

Table 3.4 and Figure 3.5 show just how massive oil rents are in the Gulf states: in covering the years from 2012 to 2015 inclusive, the earlier couple of years shows the figures at a time of relatively high oil prices, while by 2015 oil prices had plummeted to very low levels. Even in the latter case, however, oil rents constituted fully *one-third* of the Gulf's entire GDP, and over *two-thirds*, a remarkable 68.4 per cent, of total GCC state revenues. This is before including any non-oil rents, and without considering the fact that many non-oil parts of the economy, such as many major state-owned firms, were established as a result of the investment of oil wealth. As a share of GDP, these numbers indicate why the impacts of oil wealth reach into virtually every corner of the Gulf's economies. The size of rents as a share of state revenues highlights not only their importance, but the susceptibility of government budgets to sudden fluctuations in price. They also highlight the size of state spending as a share of overall GDP, which

is higher than the figures for most of the more diverse, developed economies elsewhere in the world.

Table 3.4 Gulf states' government reserves, 2012–15

As a percentage of GDP:				
	2012	2013	2014	2015
Oil revenue	39.8	37.9	33.9	21.8
Tax revenue	1.7	1.6	1.7	2.0
Other non-oil revenue	4.9	6.2	6.2	8.0
As a percentage of state revenues:				
	2012	2013	2014	2015
Oil revenue	85.8	83.0	81.0	68.4
Tax revenue	3.6	3.4	4.1	6.3
Other non-oil revenue	10.6	13.6	14.9	25.3

Source: Derived from statistics in Alreshan *et al.*, "Demystifying Government Revenue in the GCC", 7 (Table 2).

A result of the rentier bargain, and evident in the revenue data, is that
in the oil era, taxation in the Gulf states has been extremely limited.[16] In
recent decades there has been, for the most part, no personal income taxes
on individuals, low if any corporate taxes (usually only levied on certain
types of firms) and no other major taxes on citizens. Only in the late-2010s
have the Gulf states agreed on implementing a standardized consumption
tax, and even this has been delayed by disagreements and administrative problems. The first steps occurred with Saudi Arabia and the UAE
launching the new five per cent consumption tax on 1 January 2018; the
other four Gulf states plan to introduce the tax in 2019. Gulf taxes consist
mostly of taxes on foreign firms, customs and excise duties, a few specific
taxes (such as municipal taxes and hotel and entertainment taxes in a
few states) and government fees and charges for services. The extremely

limited taxation obligation in these states is core to the allocative bargain between state and society, where the state distributes a share of oil or other rent income to society, through its spending and with little if any taxation, and in exchange requires of society their political acquiescence and their acceptance of the existing political and economic order. Rentierism is, put crudely, a case of "no taxation and no representation" or something similar.

Figure 3.5 Gulf states' GDP with percentages captured by the state (2012–15 average)

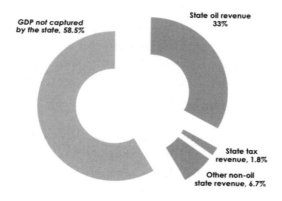

Source: Derived from statistics in Alreshan, *et al.*, "Demystifying Government Revenue in the GCC", 7 (Table 2).

Since the 1950s or so and especially since the first oil boom of the 1970s, this arrangement has provided considerable durability to the Gulf's political economies and given Gulf leaderships considerable autonomy from society. Yet oil is a finite resource, and so there is a vulnerability lurking in the rentier arrangement. While the vastly reduced need for Gulf states to raise revenue through taxation may appear to be a blessing, when states decide that they do indeed want to introduce broader or higher taxes – whether to raise or diversify revenue, undertake nation-building and enhance the meaning of citizenship, or to indicate the need to begin a transition to a post-oil economy – this can prove difficult. It makes the state appear to be amending the rentier arrangement. Society has usually become accustomed to enormous rent distributions, and if they feel disadvantaged by such reforms, may demand new political influence or freedoms in exchange. The Gulf states are, therefore, in a reform predicament: once established, a rentier arrangement is very difficult to disassemble and replace with a taxation-redistribution arrangement, with states deterred from reform by the political risks inherent in attempting it.

The Gulf also varies from developed and diversified economies such as the OECD ones in their patterns of state expenditure. The developed economies, relying on taxation for most state revenue, and redistributing large portions of that money, spend heavily on welfare benefits and aged pensions; in 2015 average EU spending on social protection was 19.2 per cent of GDP. This is substantially larger than spending on health (7.2%), general public services (6.2%), or education (4.9%), and other areas such as economic affairs, infrastructure, and defence accounted for still less.[17] The profile of Gulf state spending is very different. Typically, Gulf states spent most on education and related areas, health, defence and security, and (albeit more when oil prices are high) on infrastructure.[18] When this spending is conglomerated, the highest single proportion of it is on wages for the personnel who work on implementing these government policies and delivering services; an enormous cost, and a reducible one given the high wages, overstaffing, and skills shortages that characterize the Gulf public sector's citizen workforce. In contrast, Gulf spending on social protection needs to be only a fraction of the EU states because of the Gulf's rapidly-rising and youthful population, and because transfers to citizens more often take the forms of employment, subsidies, and of course an absence of taxation, and are less commonly done as welfare payments.

There are several unique issues with state spending, raising questions about the long-term viability and effectiveness of how budgets are allocated. One aspect of more recent budgets, and a laudable and understandable goal, has been the emphasis on spending that will foster the private sector and develop the economy by improving social overhead capital such as infrastructure. The money that has gone to ports, airlines, tourism infrastructure, major public transport initiatives, telecommunications, and arguably even real estate have this as at least one underlying goal, often the primary goal. There are also more direct allocations to business, in some cases preferential treatment for the private sector when awarding government contracts, and flow-on transfers of money to contractors and sub-contractors on projects, which seek the same outcome. Such spending is not surprising given the low number of jobs created by oil and gas, state goals of expanding the roles of citizens in the private sector, and ultimately the desire of governments to build a stronger productive, and taxable, base in the economy. The main question over this spending is whether it constitutes the most effective means of achieving such outcomes. The research on this question suggests that such spending has positive effects but is probably not the ideal means to such ends: income has not been as high as the large capital expenditure would predict, suggesting that there are some inefficiencies or other shortcomings in this spending.[19]

Perhaps states are more constrained with this spending than is sometimes assumed, given the trade-offs of rentierism. Specifically, spending such as on infrastructure contracts, other contracting, additional jobs in the public sector to implement new policies, and high wages for citizens are all a form of rent transfer to society. This does not preclude development being the ultimate incentive behind such spending; in fact, states probably assume that budget allocations perform a dual role of improving state support and services while simultaneously reinforcing its allocative role and encouraging societal groups and individuals to view the rentier arrangement favourably. In an economic sense, however, this spending can have negative impacts if it drives firms to line up for generous state contracts or subsidies instead of competing openly in private markets, or if it motivates individuals to seek out state employment rather than taking work in the private sector. Indeed, many see the public sector is better paying and providing an easier lifestyle than the more demanding but economically-productive private sector.

The aspect of state expenditure that is most unsustainable, and which has been singled out by states for reform, is subsidies. Until the onset of low oil prices in 2014, Gulf governments spent enormous sums on subsidies, including direct subsidizations of petrol, electricity, water and food, as well as indirect subsidies in the form of the opportunity cost of state-owned firms selling goods or services at below market rates or using subsidized inputs. When both direct and indirect subsidization is calculated, one source placed its overall cost in 2010 to the six Gulf monarchies at a remarkable $89.8 billion.[20] This did not cover some subsidies such as cheap fuel for power generation, and yet it still amounted to an average of 29.7 per cent of state budgets that year. It is little wonder that states would like to reduce this spending. Such has been the growth of energy subsidies, in fact, and the distortions created by them, that a 2011 Chatham House report made the rather remarkable prediction that, on current trends, Saudi Arabia would run out of exportable volumes of oil by the year 2038.[21] Traditionally Gulf rulers felt constrained on subsidies, assuming that citizens would be angered by any attempt to cut subsidies without some form of compensation, however the majority of funds spent on subsidies ultimately are transferred to people with above-average incomes; that is, to people who don't need price support. Sustained low oil prices have now provided the excuse that these leaders needed to begin addressing the subsidies problem. The UAE had made some reforms as early as the late 1990s, and Bahrain starting in 2007, but the pace accelerated from 2012. Crucially, Saudi Arabia, while late to act on subsidies, also now appears to be undertaking genuine price reform. In April 2016 it announced by royal decree a range of medium-term reforms, including rises in the price for gasoline, and gradual increases in the prices for water, electricity, and other goods over a number of years.[22] If genuine subsidy reforms succeed, they will bring significant economic advantages, even if in the interim some firms, especially state-owned ones, will suffer from shifting to market prices for, in particular, their energy needs.

Government spending, but even more so the reliance on oil and gas exports, is also closely linked to the issue of inflation. A modest rate of inflation is generally treated by economists as a positive indicator of an energetic economy. However excessive rates of inflation have a negative impact on growth, impacting investment, productivity, and consumer confidence. Various studies have suggested annual inflation rates of eight per cent and ten per cent as non-linear points at which inflation has a sharp negative impact on growth, although at least one other study put the rate markedly lower, beginning at under 5 per cent.[23] For rentier economies like the Gulf, oil price booms have been especially dangerous for inflation, encouraging states to spend more freely in the domestic economy, as well as to increase transfers, subsidies or wages, which typically encourage higher levels of consumer spending and feed inflation.[24] The two main periods of very high inflation in the Gulf monarchies coincided with oil booms, occurring roughly over the mid-late-1970s and again from 2003 to around 2010, while periods of low oil prices such as in the late-1980s and the 1990s saw inflation at modest levels. While inflation also has been driven by external inflationary pressures, which pushed up the costs of imports and foreign labour, high oil prices were a driver as well. Generally, such pressures have been handled reactively, with governments lacking much ability to address inflation pressures from abroad, and tempted by economic but especially political considerations to increase budgets as rents flooded into the economy, even if this created inflationary pressures.

Where governments did have more scope to address inflation, but for a variety of reasons chose not to, was in the fact that inflation has also been driven by their currencies being pegged to foreign currencies. The GCC currencies are pegged to the US dollar, except for Kuwait, which since 2007 has pegged to a basket of key currencies. The decision to peg currencies was driven by the fact that it provides predictability in exchange rates and reduces the likelihood of sharp changes in inflation. However, the downsides are significant, too. Generally, because a peg means that domestic interest rates cannot deviate from the foreign one to which the currency is tied, central banks surrender considerable control over bank credit, money market liquidity, and ultimately economic growth. The Gulf states have typically accepted this trade-off, making the currency peg the underlying basis of their monetary policy over the long term, although on a couple of occasions, most notably during the 2008 global financial crisis, they have acted more independently on interest rates so as to ensure the stability of their financial systems.

However the downside of fixed currencies was demonstrated in the second period of inflation in the 2000s, when the pegs undermined the Gulf's states' ability to counter inflation, since their currencies were in effect tied to US monetary policy: this was at a time when the US economy and the Gulf economies were moving in different directions; with the US in 2008 cutting interest rates as the global financial crisis unfolded and threatened a deep recession, while the Gulf economies were still booming from recent high oil prices. This also highlighted the risk for resource economies of asset bubbles emerging, since the boom of the 2000s brought with it first a stock market bubble in the early/mid-2000s and then a property price bubble in some economies, most famously in Dubai in 2008–09.

In effect, with a pegged exchange rate, the only way to fight inflation and the pressures that create asset bubbles is to absorb its effects in the domestic economy. For the Gulf in the 2000s, this would have meant massive cuts to subsidies, employment, and public works spending, which at the time, arguably, was simply not politically practical nor, on balance, economically advisable either. In particular, the argument from the Gulf at the time was that a floating exchange rate is advisable where diverse and productive exports characterize an economy's trade profile, while given the Gulf's reliance on oil exports, a floating exchange rate would be highly volatile, damaging inward capital flows and investment and thus harming non-oil parts of the economy. Table 3.5 shows the variations in inflation rates, which loosely coincide with high and low oil prices as well.

There was a hope back in the 2000s, when the GCC was planning for a single currency, the *Khaliji* (from the Arabic word *al-khalīj*, meaning "the Gulf"), that this might help with controlling inflation, as well as addressing other issues with monetary policy. This would have been unlikely: the

Table 3.5 Gulf states' inflation rates, 2000–15

	2000	2001	2002	2003	2004	2005	2006	2007	2008	2009	2010	2011	2012	2013	2014	2015
Bahrain	-0.7	-1.2	-0.5	1.6	2.4	2.6	2.0	3.3	3.5	2.8	2.0	-0.4	2.8	3.3	2.7	1.8
Kuwait	1.8	1.3	0.9	1.0	1.2	4.1	3.1	5.5	10.6	4.6	4.5	4.9	3.2	2.7	2.9	3.3
Qatar	1.7	1.5	0.2	2.3	6.8	8.8	11.8	13.8	15.1	-4.9	-2.4	1.9	1.9	3.1	3.1	1.9
Oman	n.d.	-0.8	-0.3	0.2	0.8	1.9	3.2	6.0	12.1	3.9	3.2	4.1	2.9	1.2	1.0	0.1
Saudi Arabia	-1.1	-1.1	0.2	0.6	0.3	0.7	2.2	4.2	9.9	5.1	5.3	5.8	2.9	3.5	2.7	2.2
UAE	11.5	-2.3	3.8	4.1	8.5	16.5	12.0	12.5	18.5	-15.2	12.5	13.8	1.6	-1.5	0.0	-14.5

Note: Figures for Bahrain, Kuwait, Oman, Qatar and Saudi Arabia are the percentage change in consumer prices over the year before: this figure is measured by a consumer price index, which reflects the annual percentage change in the cost to the ordinary individual of a basket of goods and services. The figures for the UAE are GDP deflator figures, which are determined by the ratio of GDP in current local currency to GDP in constant local currency.

Source: Derived from data from the World Bank's *World Development Indicators*, https://data.worldbank.org/country (accessed 26 October 2017).

currency would have been pegged, and unless the countries using it could coordinate their economic policies, a single currency alone would have had little impact on reducing inflation overall.[25] The *Khaliji* was not implemented anyway, and its prospects for the moment are almost non-existent. At the economic level, the GCC economies had very different underlying economic conditions, which in turn led to diverging inflation rates: then as now, they "pursue different fiscal policies, their indigenous labour markets have different rigidities, their housing markets vary from surpluses to shortages, and their needs for food imports relative to domestic production vary".[26] Beyond inflation, wider economic issues were pertinent, especially the limitations of economic integration among the GCC member states;[27] this is now even more the case after the 2017 Qatar crisis. There are also variations in country risk, financial and capital flows, and fiscal priorities. While five of the six GCC currencies were pegged to the US dollar, which might make it seem easier to converge their currencies into one, these other variations made it extremely challenging.

Just as important as economic hurdles were the political ones. Oman withdrew from the single currency process in 2006, followed by the UAE in 2009, complaining that the main institutions of monetary union, along with many other GCC initiatives, were to be based in Saudi Arabia and would presumably therefore be dominated by Riyadh. The GCC–Qatar crisis that began in June 2017 has made the prospects for a single currency even more remote; in fact, the future of most economic integration goals, and even of the GCC itself, is now open to question. Saudi Arabia could yet lead a group of certain other states towards a single currency – Bahrain and Kuwait would seem the most likely ones, but perhaps if Saudi–UAE relations improve further, the UAE could rejoin the process too – but the necessary political will seems absent. The Eurozone crisis after 2008, and the political risks that accompany economic reforms such as fiscal policy alignment, make even this more limited currency union appear formidable.

Central banks in the Gulf are reasonably professional in terms of their staffing and experience, but by various measures – political independence, economic autonomy, transparency, the legal basis of their operations – they lack independence from the political elite and sometimes from other institutions. The Saudi and Kuwaiti central banks are under tight control by finance ministers; the others have broad instrument independence. In other respects their autonomy varies too: there are significant differences in, for example, whether the central banks are permitted to hold public debt, as there also are in the rules over whether governments can capitalize their central banks. The accountability and transparency rules for the banks also vary: Bahrain's central bank publishes audited financial statements, Kuwait and Oman have their statements audited but do not publish the reports, while the Saudi and UAE central banks are not required to have any independent audit. This is consistent with the weakness and limited autonomy of most political institutions in the Gulf. Moreover, other tasks that routinely fall to central banks, such as regulation of the banking and finance system, and sometimes stock markets and debt markets, have largely been retained by governments and finance ministries, and at any rate, the banking sector in the Gulf is dominated by a small number of large, domestic, and mostly state-owned banks.[28]

Since their currencies are pegged, and the central banks thus most often pursue their goals through interbank rates, asset price policies, and the like, arguably the large rent surpluses of the 2000s also made the task of central banking easier until well into the 2010s. The central banks' remits have traditionally been seen as relatively modest, therefore, although giving the banks greater autonomy and reach would arguably be beneficial, helping them counter some of the negative impacts in boom periods such as 2003–14 and allowing them to more effectively and nimbly handle the impacts of oil bust periods, such as in 2014 and the years following. This is why governments have dominated policy initiatives to address low oil prices since 2014, and why, for the moment, the GCC economies remain no better equipped to handle another oil boom than they were in the 2000s.

MIGRATION AND THE GULF'S LABOUR MARKETS

One factor in the Gulf economies which is of particular economic importance, and which is unusual among higher-income countries, is their reliance on expatriate workers in the labour market. The GCC attracts enormous numbers of migrants, from the unskilled to highly skilled, to work across almost the entirety of the subregion's economies, although foreigners predominate in the private sector rather than the public sector. The majority come for specific blocks of their working lives, whether a few years or sometimes for much longer, while a smaller number are intergenerational, having been born in the host country to expatriate parents. In almost no case, however, are such workers given citizenship or a similar status; in fact, the Gulf's treatment of foreign workers is a policy which has attracted considerable negative public attention and criticism in recent years. In nearly all cases, foreign workers are motivated by financial incentives – wages and salaries are set to ensure that, regardless of the economy from which they come, they will earn considerably more in the Gulf – although among poorer workers, conditions are oftentimes very poor, and the decision to go to the Gulf may be made as much by the family more widely than by the individual him- or herself.[29]

This reliance on expatriate labour has had several economic and political goals and impacts. As already noted, at the political level it has traditionally been part of the rentier arrangement with, in effect, governments outsourcing the working class, letting citizens avoid having to take poorly-paying or low-status jobs. The government has typically focused on creating employment for citizens in the public sector, whether in policy departments or institutions such as state-owned firms. The dual nature of labour market terms and conditions reflect these goals. Citizens enjoyed, and continue to enjoy, wages that are higher than most foreign workers can demand, even those in very specialized or highly-skilled roles, as well as having very generous conditions and highly secure tenure. Foreign workers, meanwhile, did not enjoy such benefits. Their salaries typically have been set, in large measure, against what they could command in their home economies, paying enough to motivate them to come to the region to work, but with yawning variations across different nationalities. Moreover, the rights of foreign workers are strictly curtailed. Those working in unskilled or semi-skilled roles are denied the right to unionize or organize, and all of them are constrained by the *kafala* sponsorship system, which places them under the control of the individual or company who has sponsored their visa. The idea of *kafala* was to avoid domestic labour market competition emerging: workers cannot normally move jobs to a new sponsor or work for a competing firm for a period of time after leaving their sponsor's control, without the permission of their existing sponsor. Sponsors typically, but not always, hold the worker's passport or have control over his or her ability to leave the country. The *kafala* system also opens workers and their families up to abuse, and in fact the most common criticism of it has been over the mistreatment, including the physical abuse, of workers.[30]

At the economic level, there are several goals behind this reliance on foreign labour. Arguably the most important two, interconnected ones are to constrain both exchange rate pressures on the economy and the rate of overall wages growth, which helps to control inflation in periods when large volumes of resources rents are coming into the economy.[31] Relaxed migration policies mean that, in times of boom, the labour market does not have to adjust to skills shortages or overall labour shortages, while remittance outflows back to workers' home economies also helps reduce upward pressure on the exchange rate. When rents subsequently fall, workers can simply be retrenched and will leave the economy, and do not have to be paid unemployment benefits, retrained, or otherwise absorbed elsewhere in the economy. The other economic goal of importing workers – skilled ones, at least – was that earlier in the oil era, the Gulf's domestic labour markets lacked the skilled workers that these rapidly-developing economies needed. It was expected that expatriates would train or otherwise transfer their skills to nationals, enhancing the capacity of the workforce over time. This occurred to only a limited extent, however, and to varying degrees the GCC's governments began introducing workforce nationalization policies after the 1980s, to try to create employment in the private sector for citizens. These policies have been broadly similar in their profiles, covering initiatives such as closing or restricting some areas of the economy to foreign workers, setting required percentages of nationals to be employed by firms, increasing the costs of hiring foreign workers, policies to move more (citizen) women into the workforce, and trying to improve and modernize education and training. However, given the enormous supply of foreign labour, citizens' preferences for public sector employment, and the much higher average wages in the public sector, these policies have had limited success.

As a result, and since the skills transfers to citizens has been at best very modest too, certainly insufficient for the needs of these economies, the numbers of foreign workers in the Gulf has continued to rise. Yet governments still persist with labour market nationalization, and indicators of labour market problems, such as youth unemployment rates, have been and remain frustratingly high. In fact, the proportion of the overall population of the Gulf that is foreign has risen consistently and strongly since 1960, increasing over three-fold in the 1960–2005 period, with only a brief decline and stall in the early/mid-1990s.[32] The sources of foreign workers has also shifted, with the poorer Arab countries having supplied the bulk of the Gulf's workers in earlier decades, but with South Asian workers becoming increasingly numerous and a larger share of the foreign workforce from the early 1990s onwards.[33] Since 2005, these figures have not markedly changed, and continued reforms towards nationalization have not resulted in substantive shifts, much less transformations, in the Gulf's labour markets.

What this ultimately means for a description of the Gulf's economies is that, even after more than four decades of heavy reliance on expatriate workers, the GCC labour markets remain both dualistic and reliant on foreign workers, and are in these respects underdeveloped compared to the labour forces in comparably-wealthy but more diverse economies. In the short- and medium-term, this suits both Gulf leaderships and businesses. The reliance on foreign workers has always been driven by employers, who apply for visas or permits for foreign workers, and nationalization policies have only tinkered with this process, or sought to create incentives to employ citizens. They have not acted to drastically cut the ability of employers to recruit from abroad. The Gulf states' leaders, increasingly sensitive to criticisms about the treatment of expatriates, regularly claim to be reforming the labour market and especially the *kafala* system, but ultimately the weak position of foreign workers, constraints on their mobility within the workforce, and structural problems with worker productivity all mean that fundamental flaws exist, and are perpetuated, in the Gulf labour markets. The mere presence of reform initiatives and long-term state policies that imply a need for substantive labour market reforms have not been sufficient catalysts for change.

Of course, none of this precludes migrants from impacting on the Gulf, in both material and non-material ways. Gulf identity has, at least superficially, been changed by their enormous foreign populations, with long-term migrants in particular, while almost never obtaining citizenship, forming long-term communities that constitute a specific (sub-) group in the host societies. One study of Kuwait argued that members of these communities do not become "Kuwaiti", either culturally or in law, but nor do their original cultural features remain unchanged by the experience of living in and interacting with the host society. An Indian (or any other) expatriate may therefore become, for example, "Bombay-Kuwaiti," with unique social ties, kinship patterns, and certain cultural practices that are new and unique.[34] These communities are hybridized cultures, not (usually) cosmopolitan or culturally-rootless groups even though they are internationalized by their location and employment, and exposed to new experiences as a result, ultimately, of their exposure to globalization. These communities exert almost no direct political influence, and have strictly limited economic power as well, since they normally live separated from the host society and usually from other groups. However, their sheer size within the host society and their impact on the urban geography of Gulf cities (as examples, by creating suburbanization, new local public transport links, and new businesses to serve them) are not inconsequential.

THE INTERNATIONAL DIMENSION

A final dynamic that has been central to defining and shaping the Gulf economies is their position in the international economy, and the international variables that exogenously influence their economic performance. Over the past few decades, the GCC governments, like most others, have sought to integrate their economies more closely with the international economic system. This has been partly driven by the goal of economic diversification, but also is a product of the normative economic assumption that a more international economy – one that trades widely, invests abroad, attracts investment inward, and is open to the world in a more general sense – will be more competitive, productive and wealthier. This has occurred, in the case of several of the Gulf states, concomitant with more activist foreign policies, in which economic and commercial methods and goals have been made central to diplomacy and security; while foreign policy activism is probably a secondary aim of international economic integration, it should not be ignored.

The GCC states' international trade profile is narrow in its range of exports, broader in its imports, and relatively broad and increasingly diverse in its foreign trade relationships. Gulf exports are, as already discussed, dominated by oil and gas. As shown in Table 3.6, around half of all exports from the six GCC states in 2013 were "mineral fuels", a category which includes oil and natural gas, and which amounted to some $319 billion. Considering that 2016 was a year of low average oil (and gas) prices, this is a remarkable figure, and an insight into the size of the hydrocarbon sector in the region. Moreover, the GCC states also exported large amounts of chemicals, plastics, and other products derived from oil and gas. The values for some of these are not published, but they are an important component of the downstream oil and gas sector nonetheless. This profile makes it obvious why the Gulf's governments are eager to diversify their economies and expand the non-energy sectors. That said, the region also exports a number of other products, including in 2016 almost $44 billion in pearls, nearly $20 billion in machinery, and almost $17 billion in metals and metal products. The scope of the GCC's exports is not very diverse, it must be stressed, but sectors beyond oil and gas do exist and in certain cases are globally competitive. Yet as a share of global non-oil trade, the Gulf's position is weak. Arguably, the focus on oil and gas has been at the expense of more diverse economic production. In 2015, the GCC's total trade amounted to $649.6 billion out of a global total of $16.8 trillion[35] – or less than 3.9 per cent of the world share, which includes their oil and gas exports, which are a large share of the GCC's exports.

Table 3.6 Gulf states' composition of trade and major trading partners, 2013

TOTAL GCC EXPORTS		TOTAL GCC IMPORTS	
Country	% share	Country	% share
Taiwan	15	China	13
China	13	United States	13
Japan	12	Germany	7
United States	12	Japan	6
India	9	South Korea	6
South Korea	9	UAE	5
Singapore	2	India	4
South Africa	2	France	3
Thailand	2	Italy	3
Others	24	Others	40

Source: Author's calculations, using data from *Knoema*, "GCC Exports and Imports by Trade Partners", updated 11 February 2016, https://knoema.com/rorzjsg/gcc-exports-and-imports-by-trade-partners (accessed 19 January 2018).

Given the global geo-economic importance of oil and gas and the nature of the trade in them, the GCC exports hydrocarbons very broadly.

No single part of the world dominates its total exports, although the importance of East Asia has grown since the 1990s. As can be seen from Table 3.6, the GCC's top export destinations are, in order, Taiwan (15% of all exports), China (13%), the United States (12%), Japan (12%), South Korea (9%), and India (9%), with the remaining 30 per cent spread widely across Europe, Asia, and elsewhere. The region also imported goods from an equally-diverse range of countries, including the United States (13% of all exports), Korea (13%), China (7%), Germany (6%), Japan (6%), India (4%), and Italy, Switzerland, and France (3% each) and a range of others. This diversity reflects the needs of the Gulf economies and, of more concern, the limited domestic capacity in so many areas, from foods and foodstuffs, where the Gulf's limited capacity is quite obvious, to vehicles, aircraft, specialized machinery, and various other goods where it lacks the expertise or economic size for a sustainable industry.

Several points are important to make with regard to trade. The Gulf has typically had a positive trade balance, the result of the dominance of hydrocarbons. Even when prices are low, the rent component in the oil price is substantial enough that the exporting states are making large sums of money. That said, the trade figures – whether for oil and gas, or across all products – vary considerably among the different Gulf economies. As already discussed, Saudi Arabia and the UAE dominate the GCC economically. When oil and gas prices are high, these two countries, along with Kuwait, tend to have the highest trade surpluses because they disproportionately account for the GCC's oil exports. Bahrain and Oman struggle, and in recent years have typically run trade deficits as their oil exports decline and they seek to diversify into other areas. Qatar has normally had a trade surplus, but is susceptible to sudden price shocks because of its large oil and especially gas sector, and is also importing heavily as it invests in infrastructure, such as projects in preparation for the 2022 FIFA World Cup. The GCC–Qatar crisis which began in June 2017 initially seemed deeply threatening to Qatar's economy and trade performance, however it survived the initial year of the crisis remarkably well. Its economic growth in 2017 slowed to around 2.1 per cent – no small feat given the scope of the boycott against it – while its fiscal deficit fell (to 6%, from 9.2% in 2016), while the fall in bank deposits and real estate prices seem to have been only short term.[36] Its long-term prospects are bright given its colossal gas reserves; indeed, it is higher oil and gas prices, combined with investment for the 2022 World Cup, that appear to have helped its economy remain so buoyant in the face of the embargo.

Furthermore, the Gulf's trade relationships have become more diverse and sophisticated in the past couple of decades. In the first oil boom of the 1970s, the region's imports and investment relationships were overwhelmingly with the major developed economies of North America and Europe. This has since shifted markedly, to the much more diverse profile of the 2010s. This stems in part from the rising power of new economies such as China, India and some other emerging economies, but alone does not fully explain the shift. It is also the result of a more open trade environment globally, and of the Gulf states easing many of the restrictions they once placed on trade and investment. This diversification of trade (and investment) is likely to increase further in the future, as the Gulf states actively seek out new export destinations as part of their diversification efforts. Individually, the Gulf states have already pursued free trade agreements and other arrangements to promote trade and are likely to increase their focus on this in the future. Each of the six Gulf monarchies have trade agreements with the United States, for example. These vary from free trade agreements (FTAs), of which Bahrain's, commenced in 2006, was the first, followed by Oman's, signed the same year, to trade and investment framework agreements (TIFAs) such as the ones that guide the US–Kuwaiti, US–Saudi, and US–UAE trade relationships. The TIFAs are less comprehensive than the FTAs, but are still important in guiding relationships, resolving disputes, and arguably are a step towards a FTA. The Gulf states have an array of such bilateral agreements. Saudi Arabia, for example, has 36 different bilateral agreements, on top of its involvement in an assortment of multilateral processes. Kuwait has an even larger list of various bilateral agreements. Overall, such arrangements demonstrate a transformation in the trade and investment approaches and goals of the

Gulf states over the past couple of decades, signalling a strategy of greater economic openness and (selective) reform.

The GCC as a bloc, however, has been less successful in establishing free trade agreements. It has made a handful of free trade agreements, such as with Singapore in 2013, but otherwise the list of successfully concluded agreements is not a long one. It has been pursuing other FTAs, for example with the European Union, Japan, China, India, Pakistan, Turkey, Australia, Korea and others, but these have been arduous processes and have very contrasting prospects. In pursuing these agreements as a bloc, the GCC is hampered by its low taxation environment, which makes it difficult to arrange the reciprocal tax agreements that usually accompany an FTA, as well as high transaction and transport costs in the region. After the Qatar–GCC crisis began in the summer of 2017, the future of the GCC itself became increasingly uncertain, meaning that the prospects for on-going talks eventually delivering FTAs are also much more uncertain than they were as recently as 2015 or 2016.

Assuming that the Gulf states focus on enhancing trade and investment at the bilateral level rather than through the GCC (or any other, probably smaller bloc), their prospects are likely to come from a mix of their recent trajectories and by how their reform and development strategies are perceived abroad. The UAE and Saudi Arabia seemingly have the strongest prospects in this regard. The UAE's extensive diversification efforts since the 1990s and the "first-mover" advantage it has gained marketing itself as a regional hub bode well. Saudi Arabia has its large overall economic size underwriting it, especially the value of its oil reserves and exports, while its *2030 Vision* strategy has, at least initially, generated enthusiasm among potential investors and trade partners. Qatar has also established a strong economy, backed by gas revenue and state support for key industries and firms, and is in a strong position provided that its relations with Saudi Arabia, the UAE, and some other Arab states can be repaired after the 2017 crisis. The other three Gulf states arguably face a more difficult challenge, since Bahrain and Oman lack the hydrocarbon resources to underwrite the sort of state-led opening that Dubai, Abu

Dhabi, and Qatar have done, and since Kuwait continues to have difficulty in attracting foreign investment and diversifying away from oil. Bahrain now attracts a much greater perception of political risk than it did prior to the 2011 protests.

While struggling to carve a stronger position in global investment, the Gulf attracts a disproportionately large share of the investment that flows into the Middle East region. In the 2000s and 2010s the GCC states typically received between half and three-quarters of annual inward investment to the Middle East,[37] a sign of its relative political stability and stable economic environment. The initiatives launched by Gulf states to encourage investment, especially free trade zones, have also been important: at a minimum, these offer simple ways around restrictions still in place in other parts of the economy, while at best, they offer deliberately attractive, long-term incentives for major productive investment projects. While some issues remain with the regulation of investment, and the political risk perceptions of potential investors, this is a substantial transformation from the policies of these states on inward investment prior to the economic openings that they commenced in the 1990s.

In terms of outward investment, the Gulf became an increasingly important source of international investment, especially during the third oil boom of 2004–14, and then during the global financial crisis that began in 2008, when investment from many other parts of the world collapsed. In the final years of the 2000s, China and the Gulf states were among the few sources of investment at a time when international sentiment was otherwise extremely negative and cautious. The Gulf states continue to provide the overwhelming majority of investment coming from the Middle East region, typically accounting for 80 per cent or more of the region's total outward investment.[38] This is in marked contrast to the outward investment from the Gulf during the earlier oil booms of roughly 1973–84, when much of their oil wealth was squandered on portfolio investment in developed economies or on wasteful or poor-quality investments.[39]

In terms of inward investment, the Gulf, and the Middle East more broadly, is peripheral, struggling to attract substantial interest. The Middle

East in total received only $43 billion in 2014, and the GCC states only $22 billion of this. These figures were a tiny proportion of the global total that year of $1.23 trillion.[40] The GCC's economies are more attractive than many other Arab economies, which are usually poorer, less transparent or more politically risky. However the GCC economies are typically considered by international investors to be "frontier" markets – economies that are potentially attractive but which are not yet even considered "emerging" – with only Saudi Arabia, the UAE and sometimes Qatar considered as "emerging".[41] For the Gulf states, changing such international perceptions of their economies is a long-term project, made more complex and challenging by the limited economic integration between them and the continued perception among some investors that they are difficult places in which to commercially succeed.

The Gulf's investment role has also been enhanced by the prominence of their sovereign wealth funds (SWFs). As already noted, SWFs are state-owned investment funds that invest public money, most often oil or gas revenue, seeking a risk-based return on the investment. SWFs sometimes are used to address some of the economic effects of a large oil and gas sector, by offsetting some of the currency pressures that resource economies face, and by looking for investment returns and income not linked to the price of oil and gas. Other SWFs are designed to put aside a share of oil wealth for future generations.[42] Table 3.7 lists some of the main funds of the Gulf states.

These funds usually focus on investing abroad, avoiding the energy sector, and accept a risk-based return on investment. Although SWFs garnered some concern as they became more common and globally prominent in the 2000s, some of the Gulf's SWFs are much older: the Kuwaiti fund dates back to 1953, while the largest of the Gulf funds, the Abu Dhabi Investment Authority, was established in 1976. The concern about SWFs was mostly over transparency and the risk of political influence in their investment decisions, issues which remain but which are starting to be addressed by international agreements. The evidence of SWFs exerting such political pressure is actually very thin. If the funds serve any political purpose, it is instead a *domestic* one. They demonstrate to society that the state is an effective, long-term manager of oil wealth and that it is thinking about development beyond the oil era, which may enhance the state's legitimacy in some eyes. Economists debate the importance of SWFs, especially as funds for future generations, but there are positive economic aspects of them, especially in their macroeconomic stabilization role and where they provide for non-energy development opportunities.

Table 3.7 Gulf states' sovereign wealth funds, 2017

Country	Fund	Value $bn
Bahrain	Bahrain Mumtalakat	10.6
Kuwait	Kuwait Investment Authority	524.0
Oman	State General Reserve Fund	18.0
	Oman Investment Fund	6.0
Qatar	Qatar Investment Authority	320.0
	Qatar Abu Dhabi Investment Company	2.0*
Saudi Arabia	Saudi Arabian Monetary Agency foreign holdings	515.9
	Arab Petroleum Investments Corporation	5.7*
	Sanabil al-Saudia	5.2*
	Public Investment Fund	223.9
UAE	Abu Dhabi Investment Authority	828.0
	Mubadala Development Company	125.0
	Investment Corporation of Dubai	209.5
	Ras al-Khaymah Investment Authority	1.2
	Dubai International Capital	13.0*
	Dubai World	100.0*
	International Petroleum Investment Company	63.5*

* Figures from mid-2015 (either April or June 2015); all others are as at December 2017.
Source: Author's calculations, using data from various sources.

Given all this, over the past three decades the Gulf has changed in some very significant ways, but not in many others, and its economies occupy a somewhat conflicting position within the global economy. Its global importance as an energy supplier is as strong as ever, and even with the rise of unconventional oil and gas, the Gulf's sheer supply of cheaply-accessible hydrocarbons means that it will almost certainly continue to occupy a prominent place in the global energy system for as long as oil and gas retain their geo-economic importance. The dominance of oil and gas in the Gulf's economic profiles is also a source of stasis. They are all fundamentally rentier economies, and are all, if in slightly differing ways, (new) state capitalist as well. This is why they have opened to trade and selectively to the forces of globalization, while also eschewing the neoliberal economic reforms that many of the Arab republics adopted from the 1990s onwards. The economic structures of the Gulf have also sustained political systems and political cultures that share many similarities, even if upon closer inspection there are important variations in the distribution and uses of power too.

This does not mean that the Gulf states have been immune from change, nor indeed that changes cannot come from within their political-economic systems or from the top down. They have initiated reforms, predominantly in the economic sphere but also with social impacts, and specific and quite significant social reforms are now being aggressively implemented in Saudi Arabia, under the influence of the crown prince, Muhammad bin Salman. At least to date, economic reforms have been somewhat successful, perhaps a little gradual, but on the subregion's own terms and, thus far, with little negative political impact. Social reforms have also been cautious, but may accelerate, especially if they are introduced with the intention of avoiding substantive political liberalization. However, the future of the Gulf's reforms, and of their political economies more generally, is far from certain. With the 2011 Arab uprisings, the post-2014 period of low oil prices, and new international dynamics in the region, much will come down to how leaderships decide to act, whether with each other or in their relationships with their societies. It is to the question of political structures and processes, and how these relate to, impact, and are influenced by economic factors, that the next chapter turns.

4

The form of the Gulf political economies

The Gulf economies are the product not only of hydrocarbons, geography and fate. All economies are the product of political structures and dynamics, too. Economics and commerce are, in fact, highly political affairs. States and regimes – the ruling elites at their summit – play critical roles in setting both the landscape and the climate in which economies operate and perform. The components of the state, such as leaders, political elites, institutions, state-owned firms, and others, are integral to understanding both modern economic history and a country's economic profile. Non-state actors and societal forces engage and interact with the state and its components, and are critical too. Actors such as the business community, the clergy, tribes and families therefore also play important roles in the Gulf. Finally, political externalities shape the Gulf's economies, whether by the actions of specific actors such as foreign states and multinational firms or as more opaque but also important forces such as globalization.

It is these various political and social actors and forces, and the dynamics created by their interactions with each other, which are the focus of this chapter. The intention is to add to the economic profiles outlined in the previous chapter, by examining the political dynamics and recent histories of the six Arab Gulf states. In conglomeration, the two chapters seek to construct a more detailed and nuanced outline of the *political* economies of the Gulf. Politics and economics overlap strongly in the Gulf: the former is crucial in setting the scope and limits of economies, while economic structures and outcomes have important, sometimes profound, impacts on politics. For all the economic change that the Gulf has seen in recent decades, and the further reforms planned, the nature of their political systems has meant that ruling families and key elites have been able to ensure political continuity and a systemic durability, even in the face of social, technological, and other changes.

STATES AND REGIMES

Nation-states, and specifically the political entities at the summit of a nation-state's political structure, arguably have been the foremost lens through which Middle Eastern politics has been analyzed in recent decades. In the case of the Middle East, and within that the Gulf, the most obvious of these is that states have distinctive histories and structures, and behave in (somewhat) different ways, compared to other states elsewhere. As new creations (with the exception of Oman), they derive legitimacy and support from historical precedent, ethnic and religious claims of legitimacy, and the dispersal of oil income and welfare. Despite vigorous competition from ethnicity, religion, and local identities, Gulf people increasingly identify themselves by their citizenship or membership of a nation-state.

Perhaps most important in understanding the nature of the state in the Gulf, moreover, is the complexity and opacity of, and interlinkages between, the state and the "regime". It should not be assumed that the two can be examined as parallels, much less interchangeably: the core directing set of actors within the state is not the same type of "government" found in, say, constitutionally-formalized western systems. The term "regime" is used here for the network of elites, often connected to a ruler by opaque or informal political links such as clan, family, or business, that in conglomeration dominates the mechanisms of government and decides key policies. If such mechanisms are not formalized in government structures, then the elites in this system are best understood as constituting a "regime". This is very different to them forming a state, or even a government, even though they may overlay and link to formal political structures and processes. But this is why state, government, and regime are different things, and should be distinguished. To do otherwise risks, as examples, overemphasizing formal mechanisms, ignoring crucial but opaque interpersonal relationships, or confusing formal and informal discourse.

Often, states are relatively weak, but strengthened by strong regimes and elite networks, and controlled (if often with substantial delegation) by a ruler. This structure, "neopatrimonialism",[1] typically takes the form of various levels of patron–client networks, in which a patron supports his or her (usually his) clients with patronage and opportunities in exchange for loyalty and information. A ruler will have such networks, typically consisting of other royals, members of key families and tribes, and perhaps personal friends, with these clients in turn acting as patrons to a further layer of clients below them. The most effective leaders and patrons keep a tension between their clients, to keep them preoccupied and less able to collude with each other. The leaders that most effectively utilize neopatrimonial tactics are typically charismatic, consultative, if only at a basic level, and willing and able to compromise to the extent that basic elite cohesion requires. The most effective clients are those that are willing and able to protect their patron's interests, keep him or her informed, and allow the leader to hold the limelight. Patrimonial tactics date back centuries in the Middle East, but as modern state structures have emerged, and institutions and formal political mechanisms have been incorporated into these patterns of control, it has become more sophisticated and hybridized with other political tactics, and in such forms is best described as *neo*patrimonialism.[2]

Casual observers of the Gulf sometimes mistakenly assume that its political systems are all fundamentally the same. At a cursory level, there are many similarities between them. Their social and religious traditions, their customs, and some aspects of their histories are shared to a considerable extent. Oil wealth has delivered standards of living that appear, on the surface, loosely similar. They are all monarchies. However, on closer inspection their similarities are less marked. The exact form of dynastic rule varies, from emirs to kings to a sultan. Many social structures and cultural traditions appear similar, but often can be differentiated by people's clothing, food or the dialects of Arabic spoken. The majority of Gulf citizens are Muslim, but there are significant sectarian minorities. Oil wealth has made all six Gulf economies wealthy, but there are economic variations across and within them, too.

Chapter 2 laid out the different historical origins of the Gulf's ruling families, and the different societies over which they rule. There is a notable difference between, for example, a ruling family that comes from similar social origins as key tribal or other social groups, as is the case with Qatar's and several of the ruling dynasties of the UAE, compared with a ruling family that gained much of its territory initially from conquest, as in Saudi Arabia and Bahrain. The variations between ruling elites and social forces in these states are stark: Qatar and the UAE have some basic social divisions, derived from family or tribal rivalries, but this is minor compared to the cultural differences and historical experiences across much of contemporary Saudi Arabia, from the Shia populations of the northeast, to the more cosmopolitan Hijazi population, to still others. In Bahrain, many among the Shia majority see the Sunni Al Khalifa ruling family as having taken power, and continuing to hold it, by force.

The structures of the Gulf's ruling families also vary. Those of Saudi Arabia and Kuwait are expansive. Saudi Arabia's has as many as 10,000 adult members, and by some estimates up to 20,000 in total, although the estimates vary greatly.[3] Certainly, there are perhaps 2,000 royals occupying positions in the state structure or in public life, suggesting that overall the family's size is over 10,000. Qatar's royal family is probably of a similar size – again, only loose estimates are available – but given that country's small population, this makes the family a large share of the population, and its members feature in politics and business accordingly.[4] These are the larger of the Gulf's ruling families, but in all of them there are family members spread throughout the state, stabilizing the system and linking the monarch and elite to society.[5]

The variations in the titles adopted by Gulf rulers reflect their claims to power. Emir, king and sultan have different meanings and political connotations. The term *Emir* (or *Amir*), literally meaning "lord" or "commander" and commonly used as the title for a "prince", has an implication of both administrative authority and nobility. A ruler who takes this title may send a message of possessing strong and legitimate, but not absolute, authority. It is the title taken by the rulers of Kuwait and Qatar, and others in the past. In the UAE the title *Sheikh* or *Shaykh* is used for the ruler, who also has the modern position of president. Sheikh is the usual honorific title for the head of a tribe or large family, but is also used as a term of respect. It, too, has an implication of strength and legitimacy, but due to tribal tradition, also implies a leader who is accessible and consultative. In Oman, the ruler uses the title *Sultan*. This has various meanings, too, but politically it suggests a dynastic ruler who has very powerful authority over a territory. It has a connotation of religious authority as well, although not to the level of a *Caliph*, the term for the head of a religious community or for the Muslim world overall and which arguably carries the most authority of any traditional title.[6] Since the abolition of the Caliphate in Turkey in 1924, however, there has been no widely recognized Caliph of the (Sunni) Muslim world.[7] Finally, the rulers of Saudi Arabia and Bahrain use the title of *Malik* ("King"). Historically some rulers avoided this title, believing that it conveyed earthly power but not legitimacy, religious sanction, or humility. The revolutions and coups that removed kings in Egypt, Iraq, Libya and elsewhere in the mid-twentieth century reinforced that image. Technically the Saudi monarchs dropped the title in 1986, adopting the more pious-sounding prenominal "Custodian of the Two Holy Mosques" instead,[8] but in practice the term king has retained wide usage. In contrast, Hamad, the ruler of Bahrain deliberately adopted the title of "King" in 2002 (having previously been "Emir"), in an attempt to cement and assert his power.

The monarchies vary in their structure and patterns of rule in minor ways – say, in the form of succession adopted or the complexity of family politics – but what makes them all very durable is the way in which the regime exerts effective control over the state by placing family members into key state positions. This tactic began in Kuwait in 1938 but has now spread across the Gulf. It allows the ruler to coopt his relatives with state jobs, while forming a comparatively loyal, family-dominating regime deep into state institutions. Economic capacity is critical: oil wealth, for example, provides the income for a ruler to use in coopting both the extended family and society more widely. Family dynasties add an additional layer of political support and protection for a system that otherwise would be closer to a purely allocative one. No such system has been overthrown in modern times in the region. Where monarchies have fallen, as in Iran in 1979 or Egypt in 1952, it was arguably the lack of such a system, and the fact that the leader was relatively isolated from both the state apparatus and societal forces, that explains why.

The extended family also creates certain political risks for a ruler, however, and is not necessarily unquestioningly loyal. A successful ruler will have to consult with the family, not only with the members who form part of his neopatrimonial network, but also more widely, requiring at least occasional concessions to the family. To ignore or marginalize them is far more risky, but the large royal families can be very complex and messy. The Qatari ruling dynasty, the Al Thani, has had a particularly conflict-ridden history, at times demanding handsome shares of the emirate's oil income in exchange for their loyalty.[9] Its various branches continue to offer greatly varying levels of support for the Emir. It has been argued that intra-family factionalism and rivalries are the key source of Qatar's transformation under Emir Hamad (r. 1995–2013).[10] On occasion, particular members of a ruling family will oppose a ruler's particular decision, or even oppose the ruler himself. This is normally managed by mobilizing large branches of the family and senior figures against the individuals concerned. The hope is to negotiate an acceptable outcome that restores family unity; failing this, a ruler will instead seek to form a dominant faction which will then push the renegade faction out of politics – and sometimes even into exile.[11]

In these systems, the royal family members vary greatly in their distance from and access to the ruler, which is the deciding factor in their level of influence and access to patronage. The clout of their specific branch of the family, their political nous, and what advantages they can offer to a ruler also set the scope and limits of family members' power. In the past royals were often given the most crucial government roles, but this has become less common as more technocratic cabinets have become preferred. Royals are also routinely granted commercial or business opportunities, partly to control them – favours granted in the business realm can easily be withdrawn, if necessary – and partly because such opportunities are easily segmented and thus shared widely. Favours such as a monopoly over the importation and distribution of a particular prod-uct, or the chance to partner with an especially promising foreign investor, are commonly used. Royals play an important commercial role in Saudi Arabia, for example. Many grew immensely powerful and wealthy in the mid/late-twentieth century, and only in the 2010s, as more ambitious reforms are being planned, is this perhaps changing.

POLITICAL INSTITUTIONS

While ruling families are at the core of Gulf political systems, power is shared and decisions negotiated, especially in the Gulf's softer forms of authoritarianism where agreement and cooptation are preferred over coercion. The roles of formal political institutions, and of less formal polit-ical and social actors and forces, are important too. As they sit at or near the summit of politics, institutions are essential in implementing a leadership's policies, maintaining order, managing state ownership and regulation and as consultative or collaborative bodies such as legislatures. As institutional extensions of a leader's power, they support regime maintenance, while appointments at their senior ranks usually are useful tools for cooptation. The Gulf's political institutions followed a different path to the Arab repub-lics in their development. Modernization was undertaken above all by large-scale capital works and the expansion of state services to the popula-tion, with the majority of jobs held by foreign workers rather than the indig-enous workforce. Nationals were coopted instead by the free education they received and by public sector employment. This is in contrast to the republics, where rapid military and bureaucratic modernization was predominantly used for economic nationalist purposes and for populist ends.

This had enduring impacts for the Gulf's institutions. In public sector departments, excessive employment led to high levels of redundant labour. In earlier decades this was a cost the Gulf states could absorb. This is less the case now, however, and yet the (citizen) workforce remains clustered in the public sector, poorly equipped to shift into the private sector and with many people unwilling to do so.[12] Certainly, many state-owned firms are world class, in particular because they were not used for populist, non-economic goals and therefore are relatively efficient, often profitable and for the most part have not been encumbered by political interference.[13] Instead, they are a focal point for investing oil wealth (and being *seen* to be investing it wisely), for redistributing wealth through indirect means such as public offerings of shares, and by generating wealth in non-energy sectors.[14]

The Gulf's militaries have been broadly supportive of the political systems they serve. This is the product of the relatively small militaries possessed by the Gulf monarchies, done in part as a way to "coup-proof" their systems, as well as due to the relatively young age and limited institutional history of most militaries.[15] The small but professional officer class in these systems, and its penetration by royals and figures from elite families and tribes, is another feature. Finally, the "reliance on groups with special loyalties to the regime and the creation of parallel military organizations and multiple internal security agencies"[16] has also been important in constraining the political reach of military leaders. Gulf rulers have nonetheless still had to be cognizant of military matters, including the mood of the senior officers, and have at least partly followed the approach set in other Arab states where multiple military and security agencies exist, with part of their purpose being to balance, compete with, and watch over other such institutions. Security responsibilities are sometimes split among different ministries, therefore, as in Kuwait, where policing and defence are separated by ministry, while the intelligence streams of each have separate lines of reporting. Some states keep a royal guard, and sometimes special forces, as separate bodies or branches of their militaries: Oman keeps a royal guard and special forces as separate service branches to the army, while Saudi Arabia has a national guard that is separate to its main army.

The power of specific ministries also varies tremendously within and across the Gulf. Power is somewhat predetermined by role. The power of bodies with finance roles is difficult to deny, for example, and a certain power comes from defence or interior ministries because of their centrality in ensuring both national security and regime security. In other cases, power shifts can sometimes be ephemeral, the result, say, of a relative rise or fall in the influence of a particular minister or official. The successful maintenance of longer-term power typically comes from the clientelist structures that permeate various institutions. One study of Saudi Arabia[17] demonstrated this clearly, showing how the rapid creation of state institutions allowed for segmented patron–client networks to arise, with impacts on the efficiency and relative power of various departments and agencies as allocations flow downwards from the political elite. This is classic neopatrimonialism. Within institutions, there are also opaque links between actors within institutions and societal groups which they represent or with which they establish relationships of convenience. Again, layers of patron–client dynamics and weak coordination and information-sharing horizontally within and across institutions, is a standard outcome of neopatrimonial structures. In such systems – not only in Saudi Arabia but across the Gulf – policy-making is messy. Power comes from above, but elites are influenced from below by competing, often fragmented actors whose impact varies from indirect influence via personal networks, to greater power held by specialists, to cases where an actor is one of several "veto players",[18] able to oppose a reform or shift because of conflicting rules, or a lack of coordination or follow-up from above, or by simple inaction.

There are other institutions that play certain roles in Gulf politics, albeit with less power than might be assumed. One example is legislatures, another is local or provincial governments. By most measures, the importance of these bodies has grown in recent years as new parliaments or consultative bodies have been created or their roles expanded, and as some government tasks have been devolved to local government bodies, as in Saudi Arabia. In some cases electoral politics has been introduced or expanded to these institutions. Generally, however, they exist not to devolve real power, but for the appearance of reform and for consultative ends. Brumberg has argued for a concept of "pluralized autocracy",[19] or sometimes similarly argued as being "illiberal democracy",[20] a form of regime maintenance in which the state creates a permanent mode of pluralization, but not democratization. The means of democratization are actually the ends in such a system, with institutions or elections acting as a controlled outlet for popular demands, or as new consultative channels, but with the political status quo maintained and genuine political reforms avoided. Arguably the reforms in Bahrain since the early 2000s are an example, with a veneer of democratization masking the fact that precious little real power has been transferred to the legislature or the people.

All of the Gulf states have some sort of national assembly, but many are only consultative bodies, with appointed rather than elected members, and often with very limited powers. Saudi Arabia and Qatar are examples. Even where a body does possess strong powers on paper, as with Oman's (elected) Consultative Assembly, it may choose not to exercise these powers. Somewhat paradoxically, it is Kuwait, arguably the most rentier of the Gulf states, that has the most influential parliament. It is a unique case, however, and the parliament exists not because of top-down reform but from some mix of the regime's wanting to keep a broad societal base happy and maintain a consultative mechanism with society, and because the regime is unable to guarantee society protection from external threats such as that from Iraq.[21]

STATE CAPITALISM, NATIONAL OIL COMPANIES AND OTHER STATE-OWNED FIRMS

While many institutions in the Gulf are weak, this is far less the case with key state-owned firms, especially the national oil companies (NOCs). The nationalization of oil companies around the 1970s or so greatly enhanced their power, as well as transforming the global oil industry. In the domestic sphere, NOCs are extremely powerful because they are the vehicles through which states and regimes obtain the bulk of their income, with that income then used, largely in lieu of taxation in the case of the Gulf, to provide for society's needs and to maintain the political order.

The NOCs are the core of the Gulf's "new" state capitalist systems. The new state capitalism of the contemporary Gulf states is different to earlier forms of state capitalism. It is not the product of a state elite coming out of revolutionary politics, nor do its elites see the private sector as ideologically incongruous with the state. Nor is it a variety of the state-led Asian "developmental state" models:[22] even if some similarities exist, fundamental contrasts such as rentierism and reliance on expatriate labour in the Gulf differentiate them strongly. The Gulf's new state capitalism is a risk-tolerant, internationally-oriented form, (selectively) friendly towards the private sector. It is even "entrepreneurial"[23] in the sense that its ownership of firms and industries has not just been motivated by domestic social or political considerations, but by states seeking to make these firms efficient, profitable and innovative. Such systems allow the state to avoid both unpopular and politically-risky neoliberal economic liberalization and the trap of *dirigisme*. It is by this new state capitalist structure that Gulf leaderships move beyond rentierism as a simple and relatively blunt mechanism of cooptation and control, to a more nuanced form of late-stage rentier politics. It is a means for the ruling elite and its clients and supporters to manage the economy, allocate and share wealth, and control neopatrimonial elite linkages. Rentierism is still important in providing the funds that create and underwrite state-owned firms. New state capitalism supports rentierism by using rents to create alternative, non-rent sources of income for the state and because it diversifies the economy, stabilizes state incomes, and creates jobs in non-energy areas.

The NOCs are pivotal cogs in these systems in obvious ways. Their histories, covered briefly in Chapter 2, suggest some of these, particularly the role they played in supplying oil revenues to states and letting states more effectively plan both their oil policies and, above all, their broader economic and development strategies.[24] At this level, the Gulf's NOCs share basic features in terms of their political-economic roles. Where they vary somewhat is in the detail of their relationship with the state that owns them. Some, such as Saudi Aramco, operate in an environment where the state's policy role and the NOC's strategy role are relatively clear; this is true also with the Abu Dhabi National Oil Company (ADNOC), although its position reporting to the Abu Dhabi government, rather than the federal government, is in contrast to the Gulf's other NOCs and means that its relationship with the (federal) oil ministry is different to most other NOCs.[25] In some systems the NOC has political influence within the bureaucracy, and is not merely a servant of policy-makers, where it provides advisers and technical support to oil ministries or other public sector institutions.[26]

As a generalization, Gulf NOCs are well-managed at both the strategic and operational levels. This is perhaps unsurprising in light of their central position in new state capitalism, which encourages states to maximize the incomes derived from the oil companies while ensuring the long-term viability and profitability of these firms. They typically have boards of either directors or advisers, but the membership of that board, and how well-represented key political actors are, varies. This has not precluded political interference in the NOCs, however, and while they enjoy substantial autonomy on paper, they are sometimes subjected to interference or requests of a political nature through informal mechanisms. There is also no guarantee that NOCs will not suffer from redundant labour (excessive numbers of staff), as they are often required to be at the forefront of national employment programmes. Ultimately there is a balancing force at work: states rely upon NOCs for income, and thus ultimately for their capacity, and the NOCs rely on state power and authority for their operations and autonomy, and as guarantors of their international influence in the global energy sector. The NOCs also derive power and influence from the economic nationalism that drove their nationalizations and continue to shape popular and elite perceptions of them.

The NOCs roles do change and sometimes stray from their traditional focus. One example of this was Kuwait Petroleum Corporation's (KPC) investment in BP shares in 1987–88; at one time KPC owned almost 23 per cent of BP.[27] KPC was eventually required by the British government to divest substantially from this position, and the investment was arguably driven by a complex set of Kuwaiti motivations, but it is a reminder that NOCs are not necessarily passive and unchanging firms operating only at the whim of rulers, nor actors lacking completely in agency. A second way in which, more recently, NOCs have diverged from their traditional role is where they are managing gas contracts as well. Due to the enormous costs of gas investments and the need for long-term supply contracts to ensure the financial viability of a new gas train, such projects are typically run as joint ventures between a NOC and an international oil company (IOC). This has become an important force drawing together NOCs and IOCs into strategic alliances, where previously they had held more separate roles in the supply chain, and had sometimes acted in opposition. Saudi Arabia began this trend, with the Saudi Gas Initiative in the 1990s;[28] Qatar has increasingly dominated it as they developed their gas industry in the early twenty-first century.[29] Rulers have accepted this because of the relatively less political nature of gas compared to oil, and because of the foreign policy benefits that come from partnering with energy-thirsty gas importers in East Asia and elsewhere.[30]

The NOCs are crucial as sources of state income, but state-owned firms in other sectors also play important roles in generating income and employment, and even in national branding strategies and foreign policies. They share certain features in common with the NOCs, including that they are generally well-managed, with their leadership typically given a high level of autonomy by the political elite. They are expected to operate efficiently, and in most cases profitably, oftentimes in competitive environments. They are risk-tolerant. They are increasingly becoming multinational in their strategies, investing abroad or engaging with the global economy.

A range of businesses across the Gulf are state-owned, or floated on a stock market but majority- or substantially state-owned, from airlines, to telecommunications firms, to many financial services firms, to defence and security companies. Perhaps the most obvious example is in the petrochemicals sector. Since this is closely linked to the oil and gas industry, it is not surprising that the state would seek to tightly control it, but these firms are also state-dominated because they tend to be highly profitable and are an area in which the economy is especially competitive. A flagship Saudi firm, for example, is Saudi Arabian Basic Industries Corporation (SABIC), a globally-competitive and increasingly internationalized petrochemicals and industrials firm. It is publicly-traded, but with the state retaining a 70 per cent stake in it; more than double what is typically needed to be considered a controlling interest. Other state-owned firms in Saudi Arabia are similarly state-controlled but floated: the state still holds 50 per cent of the Saudi Arabian Mining Company (Ma'aden), and the National Commercial Bank, among many others.[31] Similarly, a large percentage of Dubai's major firms are state-owned businesses controlled by either the Dubai World or Dubai Holding groups, and in Qatar the story is similar.[32] Some major firms have some direct state ownership, such as Qatar Telecom (Qtel), with 50 per cent state ownership, or Qatar Cement, with 43 per cent, among many examples. Alternatively, others are substantially owned by firms that are themselves state-owned or controlled. The Qatari sovereign wealth fund (SWF) owns 50 per cent of Qatar National Bank (QNB) and smaller portions of other financial institutions, while Industries Qatar is 70 per cent owned by the NOC, Qatar Petroleum (QP). In Kuwait, Kuwait Investment Authority (KIA), the SWF, holds significant minorities in the mobile telecommunication company Zain, Kuwait Finance House, Gulf Bank, Kuwait Cement Company, and others. The Public Institution for Social Security also owns shares across a range of firms. While direct state ownership is less common, the national airline Kuwait Airways, is state owned; even if plans to privatize the airline are realized, the state would still maintain a minority ownership of the new firm.

Thus, albeit with some strong conditions, the Gulf's state capitalist structure is business- and market-friendly, but with the state retaining overarching control. In many cases, such as with financial or telecommunications firms, there are multiple firms operating in the sector and thus the commercial environment is ostensibly competitive, but the state, its investment vehicles, or other state-owned bodies will own parts of these firms. Thus, a particular sector may, in fact, be less genuinely competitive than first appearances would suggest. The political advantages of this arrangement, so common in new state capitalist systems, include the largesse and commercial opportunities the state can dispense through these firms, whether as jobs within them or as contracts for major private sector actors (whether firms owned by royals, old merchant families, or international interests) to supply or partner with them.

New state capitalism is also advantageous to a state's foreign and security policies. As a protective strategy, the Gulf states conduct foreign policy with a strong set of economic goals and interests in mind. Rulers seek the "mobilization of different parts of the state apparatus in search of a common objective"[33] far beyond what only a foreign ministry could achieve through simple diplomatic efforts alone. State-owned firms are important actors through which states conduct national branding initiatives. Qatar is famous for having done this very effectively in recent years, although the fact that Dubai has become almost a household name abroad shows how effective its efforts since the 1980s at national marketing and public relations have been. State-owned firms may assist with overseas lobbying. Their activities – such as an airline adding a new route to an emerging destination, even if not (yet) profitable – may also supplement more conventional trade and investment policy activities, foreign aid, and other economic aspects of diplomacy. At the domestic political level, the international activities of state-owned firms, along with those of sovereign wealth funds (SWFs), serve political purposes as well, suggesting to society that the state is mature, long term in its thinking, willing to engage with the global economy and responsibly spending the country's oil wealth.[34]

MERCHANTS, BUSINESSPEOPLE AND MULTINATIONAL FIRMS

The Gulf's new state capitalism does not preclude the existence of a genuine and sizeable private sector. In fact, it relies upon them and grants them a substantial degree of freedom. To be sure, "GCC capitalists remain an appendix to the state in an analysis of the fundamental drivers of growth in Gulf economies – especially if the structural role of the bourgeoisie in tax-based economies is taken as a yardstick".[35] State expenditure dominates capital formation, and the private sector is excluded from a range of economic sectors and roles. That noted, there is a substantial private sector in all the Gulf economies. They account for a minority of overall GDP, but given the preponderance of oil and gas in these economies, as a share of non-oil GDP the Gulf's private sectors are much larger. Over the 2002–12 period – a period dominated by a long oil boom – they were a majority of non-oil GDP in Bahrain, Kuwait, and the UAE, and close to half of non-oil GDP in Qatar; only in Oman and Saudi Arabia did they account for a clear minority share of non-oil GDP.[36]

The private sector consists of various groups of actors and forces. The most established of these, albeit one whose power is in decline, is the traditional merchant families. They usually have long-established commercial interests, and often a history of working with the ruling family. In Saudi Arabia, the merchants' influence in the past was particularly strong, with the wealthier and well-connected ones in the western Hijaz part of the Kingdom having been especially important sources of support for the ruling Al Saud family, given their local influence.[37] Key merchant families have been consulted at times of important political change, such as in 1962 when the royal family was preparing to remove and replace King Saud with his rival Faisal. Once the Saudi rulers had oil income, this became an important mechanism for elite cooptation. Many merchants originally made their money from foreign trade, but as of the 1950s, they increasingly found wealth in rentier-related activities such as government contracts, as suppliers to state-owned firms, as intermediaries, and as representatives of foreign companies, sometimes further benefitting from government loans or other support. The state often doled out advantages to favoured families and businesses, for example by offering concessions – in effect monopolies – to them in a corner of the economy. Later, as the economy became more developed but also more competitive, wealthy families found opportunities in the stock market, new areas of foreign trade, or in newly-opened parts of the economy.

The business–government relationships in other Gulf states share many similarities with the Saudi case. In Abu Dhabi, Bahrain, Oman, and a lesser extent Dubai, Sharjah, and elsewhere, pre-oil bargains between rulers and merchants created what Valeri has called an "oligarchic pact" of mutual support and symbiosis.[38] His argument is that this began changing in the oil era, even though the original pact survived, and is now entering a further period of change as royal families themselves become extensive commercial actors at the expense of traditional business families. This may be true, although there are some variations among these cases. In Bahrain, merchant families are closely tied to sectarian politics, often chosen for their willingness to support the ruling Al Khalifa dynasty and, in the case of some key Shia ones, as symbols of the opportunities offered by the Al Khalifa to the Shia majority. In other cases, especially the key trading hubs of what is now the UAE, merchant families have a history of close ties to the ruling elites and have engaged very effectively with them, making it perhaps less likely that the political elite would abandon them for commercial opportunities. As reform imperatives become yet more urgent in the coming years, perhaps both traditional and royal commercial elites will find the state less willing to guarantee their privileged positions.

Kuwait and Qatar are a little different. In both, the merchants historically enjoyed an influential role. Those in Kuwait had close ties to the ruling Al Sabah family, which relied on the merchants for income and at times financial and political support. In Qatar, the merchants were a smaller and weaker group, but financial troubles at times made the Al Thani dynasty's survival reliant upon loans or other help from a handful of wealthy merchants. This was particularly true of the collapse in the pearl industry in the early 1930s, which tested Kuwait's economy but nearly destroyed

Qatar's. Kuwait's merchants were larger in number, more adaptable, and more politically influential, and so handled the crisis better than Qatar's. Oil had a varied impact in the two economies: it allowed both regimes to gain autonomy from the merchants by buying them off with a share of the oil income, reducing the political power of the Kuwaiti merchants, while in Qatar, where the merchants were so much weaker, the extended royal family was of far greater concern to rulers, and new business elites emerged as oil wealth grew. The Shia always played an important role in Kuwait, one that has grown in recent decades as new Shia's commercial elites have emerged. This demonstrates both the importance for Kuwaiti rulers to manage sectarian differences in society – a minority of perhaps 35–40 per cent of Kuwaitis are Shia – but also shows how these new Shia merchants are, like others before them, reliant on the state in such rentier systems.[39]

While the large families of Saudi Arabia and the UAE dominate in the Gulf's commercial sectors, including in intra-Gulf trade and investment, in recent decades the merchant classes of all the Gulf have evolved to broadly share a number of characteristics.[40] Perhaps most important, they remain tightly linked to the state; in effect, to the new state capitalism of these economies. They have expanded their roles into new economic sectors in similar ways and under roughly similar political guidance, with the state keen to support economic diversification and business families eager to spread their risk widely and to gain footholds in new sectors and industries. These families also play an increasing role in finance. While state-owned banks remain dominant, especially in retail banking and sometimes commercial lending, too, big families have started to engage in more sophisticated commercial activity, for example in borrowing, raising capital on stock markets, and creating private equity ventures.[41] While arguably the merchants remain weaker than they would otherwise be, were it not for rentierism and the royal dominance at the highest levels of the state capitalist systems, and while for the foreseeable future these families will have to continue to defer to the state on important matters, their role – and certainly their potential – seems broader than it was a generation ago.

In more recent decades, the power of merchants has waned, if only relatively, as the Gulf economies have opened up and as rulers have sought to build more globalized, competitive private sectors. Some newer commercial actors are simply from emerging families, and have made their money much as traditional merchants have consolidated theirs, by linking to the state and its distribution of oil rents. Others have gained a foothold in new sectors of the economy, such as tourism, new information technologies, retail and business services. Some of these actors are old elites in a new guise: royals, as noted, or members of notable families. Others are technocrats or public sector workers who pursue business as a side interest. Still others, if modest in number, are genuine entrepreneurs seeking to focus their careers in the private sector. In nearly all cases, businesspeople need to have what is called in Arabic *wasta*. This roughly translates as "intermediation", and refers to the political connections, access, and support from inside state institutions that is regularly, even routinely, required so as to bypass regulations, prohibitions, or simply red tape and to get business done effectively. As much as these economies have grown more sophisticated, they are still very personalized as well.

Wasta is often conflated with corruption, although it is not the same. *Wasta* can be any form of intermediation or intercession by a third party; for corrupt purposes, very often, but it is also used for other purposes such as conflict resolution. Still, it raises the question of corruption in the Gulf states. The Arab Gulf monarchies typically rate better that the Arab republics on measures of corruption perception, such as Transparency International's Corruption Perception Index (CPI); in the 2017 ratings, the Gulf states perform well above the Middle Eastern average. All but Bahrain register in the top half of the list of 180 countries, and several are nearer the top, such as the UAE (21st), Qatar (29th), and even Saudi Arabia (57th).[42] The states beyond the Gulf, on average, fare much worse: Tunisia ranks the highest, at 74th, and along with Morocco (81st), and Israel (32nd), are the only non-GCC states in the top half of the list. Corruption occurs in the Gulf monarchies, but not with the frequency and embeddedness with which it is found in key republics such as Algeria

(112th), Egypt (117th), or Syria (178th). However, while overt financial and other corruption may be less common in the Arab Gulf states, their political economies are still lacking in transparency and are heavily reliant upon patronage. Their rentierism and neopatrimonial elite politics encourage opaque leadership-elite dynamics and wider unaccountability, while the large rents and relative wealth of these economies acts to discourage the smaller-scale financial corruption that is so common in poorer and middle-income republics.

Foreign businesses also play a role in the Gulf economies. As already discussed, NOCs often link with multinational energy firms, especially in gas-related joint ventures. The multinational firms are not usually permitted ownership in the sector, but they still exert some political impact as investors and through other forms of influence. Other international firms typically enter a Gulf market in one of two ways. One is by a 51/49 partnership with a local, well-connected businessperson, who will hold a 51 per cent share in the investment but take care of navigating the commercial environment. Otherwise, for firms that prefer complete ownership of a project, most Gulf economies have free zones of some sort that permit 100 per cent foreign ownership in a project and typically offer other advantages. These may be literal, physically defined free zones located at a port or other specified area. Famous examples include Jebel Ali, near Dubai, the Gulf's first free zone, but since then the UAE has created some 45 free zones of various types. The other five Gulf economies have all created free zones, too, typically with a sectoral focus. The resulting transformation of their economies and the urban economic landscapes of the Gulf coast in the past two decades or so have been dramatic. Other free zones are not a physical space but simply a policy framework in which firms in a particular sector can operate with certain freedoms or advantages. By various means, Gulf governments have sought to attract new foreign investment in recent decades, with similar motivations as those driving their support for the (conditional) development and expansion of the indigenous private sector – diversification, job creation, and technology and skills transfer.

128

RENTIERISM AND SOCIOECONOMIC FORCES IN THE GULF

There is a general assumption by many observers of the Gulf that society exerts very little influence over Gulf politics. Early rentier state theory made oversimplified claims about the passivity of society, arguing that the state had almost absolute autonomy from society provided it could distribute an adequate amount of rent to coopt it. Early rentier proponents claimed, for example, that the state, "being independent of the strength of the domestic economy, does not need to formulate anything deserving the appellation of economic policy", and that since loyalty is "to the system, not to individuals in power", there is no democratic imperative on the state from societal forces.[43] Politics in these countries was, of course, always more complex than this, and early rentier arguments were justifiably criticized.[44] Rentierism is best thought of as an explanation of a political *dynamic* and tactic and not, in the way that early proponents treated it, as a structural explanation for the nature of the state. Thus, the term "late-stage rentierism" or "late rentier" state, is used here. This concept has been explained elsewhere.[45] It derives from earlier rentier state theory, and concurs that allocative states are able to buy toleration by society through rent allocations, pay for repressive apparatus, and avoid democratic concessions. While the state is not democratically accountable to society, late rentierism argues that it may nonetheless be responsive to it, especially to avoid widespread opposition from forming. Further, the state has a very clear and long-term development strategy, economic policy, and foreign policy – none of which rentier theorists traditionally saw as a characteristic of the rentier state – because rents are merely a political tool, albeit an absolutely crucial one, of the state. Alone, rents are not sufficient to explain the political structure of the state.

Given this, societal power and agency exists in the Gulf and cannot be ignored. The state may well be the most important actor in the political economy, but it cannot routinely act with complete ignorance of society's wishes, nor can it challenge or undermine societal actors and forces without some form of negotiation or compensation. In Gulf societies, populations have multiple units of political loyalty to which they offer allegiance and owe obligations. The state is only one of these, albeit a main one, and ethnic identity, religion, sectarian membership, tribal affiliation, and extended family also compete with the state for individuals' loyalties and as units of their identity. The state must manage these groups and forces, a task that goes well beyond mere rentier allocation. Even when combined with neopatrimonial strategies and, when necessary, repression, the state still must usually undertake – and will typically prefer – consultative processes.

At the simplest level, the most basic social units of Arab politics are dominant in the Gulf as much as elsewhere in the region, particularly family and tribe. Along with smaller informal social units, these are what one work on the region has called "the genes of politics".[46] Group identities, including not only family and tribe but also professional, personal, recreational, religious, and other groupings form a "mosaic" of overlapping and interlocking interactions, embedded not only in society but in particular classes and wider groupings.[47] The family is perhaps the simplest of these, and membership of a particular extended family will often reflect tribal and sectarian affiliation and be important in defining traditional power structures. The senior male in a family typically dominated it, at least in terms of setting the landscape of the family; women possessed considerable power behind the scenes, but in more informal capacities and typically constrained by a patriarchal public facade. Yet the family is also a rapidly changing social unit, being reformulated as economies change, new technologies arise, gender roles shift, and other kinship dynamics are restructured or otherwise change.[48] Gender is, in fact, a good example of where social roles and state policies have met, with the latter affecting the former. Across the Gulf, state policies on higher education, employment, and business have all assisted an increase in women's public roles and positions, albeit not without opposition from traditional social groups and with substantial variances remaining in male and female public roles and power. To a considerable degree, an individual's choices and capacities remain defined by what is acceptable to the family, and especially the family patriarch: this is true particularly for women, but not exclusively so, as men, too, have roles in and obligations to the family which are unavoidable and which they are expected to prioritize.

Certain privileged individuals who are members of an elite may receive favourable treatment through their position in neopatrimonial networks, but in the Gulf states individuals and families are coopted most routinely through rent dispersements. These take several forms. Above all, there is absence of income tax, and very low taxation obligations overall. Added to this is the fact that the bulk of citizens are employed directly or indirectly by the state,[49] and employment conditions for citizens are usually very generous, with high salaries but also secure tenure. Transfer payments from the state are also substantial. In the UAE in the early 2010s, it was reported that the average Emirati male citizen received in total some $55,000 per year in transfers from the state, whether as free education, health care, interest-free loans, and even payments towards the costs of a wedding.[50] They also heavily subsidize basic household expenses such as utilities,[51] even if this would seem to be politically unnecessary, and indeed are beginning to be reduced. The situation is similar in other high-income Gulf states such as Kuwait and Qatar, and is only less-generous in the lower-rent economies of Bahrain and, to some extent, Oman, although even these economies are still highly rentier by most measures and provide subsidies and other transfer payments. More recently, in an effort to sustain but streamline transfer payments – particularly, to offset the costs for lower- and middle-income Saudis from planned economic reforms – the Saudi government in 2017 created "citizens' accounts" for direct and specific state payments to families. All these types of payments are classic rentier strategies. They are designed to ensure that the state is seen as sharing oil wealth and as a provider to society, and also serve as a routine reminder of the benevolence of the state. They are designed to boost the image and legitimacy of the state, while being at risk if a citizen chooses to challenge the state or the existing political-economic order, thereby making the perceived cost of political noncompliance expensive.

While an individual may place their immediate family first in their

131

priorities, they cannot easily escape their ties to social units such as tribe. Tribe confers obligations, sometimes defining, say, a person's marriage options, but may also provide opportunities, as when tribal affiliation can be used to gain advantages through *wasta*.[52] Tribes may have advantages such as access to a ruling family or a notable family because of the history shared by the two families, or because important individuals have carved unique relationships through marriage, commerce, or other means. Ruling families often appeal for loyalty and claim legitimacy by referencing tribal support, thus giving key tribes particular informal political influence, while tribes routinely also serve as distributive mechanisms for rent dispersements and state-bequeathed jobs and other favours,[53] all of which reinforces their political role in the eyes of the state and strengthens the social power of the tribal elite. Tribes are also important actors within political institutions, and even where tribal affiliation matters little in political practice, most individuals are at least aware of their tribal origins and linkages. Thus, tribes retain considerable informal power, and sometimes even formal influence where a ruler is compelled to consult directly with them, even if their power is limited by the state's cooptive and repressive capacities and is on the decline overall.

Finally, another informal group in the Gulf is the small informal social groups that arise through shared interests and networks. These groups vary from small gatherings of individuals with shared or aggregated interests, to larger political gatherings through which key decisions are agreed, to political associations and networks that meet for some purpose or to coordinate on shared interests.[54] Such groups can therefore cover social or recreational goals, but of most interest here are those created for a political role or purpose. Historically these groups have varied in their influence, from consultative and decision-making bodies such as the *diwaniyya* gatherings in Kuwait, to groups such as the *jam'iyya* ("societies") in Bahrain that have long crossed the near-invisible boundary between informal groups and political parties.[55] At a larger and more formal level, groupings such as chambers of commerce, businessmen's associations, and other groups not only provide services for their members, but, albeit very subtly, will also agitate for change, lobby for particular policies, or simply raise their members' profile with the state.[56] While the power of the state has risen with the region's oil wealth, an accompanying rise in the educated middle classes means that middle-class citizens have become more important to the state in recent decades. While citizens have become more reliant on the state and its wealth, the state has also become more reliant on educated professionals who are technically proficient and politically loyal. While these societal groups are all constrained by authoritarian and cooptive settings, and are weaker than in a vibrant democracy, they are important political actors and forces nonetheless. They have at least *some* agency to influence the state and at times to shape particular decisions.

The ultimate source of society's power is that the state's survival requires a fundamental level of popular acquiescence. States and ruling families need not be particularly popular, if their cooptive power is sufficient and tactics astute, however they are at risk if a critical mass of opposition forms against them. While the Gulf states have proved very durable and seen few large-scale opposition movements, there have been exceptions. The most notable of these was the opposition that erupted in Bahrain in early 2011, during the regional "Arab Spring" uprisings.[57] Bahrain's protests were partly the result of sectarian grievances, with the Shia majority unhappy at what they saw as discriminatory practices towards them by the Sunni regime, but as the protests gained momentum in February and March 2011, Sunnis were also increasingly evident in the ranks of the protestors too, angry at broken promises of political reform. The uprising only ended after an intervention by Saudi, Emirati and Qatari security forces in mid-March gave the regime the chance to focus on dispersing and suppressing the protestors. The Al Khalifa dynasty came close to being overthrown. Meanwhile, while the Bahrain uprising was the most serious at the time, there was also significant protests by the Shia minority in Saudi Arabia's northeast,[58] and smaller, predominantly anti-corruption protests in Oman.[59] What these protests demonstrated to regimes is that, while populations could be very effectively controlled by rentier arrangements, if society had significant and genuine grievances, once they gained momentum they could pose a real threat to the political order. The 2011 uprisings and protests prompted an extensive and further set of state spending including direct payments to citizens in Saudi Arabia[60] and pay rises in Qatar,[61] as well as targeted suppression of opposition forces in some states. The Saudi spending, at a total of some $130 billion, was particularly notable, and was focused on boosting salaries, building housing, and more funding for religious activities.[62] It was a reactive move by a leadership that felt threatened by the uprisings and which lacked alternate means to rapidly boost its legitimacy. This highlights Gulf regimes' continued reliance on rentierism and soft repression for their survival, while in the longer-term, the non-material grievances and desires of citizens remain for the most part side-lined.[63]

None of this applies to expatriate populations, who play no formal political role in the Gulf and are only minor informal actors, given that they are not citizens and sit outside of the rentier system. However, two exceptions arguably exist, where expatriates are politically important. The first is where they constitute a large share of the military or security services,[64] as they do most notably in Bahrain but also in Qatar, while the UAE uses foreign experts to help in the modernization of its armed forces. Expatriates in these roles may have influence, for obvious reasons. Second, foreigners are politically noteworthy, although not influential as such, by virtue of their existence in such large numbers. This can cause anxiety among citizens as to whether local cultures and values are being eroded by foreign populations; or more specifically, whether the economic conveniences of large expatriate populations are being privileged over the more opaque, but to many people more important, considerations of culture, tradition and religious values. This has been an issue in the UAE in recent years, where expatriates (but also the rise of tourism) are seen by some as responsible for a rise in gambling, alcohol availability, and looser sexual mores.[65] This is a vague type of influence, however, and generally there are few expatriates who enjoy much direct influence in Gulf politics.

EXTERNAL DYNAMICS IN GULF POLITICAL ECONOMIES

A final aspect of Gulf politics – but a very important one – is the international dimension. As much as states have led the transformation processes in the region since the 1980s and 1990s, some forces have been beyond their control, or are the product at least in part of externalities. Two particular dynamics are notable in this respect: the forces and impacts of globalization, and the role of regional politics.

Much of the scholarly debate about globalization and its impacts is hampered by argument, including the definitional fuzziness of the concept itself, but in particular over the difficulty in pinning down and attributing its impacts in and on the Middle East and the Gulf. One definitional and explanatory approach has been to examine globalization not as a holistic and homogenous force, but to separate its characteristics and impacts into categories.[66] There is an obvious economic angle to globalization, which is often given greatest focus by the beneficiaries of globalization. This includes free or freer movement of money, capital, goods, and people, with proponents of globalization often arguing for more liberal market structures. To its critics, conversely, the economics of globalization include political impacts such as reduced state power, less worker power, lower individual autonomy over one's economic life, and even exploitation. This perception of exploitation, or even the possibility of it, has seen some observers equate globalization with neoimperialism,[67] substituting once direct political and social control with an indirect but powerful economic control. More commonly, arguments that globalization is a force for largely-negative economic neoliberalism are made.[68]

Similar arguments are made about another category, cultural and political globalization. There is an argument that globalization creates a "convergence"[69] of social and cultural dynamics, increasingly linking, relating, and impacting various communities across national and other boundaries. Ultimately, the argument goes, cultures become homogenized. The idea of globalization as "deterritorialization"[70] is an aspect of this line of argument, too, "signifying disjunctures between state borders and cultural communities".[71] While sometimes assumed to be a negative thing, elements such as freer human movement, the adoption of new homelands and cultural practices, and the transfer of politics from one territory to another, are all potentially positive or at least more ambivalent than often assumed. Finally, globalization is typically defined or delineated in part by its technological and communication impacts. Technological changes since the 1980s, such as the dramatic expansion of the online world, new mobile phone technologies, and new forms of mass media have often transcended national boundaries, potentially allowing for changes in state–society relationships and, some have argued, reducing state power and providing new and greater agency to individuals and communities.

The debate over globalization was late to focus on the Arab Gulf states, which provide a somewhat unique case study. The Gulf's oil and gas wealth place it in a unique position, by no means central in the global economy, and in many ways on the margins of it, yet willing to engage with it and to accept economic change as a price for doing so. That the Gulf has transformed so markedly since the 1990s and with so little opposition or social instability, despite rapid urbanization and transformations in social relations, is quite remarkable.[72] This is in part the product of how globalization, including economic globalization, has been managed by Gulf rulers, with neoliberal economic policies mostly avoided and yet the commercial environment in general having been substantially changed and freed up. Policies such as fixed exchange rates, protectionism in certain industries, and controls over foreign ownership of land and assets have all helped maintain stability, as has the fairly effective regulation of key sectors such as banking and finance, and institutions such as stock markets.[73] These policies have limited a backlash against foreign investment in particular, and globalization more broadly, while the relative economic stability enjoyed in the Gulf has probably helped enhance state legitimacy.

Second, the Gulf has responded to economic globalization in some proactive ways. A couple of obvious examples of this are the successful rise of transcontinental airlines owned and based in the Gulf, and the new Arab media companies that have come out of the subregion since the

1990s. The airlines – Emirates, perhaps most famously, but also Qatar Airways and Abu Dhabi-based Etihad, among others – are one area where the region has responded aggressively and quite successfully, carving a role in the global economy[74] and enhancing the country's international image at the same time. The airlines are the product of state strategies to develop trade, and especially tourism and airfreight, as part of their economic diversification strategies,[75] but they are also national symbols of development and economic engagement. Tourism has remained at least partly controlled, to avoid some of its less-positive social and cultural impacts, but certain types are sought nonetheless for their economic and branding benefits.

In a similar vein, in the economic and social-cultural realms, Arab media has been transformed since the 1990s, led by the media established in the Gulf states, indicating a more positive and proactive response to globalization. Qatar's Al Jazeera is the best-known example, created in 1996 by the then-new Qatari Emir Hamad as a new, entertaining and liberal satellite television news channel.[76] It was followed by a range of others, such as the Dubai-based, Saudi-owned Al-Arabiya. These firms play several roles. They are important as commercial enterprises, including as vehicles for economic diversification. More importantly, however, they serve political roles too, helping states to set the tone for domestic political and other discourses and assisting with national branding strategies overseas. They create an image of modernity, liberalism, and social and economic vigour, even if their impacts fall short of such ideals.

These are examples of what has been a relatively successful, and by many measures impressive, transformation in the Gulf since Dubai began its reforms in the mid-1980s. Dubai is indeed the most prominent example, having become by the 2010s a global city and economic hub – one of only a handful of such cities in the world.[77] It largely led the rest of the Gulf in its strategies to be an airline hub, tourist destination, shopping city, transhipment port, free trade area (in parts), and a connected, cosmopolitan city. As Khanna notes, Dubai's state capitalism has been central to its success, exploiting a symbiosis between the state and domestic and international business. Elements of Dubai's transformation have informed other Gulf states, including Qatar and Abu Dhabi, since the late 1990s.

Third, the Gulf has responded to the social and cultural risks of globalization relatively successfully. It has not allowed for unhindered social change, and new processes and technologies have often been adapted to the Gulf cultural setting. The introduction and expansion of online technology, the expansion of travel afforded by cheaper and more extensive air links, and the more recent rise in mobile telecommunications has not led to state–society, intergenerational, or gender conflict, even if they have assisted some social actors and forces to better communicate with each other or gain a more prominent voice. The state has intervened at times to constrain social forces, including online, and there are also strong social forces for stasis in the region. The new technologies that symbolize globalization are also, by nature, fragmentary, able to create new opportunities but in so doing, allowing a great many voices to arise, creating noise and confusion. There are thus limits to the degree to which opposition can be mounted through new technologies, on top of the effectiveness of the rentierism-state capitalism structure for the maintenance of state power.

Where Gulf states' and their leaderships have been less able to manage the effects of externalities is in the regional diplomatic and security setting, where a range of regional conflicts, rivalries and suspicions have undermined subregional security and created regional uncertainty. To be sure, the Arab Gulf states have been more politically stable and economically successful than most of the republics in recent decades. Their development strategies have been more cautious and considered, cushioned with oil wealth. They have also been fairly effective at distancing themselves from many of the major conflicts that have bedevilled other parts of the Middle East: the Gulf has been only a peripheral actor in the Arab–Israeli conflict, for example, and until the early twenty-first century, much of the Gulf pursued quietist foreign policies in the broader region. The smaller Gulf states largely fell in line behind Saudi Arabia, sharing much of its conservative outlook and unable to compete with its size and wealth. This was formalized by the creation of the Gulf Cooperation Council (GCC) in 1981, a regional body of the six Arab Gulf states, intended as a conservative Sunni front against Iraq's radical Arabism and Iran's Persian nationalism and Shia revolutionary politics after 1979. While the GCC's relevance is now in doubt, after the Saudi-Emirati-Bahraini dispute with Qatar erupted in June 2017, the GCC has previously played some quiet but important roles in the region. It helped counterbalance Iraqi and Iranian influence in the Gulf, provided architecture for security dialogues among the Gulf monarchies, and was the framework for certain trade and economic initiatives. It was just as important for its symbolism of unity, arguably, than for more concrete accomplishments.[78]

This began to change in the 2000s and especially the 2010s, as shifts in the regional (both Middle Eastern and Gulf) balance of power took place. There was a shift in regional power from the republics, especially from the eastern Mediterranean region, to the Gulf, as military power became less important to regional standing and economic power rose in importance. Key republics such as Egypt and Syria entered a period of economic and political stagnation after the 1980s, while Iraq was worn down by the brutal 1980–88 war with Iran and then from sanctions and war almost continuously after 1990. Meanwhile, the Gulf had the financial resources to attempt reform on its own terms. Their relative rise in power gave the Gulf states renewed reasons to engage more actively in the region, and the confidence to increasingly do so in ways that suited their domestic imperatives and their security and economic goals.

This led to a rise of new influential states in the Gulf. An early and prominent one was Qatar, which, beginning in the late 1990s, adopted a highly activist foreign policy. This was partly a military and security strategy, seeking to build new ties with external powers and other actors such as the United States, but it was also driven by economic goals.[79] Diplomatic and economic efforts were linked more closely, so that regional and global powers would be more motivated to support the status quo in Qatar. This was especially the case with Qatari–Iranian relations, but also more widely. Put crudely, diplomatic and trade initiatives were also, in effect, a form of business development, providing new trade and investment opportunities for the country which would flow on to greater domestic political advantages for the ruling elite. From the late 1990s to the mid-2010s, Qatar played a dramatically outsized role in the Middle East, with unique policies at various times towards Iran, Israel, the 2011 NATO-led Libyan intervention, Egypt's post-Mubarak government, and the Hamas government in Gaza after 2007, among various others. Later, after Hamad abdicated and handed power to his son Tamim in 2013, this strategy would backfire, and Saudi Arabia in particular sought to rein in Qatar by diplomatic pressure in 2014 and then a more dramatic isolation and sanctions after June 2017. Qatar's foreign policy activism was followed by more active Saudi and Emirati foreign policies in the 2010s, partly in response to Qatar's rising influence. Qatar can be seen as a source of, and leader in, this recent rise of the Gulf states' roles in Middle Eastern affairs.

The above coincided with a couple of other substantial regional changes at the time. One was the 2003 Iraq War and the geostrategic changes that came in the wake of the war, including the rise in Iranian influence in the region,[80] and Saddam's removal and replacement with a Shia-dominated political order in Iraq. This, plus the mess of Iraq's economy, left Iraq relatively weak and unable to resurrect itself as a regional power. At the same time, the civil strife in Iraq, especially over 2004–08, served as a reminder of the limits of US power in the Middle East, and was something of which Iran could take advantage. Iran felt more emboldened to act more forcefully and actively in the region, both in support of Shia groups and populations and in pursuing its strategic rivalry with Saudi Arabia. Iran's rise, and the intensification of sectarianism in the region, led Saudi Arabia particularly, as well as the UAE and other Gulf states, to play a more active regional role.[81]

Finally, the Arab Spring and its aftermath raised the relative position of the Gulf in Middle Eastern regional politics. The Bahrain uprising in 2011, as already noted, prompted a Saudi-led intervention to ensure the survival of the Bahraini ruling dynasty. Elsewhere, the Arab uprisings led to the serious civil strife in Syria, which morphed into a civil war after 2012, while Yemen was destabilized to the extent that it, too, slid into civil war around the same time. Both of these conflicts became inter-nationalized, with the Gulf states playing important roles. In Syria, both Saudi Arabia and Qatar were important early supporters of (different) anti-government opposition forces,[82] sending arms and other support as a way to undermine the Syrian regime of Bashar al-Asad, Iran's only ally in the Arab world. In Yemen, fears of Iranian support for the Shia there led to the Saudis leading an international coalition to support the Yemeni government against an uprising by the Shia Houthi rebels in the north.[83] Despite a brutal air campaign against the Houthis, the situation in Yemen stalled, becoming a long-term stalemate.

These international dynamics are, in practice, beyond the control of any one single state, and in that sense the Gulf has been drawn into play-ing a more active role in the wider region and has incentives to do so. The Saudi–Iranian rivalry is beyond the scope of either party to stop, given the lack of Gulf-wise security architecture and the history of competition, and often animosity, between the two.[84] Since Saudi Arabia has the resources to play the role it does, and is seeking what it sees as a more appropriate role as an international middle power, it is motivated to be activist, espe-cially if it feels that its interests are threatened by Iran. The smaller states play regional roles that are largely the product of their small size and of Saudi and US dominance in the region. For their leaderships, US power in the region is both a reality and an opportunity. There is little they could do to influence the US presence and role in the Middle East, and they have little choice but to work with Washington if they want access to US arms, support and favours. Closer to home, they are also quite restricted in their ability to challenge Saudi dominance. Leaderships are too concerned that to do so would invite Iranian intervention in their domestic politics. Meanwhile, the isolation of Qatar in the summer of 2017 was a reminder, if one was needed, that Saudi Arabia is willing to go to significant lengths to restrain small states in the Gulf that it sees as trying to usurp or test Riyadh's dominance. Bahrain, relying as it does on Saudi support for the survival of the regime, is particularly close to the Saudis.[85] The UAE, probably seeking to carve a regional role for itself in a way that would not upset Riyadh, has been increasingly activist in recent years as its wealth has grown and as other small states in the Gulf have become influential too.[86] It has been an important ally for the Saudis, including in restraining Qatar's ambitions.

The international setting is only one dimension of Gulf politics, however. In the domestic realm the Gulf's political systems are very stable and durable. The combination of rentierism, state capitalism, and neopatrimonialism support this stability, especially when used in combination effectively. It is a robust framework because it makes attempts by institutional elites or social forces to marshal opposition highly difficult, while giving ordinary people a stake in systemic stability and a disincentive to risk their standing within it or the benefits they derive from it. Politics in the Gulf is, therefore, first and foremost based on economic strategies, supplemented with more traditional elite management. This does not preclude ruling families and elites seeking to build legitimacy in other ways: it is a foolish ruler who would choose to rely *solely* on material incentives to maintain power and support.

Where rulers and ruling families find their support waning, or even sometimes face more direct challenges to their rule, it is typically for one of two reasons. It may be the result of them being in a weak position to begin with: say if they are part of a minority, as in Bahrain. Alternatively, it may be because they have failed to protect the national interest, or are perceived as having failed. This may happen where a sufficient mass of society sees the regime as having squandered oil wealth, for example, or having failed to share it equitably, or having shifted too far from the concerns of ordinary people, especially in times of difficulty or austerity. Such challenges are rare, however, and increasingly so as the Gulf's regimes become more experienced and sophisticated in their political organization and strategies. Whether this could reverse as new challenges will emerge in the future, however, is a question that cannot be neglected and which is taken up again in Chapter 6.

5

Human factors in the Gulf economies

It is somewhat trite – but very true nonetheless – to observe that human factors are the most important element in the success of an economy. It is the labour of a workforce that adds the greatest value to most goods and services. It is because of a workforce's education, training, employment experience, and continued development that an economy remains effective and, perhaps most importantly, is internationally competitive. It is entrepreneurialism and innovation, driven by particular individuals or distilled across an organization or culture, which is most crucial in expanding and developing an economy and improving real wages. It is via positive but appropriate rates of population growth, suitable immigration policies, and other demographic change that a workforce maximizes its economic potential – and moreover, such factors are also important in ensuring social stability and in assisting societies to respond to the pressures of economic changes.

The Arab states of the Gulf possess a unique demographic profile, characterized by a range of demographic and human capital features that contain both positive and negative features. The degree of economic reliance on foreign labour is perhaps the most obvious, but important too are (indigenous) population growth rates, labour market policies, the education and training framework, and gender and intergenerational dynamics. These occur in a framework set by the political order, and by structural and historical dynamics. Culture matters too, to the extent that it shapes corporate and institutional cultures and liberates or constrains the ambitions of societal groups and forces. The purpose of this chapter is to explore some of the more important human factors that have shaped the Gulf's economies, and which will be key elements – perhaps even deciding ones – in determining its prospects in the future.

WEALTHY SOCIETIES?

As already discussed, the Gulf economies are, by conventional measures, very wealthy. Nominal GDP per capita varies by country, from upper-middle income levels in Bahrain, Oman and Saudi Arabia, to levels in the UAE, Qatar and Kuwait that are comparable to the developed OECD economies. Infrastructure, capital, and public utilities are of a high standard: to a visitor, public spaces and infrastructure generally seem physically comfortable, and state services appear to be freely available and good quality. This is partly because they have been such a prominent focus of Gulf states' development strategies, leading governments to spend handsome amounts of their oil wealth on such projects, hoping that this would lay the groundwork for further growth and economic diversification. Moreover, while these economies indeed are relatively wealthy and comfortable, their nature and features are also distinct from those in more diverse, industrialized, developed economies.

In its inaugural *Arab Human Development Report* in 2002, the UN Development Programme suggested that the Arab world overall is "richer than it is developed with respect to basic human-development indicators".[1] It is rich, of course, predominantly because of oil, and the Gulf states are relatively economically developed by most measures, making this statement less pertinent to the Gulf states. Yet even in those economies, there are weaknesses and unique or unusual structural features, including the variability of their export incomes, their relatively small non-oil economic sectors, and their weak productivity rates. Structural problems such as their limited natural resources beyond oil and gas, small (citizen) populations, and climates are important features of them, too.

Along these lines, Michael Ross, in examining the so-called "oil curse", suggested an oil-related shortcoming in Gulf economic growth: "The real problem is not that growth in the oil states has been slow when it should have been 'normal' but rather that it has been normal when it should have been faster than normal, given the enormous [oil] revenues these governments have collected."[2] He goes on to argue that the marginalization of women and the inability to handle revenue volatility are the main explanations.[3] He is applying this argument to all oil states, but a specific examination of the wealthy Gulf states alone would still find similar answers, perhaps supplemented by what Ross has elsewhere examined as the "group formation effect".[4] This is relevant here because it has a causal link to the inclination and ability of society to engage with the state: "the formation of social capital—civic institutions that lie above the family and below the state—tends to promote more democratic governance...[but studies of] Algeria, Iran, Iraq, and the Arab Gulf states have all suggested that the government's oil wealth has impeded the formation of social capital and hence blocked a transition to democracy".[5] The extent of this dynamic is contested, but rent distribution by the state does appear to have some impact. Such arguments are central to the rentier theory idea that allocative systems relieve the state of pressure to democratize.

Even more controversially, some observers have contended that rentierism encourages in society, especially among young men, an expectation of good employment from the state. This is sometimes called a "*mudir* (or 'manager') syndrome": young people bring "a concept of honour" to their decisions on whether to accept a particular job, the argument goes, rejecting manual labour and other low-prestige work, and will only accept a position of "authority, status and respect".[6] In larger rentier states such as Saudi Arabia, in particular, there are not enough of these jobs for everyone who wants one. There is probably some validity to the "*mudir* syndrome" idea, and it is heard in various forms around the region. Yet it is also overstated: most people, not just those in rentier economies, seek employment that is prestigious or which comes with status and power, particularly university graduates seeking professional or managerial careers. It is a reminder that employment is not only a source of material benefits, but also of social status, identity, and other non-material advantages. It is probably also best considered as a manifestation (one of several) of a wider problem, wherein rentierism encourages "a public attitude of apathy rather than dynamism and a weakness of the private-sector."[7]

Another problem with making blanket statements about the standard of living in the Gulf is the variation within societies in their income and access to opportunities. The state is allocative, but not equally and to all. The nature of *wasta* means that those who are members of the royal family or well-connected to it will fare markedly better than most others. People holding well-paid government jobs, especially in high-paying firms such as national oil companies, will have higher incomes than those who cannot obtain such roles. There are, as in most economies, disparities in income, plus other patterns of discrimination or inequitable distribution of wealth.[8] People in rural areas tend to fare less well than those in major urban centres, whether due to discrimination or just the reality that there are fewer well-paid jobs or business opportunities in more remote locations. There is also some discrimination against minorities. The Shia in Bahrain and Saudi Arabia often claim that the state is discriminatory towards them, including in the economic sphere.[9] Beyond cases of overt discrimination, there are other inequalities, although it is difficult to discern their exact levels and sources. Incomplete data and the problem of comparing Arab states with markedly varying economic profiles present methodological challenges. When attempts at quantitative measures of inequality are made, the data that does exist indicates that the Gulf states perform reasonably, but not by any means impressively.[10] Other standard measures of inequality, such as Gini coefficient numbers, are incomplete for the subregion. Attempts at surveying inequality within the Gulf states are, therefore, typically qualitative in their methods.

Where there are much clearer inequalities is between citizens and certain expatriate nationalities. Expatriates for the most part are paid less than nationals, even where both are doing the same or very similar work, and expatriates do not enjoy the same benefits or job tenure as citizens. Foreign workers are generally paid not at a standard wage rate, but rather at rates consistent with the salaries they could command in their home economy, which accentuates a differentiation of roles between various foreign nationalities. The Gulf's labour markets are deeply segmented, both between citizens and expatriates and also between various expatriate nationalities.[11] It is not uncommon, therefore, to find unskilled workers from poorer economies performing unskilled roles at wages that, while far better than they could command back home, are extremely low compared to other roles held by a citizen or someone of another nationality.[12] The lowest-paid workers are the most likely to have their rights breached or to otherwise be treated poorly. While several Gulf states now have minimum wages in place for expatriate workers, these are low. The better positions, when filled by expatriates, mostly go to expatriates from developed or middle-income economies. Most foreign workers in the Gulf fall under the *kafala* ("sponsorship") system, which requires them to obtain sponsorship from a citizen before being able to request a work visa. This system increases the risk of maltreatment and exploitation because of the powers it grants the sponsor over the foreign worker, such as the right to hold the worker's passport, deny them mobility of employment, and even in practice to limit their resource to legal assistance.[13] Ultimately, however, foreign workers have few powers or rights, and therefore little impact on the politics of the Gulf. Their importance stems instead from the fact that they are an essential component of the rentier bargain and for the economic benefits they provide the host economy.

THE GULF'S UNIQUE DEMOGRAPHY

Feeding into the Gulf's labour market, and indeed into its wider social structures and settings, are some particular demographic characteristics. These include relatively high population growth rates, variations within states across citizens, and the debates around citizenship, including over people's social origins and the rights of a foreigner who has married a citizen.

Demographic data is often unclear, since states may publish total resident figures, not distinguishing between the citizens and non-citizens, to give an artificially high figure for total population. These figures can also seem very high, even alarmingly so, as an influx of expatriates in a period of growth can give the impression of an extremely high population growth rate. That said, total residence figures are also useful, in that high overall population growth rates, including expatriates, are typically a positive sign, demonstrating that the economy is expanding, jobs are being created, and having a reinforcing effect because of the additional demand created by these expatriates for goods and services in the economy. Table 1.2 in Chapter 1 showed the population structures for the six Gulf states, including a breakdown of the total into citizens and expatriates. However, the total population figures can also mask changes in the demographics of *citizens*. Expatriates have virtually no direct political power or role, and only very limited indirect influence. This is deliberately so. Demographics has the greatest impact on politics, therefore, with respect to the citizen population rather than the total resident population. The Gulf's citizen populations have grown strongly in recent decades, if not as rapidly as total populations. The UAE's citizen population in the early twenty-first century was rising at about 3 per cent per annum.[14] The figure is similar in Saudi Arabia, and was especially high there in the latter twentieth century, having more than doubled over the 20 years from the mid-1970s to the mid-1990s.[15] Several other Gulf states have very high growth rates, especially Oman and Bahrain, the two that will also be the first to face the problem of the exhaustion of their oil resources.

Politically, this matters most of all for the strains it potentially places on the rentier bargain. Citizens are almost exclusively the beneficiaries of rentier allocations, and are the focus of states in their drive for support and legitimacy. However the specific rentier packages that characterize the region are the product of the 1960s and especially of the oil booms of the 1970s and early 1980s, when these economies had citizen populations that were well under half their current figure; a figure likely to almost double again in the coming 30–40 years.[16] Gulf states' energy rents have not, in general, increased at a comparable rate to the population. Even where populations remain modest in size overall, and rentier allocations on average are affordable, fluctuations in rent income still create uncertainties and risks for states and regimes. Saudi Arabia's rentier "bargain" is already under strain, with the Kingdom running budget deficits whenever oil prices are at low or middle levels for a sustained period. They ran deficits throughout the years of low oil prices from the mid-1980s to early 2000s,[17] and then fell back into deficits after the next era of low prices began in 2014. They will likely be in deficit until around 2023. If such strains are evident now, when the Kingdom has a population of around 29 million, 21 million or so of them citizens, then the challenges that will arise if the population hits 43–44 million by 2050, with perhaps 32–35 million citizens, should be deeply worrying for the regime. Indeed, this fear about the long-term viability of the rentier arrangement is arguably the main driver of the Saudi *Vision 2030* programme.[18] All the other five Arab Gulf states have modernization and diversification plans along similar lines, and probably stemming from similar political motivations.

As noted, in rentier systems such as those of the Gulf, citizens are provided with basic or fundamental benefits of citizenship. An absence of taxation, particular subsidies and free health care and education are typically provided universally to citizens. However, it is up to their social standing, family linkages, ability to build and harness *wasta*, and an array of other factors as to whether citizens can then gain further benefits from the system. Regardless, the allocative nature of these systems is perhaps the key reason why citizenship is such a protected privilege in the Gulf. It is almost impossible for a non-citizen resident to be awarded citizenship by these states, even in the case of an expatriate worker born in a particular Gulf state, sometimes whose parents were born there too. For foreigners who marry a Gulf citizen, it is not much easier. A foreigner cannot usually obtain citizenship simply by marriage, and usually will not be able to access state benefits for a very long period of time. The children of such marriages have also encountered difficulties, especially where the child's father is foreign, since citizenship is usually passed down through the father's line.[19] This is now changing, but for a long time it affected many young people's access to education, healthcare, and other benefits of citizenship.

Such policies are driven by concerns that rentier benefits would be "diluted" if naturalization were too easily approved.[20] Politically, Gulf citizenship and the emphasis on family lineage allows the state to differentiate "tiers" of citizens. Given the region's history of migration, slavery, and other movements, to have citizenship one usually has to have grandparents who were citizens, often prior to a particular date, while some states consider citizenship differently depending on how well and formally it can be substantiated. The granting and withdrawal of citizenship is also typically a preserve of royal families, giving them enormous power to grant the status as a reward and withdraw it as a punishment.[21]

THE DUAL LABOUR MARKET

As already noted, the labour markets of the Gulf are fundamentally dualistic. There is one labour market for citizens and another for expatriates. By design, the wages, conditions, and tenure of workers in each are completely separate and unlike. Furthermore, in effect the expatriate labour market is also divided along ethnic or national lines, since there is a correlation between the wages earned and the nationality of the employee. Generally certain nationalities hold different types of jobs, with low-wage workers coming from poorer countries and more skilled workers from middle-income and upper-income countries. This impacts how they are treated, and other aspects of their experiences.

The differences in employment conditions are stark. At the lower end of the labour market, such as in unskilled work in a services company or construction firm, workers are almost exclusively foreigners, often from South Asia or Southeast Asia, and receive very low wages. A typical unskilled wage in construction in the UAE or Qatar, for example, is as little as $200 per month. Sometimes wages can be lower still than this, say as a driver or domestic cleaner. For the expatriate worker, however, this may still be attractive when unemployment in their home country is high and where in, say, South Asia, unskilled wages may be as low as $50–60 per month.[22] There can be other push factors in their home societies, including lower opportunities, political violence, or family problems, while the existing, large expatriate communities may act as pull factors to the host economy. Financial and economic factors are typically the primary driver of labour migrations, but not the only one.

At middle-income levels sometimes the story is similar. Jobs in semi-skilled roles, trades, and semi-professions are filled by people from a range of countries, including some of the poorer ones that supply so many of the unskilled workers, but also from middle-income countries such as other Arab states. These workers will typically also be attracted by relatively good wages. They may also be able to save money and obtain social mobility, or simply save the money needed to get married and start a family, after spending several years in the Gulf. Expatriates from developed economies may ultimately have financial incentives driving them too, although they will be earning high salaries that permit them a comfortable lifestyle while they are living in the region, too. The safety that expatriates have in their jobs, and their freedom (or not) from exploitation, vary greatly: trade unions and other cooperatives are banned, and so unskilled workers have few ways to protest poor conditions, exploitation, or workplace safety concerns. There are some cases of them trying to do so,[23] and their countries' embassies may advocate for them or assist those in particular distress, but it is common for foreign workers who raise objections to be reprimanded and, very often, removed from the country. There is considerable risk in speaking out. Expatriates from wealthier economies are typically treated better, but only comparatively: they are still in a position of vulnerability and have relatively little power compared to back in their home country. There are cases of western workers being mistreated or running into other trouble in the region, even if these occur much less frequently than for unskilled workers.

These systems exist for reasons already discussed. Economically, the reliance on expatriates helps control wages growth and inflation and reduces exchange rate pressures. These problems are all features of the so-called "Dutch disease", where demand for an economy's resources, and thus its currency, has negative macroeconomic impacts.[24] Furthermore, all but the most highly-skilled workers are cheaper to employ than a local citizen, and can be more easily dismissed or retrenched. Remittance outflows also help alleviate upward pressure on the exchange rate. The reinvestment of rents abroad in sovereign wealth funds, reducing the need to absorb rents in the domestic economy, is motivated by the same goal. Finally, at least historically a large foreign workforce was needed because the local labour market simply could not supply the workforce suddenly required.[25] At the political level, expatriates are an element of the rentier bargain. The system outsources unpleasant jobs – most of the working class – to foreigners, and by doing so relatively cheaply, frees up funds for the state to employ citizens in higher-paying roles. It is no coincidence that most citizens in the Gulf work in the public sector. State jobs are a route for rent dispersements, and a method by which the state coopts society.

The problem is that rents are derived from non-renewable sources. At some stage, the rentier bargain must be amended, and eventually abandoned, including the tradition of widespread, secure, well-paid state employment. Population growth, the cost of state payrolls, and the need for a tax base in the private sector all will prompt changes to this practice at some stage in the future.[26] In fact, change is already happening in Bahrain and Oman, and is probably coming to Saudi Arabia too. This amendment of the employment "bargain" means that the exact profiles of these dualistic labour markets varies across the Gulf. In Bahrain and Oman, the two states where oil rents will be exhausted first, the imperative to reform the economy, including the labour market, is strongest. They have placed much greater emphasis on moving citizens into jobs that, in the other Gulf states, would be much less likely to be held by citizens. In Oman, there has been a genuine attempt at this, dating back to its *Vision 2020* strategy, launched in 1995.[27] While *Vision 2020* was not a success overall, including in its "Omanization" employment goals, overall expatriate numbers there have fallen and Omanis now occupy more varied roles than citizens in most Gulf states.[28] In Bahrain, sectarianism and the absence of a minimum wage even for nationals has meant that the Shia, in particular, have sometimes been employed in roles that, elsewhere in the Gulf, would be held by foreigners.[29]

The Omani and Bahraini examples show that labour markets can differ across Gulf economies. The seriousness and urgency with which Saudi Arabia appears to be adopting the goals of its *Vision 2030* may also signal a more transformative change there in the coming years. Past Saudi efforts at labour market reform have been abandoned or have underperformed, but *Vision 2030* has more detailed goals than previous plans, including a dramatic expansion of the private sector's role, with the aim of increasing its relative size from 40 to 65 per cent of GDP.[30] When coupled with plans for better-skilled Saudi workers and an expansion of small and medium-sized businesses, and given the pressures of a government wages bill that consumes some 45 per cent of state spending, its proposals and goals may be taken more seriously than previous plans.[31] *Vision 2030* also has the backing of the ambitious and influential crown price, Muhammad bin Salman, who appears more dedicated to reform than previous monarchs and elites. There is also the fact, true across the entire Gulf but explicitly acknowledged in *Vision 2030*, that women remain an underutilized economic resource, despite the potential to shift sizeable numbers of them into jobs currently performed by expatriates. Overall, any substantive shift in the Saudi labour market would increase the likelihood of it being copied by other Gulf states, but the task is a mammoth one.

EDUCATION, TRAINING AND HUMAN CAPITAL

Closely linked to labour market reform are the prospects for human capital. Education, training, and even the fuzzier ideas of work ethics and culture, are all important dynamics that can assist or hinder an economy. All the Gulf states have paid a great deal of attention to education, and spent vast sums of money supporting it, with an expectation that this would also innately contribute to development and economic diversification. In fact, the outcomes have been more mixed, and in some cases more surprising, than that. Furthermore, but in contrast, far less focus has been given to training and other forms of skills development, which are equally important for overall economic performance, if less attractive to a population that overwhelmingly wants to obtain prestigious, well-paid positions, preferably in the public sector. Finally, a shift in both private-sector thinking and potential workers' expectations is necessary if the Gulf economies are to move from their energy focus and develop larger, more vibrant private sectors.

The Gulf's development and support of education, including higher education, is now several decades old. Both basic measures such as literacy rates, and more complex ones such as the number of university graduates produced, have improved enormously. However modern mass education came to the Gulf comparatively late, with schooling having previously been less widely available, often conducted privately by wealthy families or coming with religious training. The first western school in the Gulf was in Iraq; the first among the six Gulf states that are the focus here was in Bahrain, set up in the 1890s by American missionaries. This was followed by a series of schools designed along British lines,[32] expanding further as oil revenues arrived. Other Gulf states began founding schools at this time, although access was not universal: while Saudi schooling dates to the 1930s, it was usually only available in urban areas and for boys, with state schooling for girls not introduced until 1960.[33] In some states modern education came later still; in 1962, when oil production began, Abu Dhabi had only 20 schools and less than 4,000 students.[34] In 1970 Oman had almost no primary education, which only began en masse after Sultan Qaboos took power that year, and higher education was even slower, with no higher education institutions in Oman prior to 1970.[35] The University of Kuwait dates only to 1966 and Qatar University to 1973, while King Saud University (originally established as Riyadh University) was only founded in 1957.

Education expanded massively once oil wealth began flowing into the region. Enrolment in the 1970s and 1980s across all levels of education expanded dramatically, jumping to levels well above those of developing economies by the early 1990s.[36] The lateness and suddenness of this education boom meant that by the 1990s there was a generational gap in education levels: people born as late as the 1970s often remained relatively modestly-educated, while those born after, including women, could typically achieve high levels of education and literacy. The number of educational institutions grew accordingly, across all levels but especially in primary and secondary, as state spending increased and as private schools opened and built their reputations. Education not only became compulsory at primary and into secondary levels, but often an expectation at more advanced secondary and even tertiary levels.

In the 1990s and 2000s, primary and secondary systems were also modernized in some of the Gulf states, both in terms of curricula and in how schools were administrated and managed. Problems remain in these systems, however, particularly in secondary schools, where there is often an emphasis on rote learning rather than critical thinking and self-teaching. As evidence of this, while governments have spent handsome sums on education, the ratio of spending to quality, or spending to student's comparative international performance, has not been very impressive in several of the Gulf states, especially Saudi Arabia and Kuwait and to a lesser extent Oman.

There remained some issues, however, including gaps in education and literacy between the sexes. While female education and literacy expanded greatly from the 1970s to the 1990s, literacy rates still lagged slightly for women, as did the mean years of schooling. However, women quickly began overtaking men in higher education achievement, a trend that was evident by 1990 but which became especially pronounced by the early twenty-first century. Women now outnumber men in higher education enrolments in the Gulf, and have a reputation for working harder and outperforming male students, too.[37] While some 60 per cent of university graduates across the Gulf are women, they cluster in the social sciences and humanities, and for a variety of reasons enter the workforce in much lower numbers than their graduation rates would suggest.[38]

The boom in higher education in the Gulf occurred soon after that of primary and secondary schooling, especially from the 1980s on, once illiteracy and basic educational standards had been improved. It also coincided with a period of low oil prices, which drove the Gulf's first substantial economic diversification policies – for which higher education was considered a crucial component.[39] This was also a period in which the impacts of high population growth rates were starting to be felt, and it was no longer realistic (or sensible) for governments to send a large share of their university students overseas for their education, as had been the earlier practice. There was an expansion in the number of universities and their size, and by the 1990s, a rise also in foreign university campuses in the region, especially in Dubai but later in Doha, Abu Dhabi, and elsewhere.

However, there are problems that inhibit the capacity and potential of education in the Gulf. To some extent this is a problem generic to the Middle East region, where "the relationship between education and economic growth has remained weak, the divide between education and employment has not been bridged, and the quality of education continues to be disappointing."[40] The Gulf fares better than the region on average, but its higher education institutions vary in quality, and certainly education has not delivered the more ambitious results initially anticipated for it, especially in preparing graduates for more advanced work in emerging fields. The growth of foreign campuses and the importation of foreign educational systems and curricula, moreover, may not be ideal for the region if simply replicated and not adapted for local needs.[41] It has been argued that a by-product of rentierism is that the combination of free education and widespread, usually comfortable public sector employment deters people from studying what the economy most needs and from taking on more challenging programmes that would lead to private sector careers.[42]

Closely related to this is the failure of the Gulf to more effectively encourage the uptake of other types of skills development, particularly training in the trades and in semi-professional fields. While university graduation rates appear, on the surface, to be impressive, if these are primarily in areas for which the economy does not have a strong need, then they signify little in terms of development. There is a preference among young people in the Gulf for professional careers, but if governments continue to fund higher education but not appropriate education and training for less prestigious career options, they are failing to meet the needs of their economies, and arguably are creating unrealistic expectations among young people as well. In particular, there is a lack of vocational training systems and opportunities, both traditional training programmes for trades and in the sense that graduates of universities enter the workforce with insufficient industrial and applied skills that they will need on the job.[43] This is not only a failing of the state, but also of business and other institutions in the economy. A 2015 study found that:

> only 27% of employers in the GCC offer work experience or internship programs to students. Correspondingly, only 30% of students say they were able to benefit from workplace experience – although there were significant differences between countries, ranging from a high of 42% in the UAE to a low of 7% in Saudi Arabia.[44]

For the Gulf states to maximize the potential of their human capital, much more is required from their educational systems, at all levels. Spending substantial sums on education is beneficial, but alone is not sufficient to guarantee economic development in the future.

GENDER ISSUES

There is an image that women in the Gulf, and elsewhere in the Arab and Muslim worlds, are in disadvantaged positions in societal hierarchies, have limited personal autonomy, and are constrained by male-dominated, conservative political systems, patriarchal family structures, and economic systems that are resistant to change. While there is a considerable degree of accuracy in many of these images, gender is a more complex dynamic than this. It is important to note also that the roles of both women *and men* are defined by historical, societal, and political forces, and that the position of women and the agency they have varies considerably across and even within various Gulf societies.[45] Women are certainly disadvantaged in a range of areas, and are underrepresented in public roles, but the extent of this and the reasons for it are complex.

Gender roles have changed considerably in the Gulf's modern history, as economic conditions and the patterns of social organization have changed. In the pre-oil era, for example, women's lives were, unsurprisingly, very different from today, defined and structured (as were men's) over many centuries predominantly by tribal solidarity and Islam.[46] Tribal and extended family networks often meant that many of the decisions about women's lives were taken by men – fathers, husbands, or other male relatives, depending on the particular circumstance and the woman's stage in life – and while women typically enjoyed significant informal power within the family, they rarely had formal or public roles. Typically, they also lacked many of the choices that they now increasingly have, such as deciding whether and whom to marry or whether or not to go to university. They were constrained in such choices by both social structures and by economic circumstances.

This, however, is only a general observation. Wealthier women may have lacked power in some respects, but they often also had servants or slaves to assist them, while more liberal families, especially those involved in commerce or trade, sometimes gave women important roles in family businesses. Women also exerted influence in indirect ways, particularly when marrying, since they served as the link between their families and their husband's, into which they moved. They could also shape the opinions and decisions of their husbands and children. Importantly, the nature of the Gulf economies at the time, based on activities such as trade, pearl fishing, animal herding and fishing, meant that men were often absent for extended periods, with women sometimes stepped in, by choice or necessity, to support the family business or to play other public roles.[47]

In the contemporary Gulf oil wealth has had a conservatizing impact.

Women are far wealthier than were their predecessors, but in many ways still just as constrained. It is in Saudi Arabia where constraints on women's agency and independence are most strict. Perhaps most famously, Saudi women were restricted from driving cars until that control was lifted in 2018.[48] The restriction reflected a male dominance over women, but also a desire by conservatives to maintain gender segregation and modesty and to limit the risk of men and women meeting in uncontrolled settings where they may be tempted into a sexual liaison.[49] However the restriction had economic impacts: hiring a driver was expensive and public transport poor, meaning that women's ability to work, run a business, or perform other roles was curtailed. The restriction was part of wider system of male control over women. Women need permission from a male guardian (a father, husband, or son) to marry, obtain a passport or travel. The oil era also saw a resurgence of male polygamy, a stricter division of labour within the family,[50] and stronger enforcement of dress codes, including veiling. However, these policies alone do not paint a complete picture of women's roles in the Kingdom. Many women pushed back against policies such as the driving restrictions, either directly by protest or civic activism. Many would say that they have far better and more equal marriages than their mothers and grandmothers,[51] perhaps because of the influence of travel, as a product of oil wealth, which has shown both men and women what marital dynamics are like in other cultures.

In the economic and commercial realms, the Saudi state has encouraged women to play more active and public roles. This has been described as "modernizing authoritarian rule" or "state feminism".[52] It commenced as early as the 1970s, with the remarkable growth in women's education, supported and mostly funded by the state. It then grew to include an encouragement of female entrepreneurship, expanded employment opportunities for women in the public sector, and women being granted new cultural roles, such as in museums, festivals and new media organizations. This has been driven by politics, including the state wanting the support of women, and more moderate men, for its legitimacy and as a counter to conservative social forces. Particular rulers have been more moderate than others, particularly King Abdullah (r. 2005–15), while since 2015, crown prince Muhammad bin Salman has been a powerful force for social reform. The increased role of women is also a product of economic necessity, especially the economic reforms pursued before and after the Saudi accession to the World Trade Organization in 2005. Women figure in economic planning as important economic agents, employees, and by implication, consumers. To date it is wealthier and middle-class women that have gained the most from these economic policy reforms, but these changes are likely to spread further in the future.

Saudi Arabia is a very conservative case in the Gulf, but many of the factors shaping and changing women's roles are present across the sub-region. In the other Gulf states, women still must operate in roles set in part by their sex, but they have typically faced less stringent controls than in Saudi Arabia. Women were not restricted from driving in the other Gulf states, for example. In the economic realm, women have generally benefited from state-led policies of social liberalization, state-funded education, and some economic reforms, even if they are underrepresented by almost any measure. Prior to the 1990s, women played very minor roles as employees, and even less so as managers or entrepreneurs. Gulf women's participation rate in the labour market is still, on paper, extremely low, although rising: at 26.9 per cent, it is barely half the global average, but this figure is skewed by the high number of expatriate workers, who are disproportionately male. Their role in the workforce has increased markedly in recent years. Over 2001–10, some "1.5 million women joined the labor force in the GCC", which is "an 83% increase from the 1.8 million … in 2001 to the 3.3 million … in 2010".[53] These numbers also mask a large number of women who work in family businesses and other roles not captured in formal statistics. There is considerable variance across countries, with Saudi Arabia and Oman having the lowest female participation rates, at below 30 per cent, and Qatar the highest, at 51 per cent, followed closely by the UAE.[54] At senior levels in business, women are very underrepresented, as might be expected, but not completely absent. The ratio of women in senior commercial roles:

[V]aries from 7 per cent in Saudi Arabia and Qatar to the highest level of 14 per cent in Kuwait ... At board level, the contrast between the GCC and the rest of the world is even more striking. In 2014, 17 per cent of board members at Fortune 500 companies were female. Shares of board seats held by females in the GCC countries in the same year ranged from 0.01 per cent in Saudi Arabia to 1.7 per cent in Kuwait.[55]

Indicators of female entrepreneurship have also improved, from measures of entrepreneurial activity to business ownership to the wealth held by women, but again the numbers remain low by international levels.[56]

In all the Gulf economies, state support has been a leading factor in women's growing role in commerce and in the labour market. This sometimes has come ahead of societal expectations. However, women themselves have been responsible for their growing economic roles. Their educational achievements often constitute the foundations for their careers, but many women are choosing to enter the workforce regardless. Among those in senior levels, a further combination of ambition, open-mindedness, and confidence appear to be the main traits explaining their success.[57] State policies vary markedly but also assist women, and include earmarking specific roles for women, providing specialized training targeted to them, and providing support for potential entrepreneurs. More general labour market policies also assist women, for example those covering maternity leave, discrimination in employment and workplace harassment.

Despite this, formidable challenges remain for Gulf women, especially those who want to build a long-term career or build a large, successful business. In a survey of women in leadership roles, one study identified four main problems.[58] The first three, and probably all four, apply beyond leadership positions, to women in other roles as well. One is the challenge of balancing work and family commitments. This is by no means unique to the Gulf, but is especially strong there given the emphasis traditionally placed on women's family roles. Second are the challenges in expanding

161

women's roles in the workforce, including presumptions about their career paths and outright discrimination at work, and traditionalism and conservatism in some families and social groups that consider women's primary role to be at home. Third are structural issues, including weak human resources policies in organizations, and infrastructure issues. Finally, there is lack of mentoring, networking, and development opportunities for women, a particularly important factor when women are reaching senior positions with few predecessors or role-models to draw on.

For female entrepreneurs, further specific problems remain, including access to capital and finance, the problem of building the necessary networks – a particular issue when *wasta* is so important to success – and the more general problem of the complexity of government rules and regulations. All this suggests that while women are playing new and more engaged roles in business and the labour market, social and cultural forces will continue to make change a slow process.

YOUTH AND INTERGENERATIONAL DYNAMICS

While the overall population of the Gulf is small relative to other parts of the Arab world and developing world, the median age is around 25 years.[59] This is very young compared to the United States (38.1 years), the UK (40.5) and Japan (47.3). The youth population's relative size varies across the region: it is especially high in Oman and Saudi Arabia, less so in Kuwait and Bahrain, and more manageable in the UAE and Qatar. Regardless, the economic, social, and other demands of a large youth population have created specific pressures on the Gulf political economies. With such growth rates, there is a risk that youth disgruntlement will lead to higher poverty rates, political instability, and a stronger lure to Islamic extremism, although to a lesser degree in the Gulf, perhaps, given its relative wealth and mostly-small populations. The main challenges for the Gulf from its large youth populations are economic ones.

The most critical challenge is creating sufficient quality jobs for young people. Youth disproportionately bear the burden of unemployment. In

Saudi Arabia in 2013, for example, the overall unemployment rate was 5.7 per cent, while the youth rate was 28.7 per cent, while Bahrain and Oman both had youth rates over 20 per cent and Kuwait 19.6 per cent.[60] Only in the UAE is the figure markedly lower (9.9%) and in Qatar low (1.5%). Youth unemployment is nearly always higher than average, since young people usually lack the nous and independence that comes from gaining work experience. However, the problems in the educational and training systems mentioned earlier are likely a major source of youth unemployment, too, with too many well-educated young people being inadequately prepared for the workforce. This is a long-term issue, because if anything:

> the emerging generation of young people in the GCC will be highly educated, and will thus have high expectations of high-status future employment. They will be increasingly technologically literate. Many will be affluent and well-travelled, and many will be educated overseas, giving them a high awareness of different lifestyles and cultures.[61]

This leads into a related issue stemming from high education levels: that young people expect a degree of autonomy, responsibility and even authority that is rare in the institutions and businesses of the Gulf. Even once they are in good employment, young people routinely express a frustration with corporate cultures that give them less responsibility or opportunity than older colleagues. As one young Qatari, working for a large state-owned firm, noted: "What was the point of sending me to study management and business overseas for six years, if I am then going to be put into a role back here and told to keep my mouth shut and do what I'm told?"[62] He contrasted his academic background with older, senior staff at the firm where he worked, many of whom lacked a tertiary education. As Gulf societies globalize and people become increasingly well-educated, this sort of grievance is becoming common. Through travel and overseas study, young people observe cultural practices elsewhere, such as young people being given considerable autonomy at work, that are not normally part of Gulf organizational cultures. Gulf firms are typically quite hierarchical and autocratic, and sometimes neglectful of human resources issues.[63] Even those who gain access to good jobs may come to feel unappreciated at work, while those who miss out on even that opportunity may become stuck in poverty.

The reform agenda in many Gulf states has sown fears among some young people that the state will not support them in the way it did their parents and grandparents, or that at a minimum, they will inherit greater responsibilities and shoulder an unfair burden. This sense of intergenerational inequity is a political and social risk, more so if it comes to pass. If young people develop a genuine and deep sense of relative deprivation when they measure themselves against their parents, then even if they maintain good standards of living, a mood of intergenerational unfairness will create new tensions which, left unaddressed, could undermine economic reform efforts and even state legitimacy. Moreover, if the rewards of economic reform are not distributed equitably, then social problems such as crime, corruption and substance abuse may worsen, or class differences become more accentuated.[64]

SOCIETIES, CULTURE AND ECONOMIC POTENTIAL

All of the social actors, forces, and relationships discussed above exist in societies that are undergoing rapid cultural and technological change. As much as globalization and new technologies are important, they are also met with resistance from forces of tradition. What ultimately flows down into society, organizations, and individual identities is therefore a modified, conglomerated set of forces shaping the Gulf's cultures and rapidly changing its social dynamics.

There is no single "Gulf culture", or even "Arab-Gulf culture", that can be reliably utilized to profile and understand the subregion. Scholars have started to explore the idea of a *khaliji*, or Arab-Gulf, cultural identity across the six Arab Gulf states. The failure of pan-Arab ideology by the 1970s allowed room for subregional identities to emerge and expand.[65]

With some unique shared cultural elements in the Gulf, certain distinctions can be made between the Arabs of the Gulf and those elsewhere. States have encouraged people to think along such lines, in the interests of undermining pan-Arabist tendencies and to create stronger intra-Gulf bonds. Yet *khaliji* identity has its limits. It is one of multiple identities, and arguably national identity is stronger, with family, tribe, Arab ethnicity, Islam and sect all competing with it as well. The variations and diversity within Gulf societies, even among citizens, may also constrain the *khaliji* identity. Divisions exist both within and across the Gulf states, including in people's ethnic origins, religious sect and lineage. There is an argument that shared socio-economic class identity is strong across the Gulf's national boundaries,[66] although the 2017 Qatar crisis showed that international politics could still undermine such linkages.

To speak, then, of Arab culture, or a *khaliji* one, or one for a particular country, is to miss the point that culture is more a conglomeration of varied cultures than something monolithic. It is also in flux, as it is shaped and buffeted by various external forces, and amended or renegotiated by internal ones. However, there is also a need to generalize at some level. Where this is arguably most useful is in noting cultures (in the plural, ideally) as something that can be a force, among many, in shaping organizational behaviour and economic outcomes. While political structures may be fairly static, they will still change if cultural values and dynamics also change. Culture and some of its subsets, particularly political cultures and organizational cultures, will shape institutions, and even state behaviour, while the primordial loyalties underlying culture can affect state capacity.[67]

In the Gulf's political economies, cultural features do indeed matter, insofar as they influence the behaviour of individuals and shape the cultures of groups, firms, organizations and societies. Culture is a factor when drilling down into the institutions and interpersonal dynamics of these political economies. One author talks about "sheiko-capitalism"[68] in reference to the Gulf, in effect describing its state capitalist structure, but linking it to traditional social structures and values. While a clumsy term, it has the benefit of implying a strong informal, personalization of business and suggesting an importance to informal relationships. As these personal dimensions of new state capitalism are its most opaque aspects, and contribute to the protectionism and favouritism that are such features of it, there is ultimately an indirect link here between some cultural characteristics and economic outcomes such as the competitiveness of firms and managerial competence and quality.

Some of the cultural features of the Gulf are clashing with economic and political imperatives, and will continue to do so. Private sectors in the Gulf are gaining greater state focus, and specific firms are becoming more globally competitive, especially the younger ones created in the last generation or so and with less access to state largesse than more established ones. This is bringing about modernizations of business practices, however the impact on business culture can be complex. With state-owned firms, in particular, an efficiency-driven market-conscious model may be the goal of the state that owns these firms and the leaders appointed to run them, but the older values of state-owned firms remain powerful drivers of managers' conduct and of the culture within the organization. The superficial elements of a firm's profile – the existence of a world-class website, the use of western job titles, even the adoption of international senior management structures and boards – may not necessarily reflect the *actual* cultures within the firm. A firm is not usually the same as one in the United States or Europe, even when similar corporate structures, job titles, or policies exist. Cultural norms will dictate practices, often in informal ways or in the style of, say, decision-making. A state-owned firm's culture of social responsibility and loyalty to employees, for example, may deter its head from making cuts to employee numbers or conditions, or insisting on new and better performance measures for staff, even if there is an overwhelming need or case to do so. A work on the national oil companies of the Gulf noted in this regard:

[I]t is questionable whether [the national oil companies] are willing to apply the actual necessary measures and working practices [to be like international oil firms]. For example, would NOC [national oil company] employees be willing to work the long hours of IOCs [international oil companies]? Would they accept cost-cutting measures that involved firing employees? The following comment was made by a Saudi Aramco executive: "We inherited a blend of our corporate culture *and* our national culture. This blend is the Saudi Aramco culture. It's a heart culture more than a think culture. We don't want to hurt people."[69]

There is, therefore, a mix of continuity and change in the commercial and organizational settings of the Gulf. Where things are also changing, if less dramatically than once prophesized, is in the realm of technology. Much has been written by both scholars and the media about the impacts of technology, especially after the Arab uprisings in 2011 appeared to rely heavily on social media to organize protests and garner support.[70] It was also a reminder of the drive for reform among young people, who are also the most enthusiastic users of new technology and media. Online communication is a great equalizer of voices and a method for empowering populations, although too many unedited and unqualified voices can also have a disorienting effect on public debate. As new technology has emerged and its importance has grown, governments in the Gulf have introduced and maintained a substantial amount of control over it, especially over political content and politically-related usage.[71] They are also competing with it, whether by using competing online and social media narratives or by dictating what is covered (or not) on traditional media. Important as new media is, therefore, it is ultimately a tool, which much like any other communications tool contains great promise but will also have to contend with attempts to constrain it by the state and other traditional sources of power.

The Gulf states have embraced new technologies and new forms of media, including social media. While, again, this may not have had a transformative *political* effect, it has been important socially and economically, and could yet prove politically profound as well. In the Gulf, Twitter and messaging tools have proven especially popular. This is perhaps a result of the tight control exerted by the state over mainstream media and social interaction in general: online messaging and other digital tools are far freer from government control than traditional media, and with the Gulf having such large youth populations, there is a large population of eager, adaptable users.[72] For young Saudis, for example, their concerns and the issues that matter to them are not new, nor is their eagerness to adopt new technologies. However, the capabilities that Twitter and other new media offer *are* indeed new. Their speed, mobility (for example, being accessible on cell phones) and breadth of features (such as the ability to send photos, videos, and links) are an advance on earlier technologies. As a comprehensive communications platform, "Twitter is changing the way people voice their opinion in the kingdom, and now because of social media like Twitter, those voices are being heard instead of censored. Social media is having a major impact on the conservative Saudi, Qatar and UAE societies."[73]

The online realm, including new media but also older forms of electronic commerce, also has the potential to dramatically change the economies and business environment of the Gulf. It has begun to do so, even though it lags behind developed economies in some respects, as one study noted.[74] Overall the Gulf has been a strong adopter of online technologies and tools. The UAE, Qatar, and Bahrain perform especially well on measures of digitization and online commerce, while the other Gulf states lag slightly behind but perform above the average level for the Middle East. The UAE has been especially successful:

> Among the Middle Eastern countries studied, the United Arab Emirates has the highest digital identification – a metric that is based on multiple indicators such as access to services, digital signature, and card features. The country is also engaged in various digitization initiatives, such as expanding broadband coverage and creating a unified smart-city platform.[75]

Similarly, Qatar's infrastructure, mixed with its small population, gives it enormous potential in maximizing the digitization of its economy.

The Gulf states also all include online and digital initiatives in their strategic development plans. These are partly framed within economic diversification strategies, but typically also include modernizing and improving services such as health and education; on the latter, several of the Gulf states have, for several years now, articulated the concept of becoming a "knowledge economy".[76] The UAE and Saudi Arabia have used this term, and have certain initiatives on it such as online government and plans to bring internet access in remote areas of their countries. The Gulf is aided in their online strategies by their well-educated population who can often operate online in English, the dominate language online. They have also invested heavily in communications infrastructure. Online initiatives typically sit alongside reforms to education, attempts to develop the private sector, and certain economic reforms to encourage investment and the introduction of new technologies and practices. There is the question, however – probably an unanswerable one, for the time being – of whether a knowledge economy can truly be formed in a rentier system.[77] In particular, the concept of a knowledge economy carries the implication of bottom-up change through societal agency and individuals operating as empowered economic actors, yet rentierism is a top-down and managed state–society dynamic. Most likely, the answer will be determined by the success or failure of economic diversification efforts, and by whether the growth in education leads, longer-term, to a more politically-engaged society.

Regardless, there remain challenges for the Gulf in further developing electronic commerce and in digitizing their economies. E-commerce is still a small sector of the Gulf economies overall. At 0.4 per cent of GDP, e-commerce accounts for a much smaller share of economic activity than it does in, say, the UK (3.5%), Japan (2.2%), or the United States (1.9%).[78] This figure is probably lower than otherwise because of the size of the oil and gas sectors, where the prospects of e-commerce may be more limited, but the level of e-commerce uptake is nonetheless markedly lower than in most other economies with similar incomes. Moreover, there is still a gap between the adoption and use of technology by governments on the one hand, and business on the other, with measures such as the level of online advertising by firms being quite low, and the legal frameworks for online commerce still weak or incomplete in some Gulf states.[79] Arguably there is also a cultural aspect as well, at least with older Gulf consumers, who prefer to shop or conduct business face-to-face, and may have difficulty in feeling the same level of trust online as they do from in-person commercial interactions. This means that firms have (and still do) usually need both a physical and online presence to succeed, as people will use online tools for certain stages of a purchase, such as comparing features and prices, but will also want a physical location where they can go, sometimes for the purchase itself and especially for things such as after-sales service. The adoption of online tools for activities such as personal banking has been especially slow, perhaps highlighting the trust issues that remain with e-commerce, plus an overall preference for cash over cards anyway in these societies.

To a considerable extent, therefore, consumer cultures are an important element of broader culture, as are other subsets of culture such as organizational or political ones. Culture, in a range of manifestations, can have a strong impact on both traditional and emerging economic sectors, and on almost any type of firm or organization. Cultural and social dynamics cannot be ignored when analyzing how the Gulf economies function in practice, and in differentiating them from economies in other parts of the world. This is not always a simple task. Too cursory or shallow an assessment of these societies and cultures is a recipe for overgeneralization. Too much emphasis on them, however, can mean underemphasizing the importance of economic factors in the region's politics or social dynamics, or undervaluing the power of states and (certain) institutional actors.

6

Making the Gulf economies: unique factors

As the previous chapters have implied, while there are many features of the Gulf economies that are generic to economies around the world or shared with certain other economies, there are also a range of particularities that are very specific, even unique, to the Gulf or to certain Gulf political economies. Some are the product of state policies, and the subregion has certainly tried its share of poor policies in the past. Many others, however, are exclusively or predominantly beyond the control of states and societies: they can be addressed to some extent by policy, and adaptations can be made in response to them, but they are also a product of fate. This chapter explores these features of the subregion and how they link to economic dynamics and prospects. It examines the very personalized nature of politics and societal interactions, past shortcomings in economic policy-making and political reform, and some of the issues that have been neglected in the past. Among the issues over which the region has little control are its geography, where the Gulf is inextricably linked to events and dynamics in the wider Middle East, and emerging threats such as from climate change, where the best that the region can do, in all likelihood, is to adapt to change that now appears all but inevitable.

"RICHER THAN THEY ARE DEVELOPED"?

As already discussed in the previous chapter, the inaugural *Arab Human Development Report* quite directly, and somewhat controversially, described the Middle East as "richer than it is developed". Sentiments along similar lines are found in scholarly work and, even more often, in mass media and other sources, where it is taken at face value that the region's economies suffer from particular, and very serious, ills and shortcomings. The region includes some of the poorest countries in the world, has pockets of poverty in even the wealthiest, and is confronted by a series of social, political, and other challenges that will have a profound impact on its future development. In the Gulf, the story is more positive, but there too there are a range of challenges and uncertainties that must be addressed.

So, is the region really "richer than it is developed"? Or more specifically, does this statement apply to the Gulf? Even if it does not, does it implicate the Gulf, because of its energy wealth, in the problems confronted by other parts of the Middle East? By any basic measure of per capita wealth, infrastructure, or other economic measures of quality of life, the answer is in the negative. As already outlined, the Gulf states have standards of living that, overall, compare favourably with most developed economies. A simple comparison of statistical economic data, however, does mask some of the more subtle, but still important, problems that lurk within these economies. Perhaps the most straightforward observation here is that there are pockets of poverty, including both absolute poverty, especially among migrant workers, and relative poverty among some citizens, especially those who are part of a minority or who lack the family or personal connections needed to do well in these political economies. As a second, somewhat related point, there are considerable variances between the experiences and potential of people within these economies. In particular, women remain greatly underutilized in these economies, resulting in lost economic opportunities. Youth, also discussed in the previous chapter, have some genuine grievances about being underutilized or underappreciated, and in many cases these complaints about their economic

172

circumstances remain unanswered. There likely are some opportunity costs incurred from youth unemployment and economic underutilization.

The *Arab Human Development Report*'s comment, however, was and remains most applicable to the non-oil economies, where human development indicators are far poorer than in the Gulf. In fact, by many measures the Gulf states perform well on some development indices. Their oil wealth is a reminder, however, of how deeply the subregion is linked to the wider Middle Eastern economies. They are important sources of employment for expatriate workers from other Arab economies, which alone is a crucial factor in increasing the interdependence between the Gulf and other Arab economies. Labour remittances are in many ways highly beneficial to developing economies, since the money is often invested, contributing to capital formation and new business activity, or boosting demand in their home economy if the money is instead spent. However, remittances are also a form of rent. The money is earned abroad, and so when repatriated, a worker's funds are in effect money not earned productively within that (home) economy. Sending workers to the Gulf is a helpful short- and medium-term economic measure, therefore, but as a solution to long-term economic development is far more debatable.[1] Beyond importing labour, the Gulf also provides aid and other assistance to some of the non-oil states, and through tourism and other activities is also important to many poorer Arab economies. In these ways, there is a correlation between oil wealth and *regional* economic performance, not just between oil wealth and the Gulf economies.

The greater issue for the Gulf, already touched upon, is about the best strategies to prepare for their post-oil futures. While this is a long-term question for many of them, which have decades remaining before their reserves are exhausted, Oman and Bahrain will confront the end of their oil reserves around the 2030s, although Bahrain's 2018 announcement that it had found tight oil and deep gas off its west coast may change this prognosis. Regardless, all the oil economies of the Gulf have started to consider and address the dilemma of hydrocarbon reliance, motivated not only by post-oil fears but also by the fact that their heavy dependence on oil and gas rents also has current impacts on their economic performance, labour markets, and state–society relationships. In doing so, the Gulf's rulers are acting in more long-term, future-oriented ways than they did in the past, especially during the first two oil booms of the 1970s and early 1980s. Long-term economic development strategies, the rise of sovereign wealth funds, and the enormous investments made in infrastructure in recent years all point to more considered long-term economic thinking by the region's leaderships.

PERSONALIZED ECONOMIES

While Gulf leaders need and will want broad popular legitimacy and support, politics in these systems is highly personalized and informal. Personal linkages are an important method of maintaining power; in the contemporary setting these are in the form of neopatrimonialism, with patron–client relationships structured in a hierarchical order down into institutions and social groups. Other social and commercial interactions take place in similar ways, with personal relationships, informal negotiation and decision-making, and reciprocal trust-based interactions given particular importance. This is partly a product of the importance of family, tribe, and other basic social units: "The main characteristic of Gulf society is that the socio-economic structure revolves around kinship", with kinship "dominat[ing] every facet of socio-economic life".[2] These kinship structures that are managed through patriarchal and hierarchical lines of authority, let people manage those below them and encourage informal lines of communication and decision-making. Extended families are central to the Gulf's social structures, and ensure their reach through various personal and business connections within their ranks, especially among senior members, and among younger members through arranged, often first cousin marriages, which remain a common, although no longer exclusive, means by which people find husbands and wives.[3] Family is an informal unit, but an extremely powerful one. Moreover, there are economic and commercial relationships across families, such as

between merchant families, or between a merchant family and a political one. These are sometimes cemented through marriages (in such cases,
typically beyond the extended family, but sometimes still within a tribe or
other social grouping). Conversely, a commercial relationship may exist
between such families because they share membership in the same tribe,
tribal confederacy, or other such broad faction.

The family is an important link to the political economies of the Gulf
because of how family linkages are utilized by ruling families. This takes
various forms.[4] Sometimes royals themselves will become businesspeople
or engage in business as a side interest, and through this will form part-
nerships and other relationships with merchant families and others. In
other cases, families with commercial interests will seek out links, both
commercial and social, as a way to build strong alliances that will protect
their interests and create new opportunities. Away from the royal family
itself, business families may ally with each other, whether within or across
other units of social organization such as tribes, as a way to share risks
and rewards, obtain financing or enter new areas of the economy. These
linkages expanded and were strengthened by the 1970s oil boom, when
state spending increased dramatically, giving ruling elites a greater power
over traditional business families as rents were dispersed and as new commercial players were able to enter the economy and become wealthy and
influential. Later, as the Gulf economies have globalized, such links have
remained important, both to solidify and insure family interests and, for
newer business families or those with very specific commercial interests,
to locate or access new opportunities overseas.[5]

This has been a particularly strong feature of post-1960s Saudi Arabia,
but is the case across all of the Gulf states to some extent. It features in
both rentierism and new state capitalism, the two pillars of modern Arab
Gulf economies, and in fact it is a key juncture at which the two meet.
With rentierism, this is because wealth is dispersed "not only through the
mechanisms of 'direct' and un-individualised redistribution ... (bureauc-
ratisation of employment, no taxation, health and education for all, etc.)
but also through individualised favours, which benefit only some citizens

to whom the regime considers itself particularly indebted".[6] Specific or targeted redistribution such as this, through neopatrimonial networks, brings state capitalism into the process. Opportunities are often provided by the state by, for example, the opportunity for a business to sell goods or services to the state, supply to state-owned firms, or partnering with a ministry of state-owned firm on a project. In Oman, the business community has done especially well, and less wealth than elsewhere has returned to the royal family (although the Sultan's family is small compared with those in the other Gulf states). The royal families in Saudi Arabia, Kuwait, and various emirates of the UAE have a range of members with business interests; Saudi Arabia's consists of perhaps 600 royals[7] from, as discussed, a pool typically estimated to total 7,000–8,000 or more. In Dubai, as in some other emirates, the royal family has close inter-family ties to business elites, through which it manages links down to more minor families. Given its small (indigenous) population, this permits an extensive network of distribution by the state of business opportunities, strengthening the bonds among Dubai's small population of citizens in a political economy that is overwhelmingly made up of foreigners.[8] Qatar is somewhere in-between Oman and the other Gulf states in terms of regime-business relations. It has an extremely large royal family relative to the population, but they are heavily supported through transfer payments and employment opportunities. While some of them enjoy commercial opportunities, these are spread widely across the business community as well to ensure a breadth of support for the ruling wing of the Al Thani dynasty.

The role played by primordial social units in the political economies of the Gulf has both positive and negative aspects. In terms of politics and regime maintenance, ruling elites have a strong incentive to share at least some commercial opportunities, and doing so through family linkages is a way of enhancing trust and reinforcing the solidarity between families that often have long histories of collaborating together in both commerce and politics. This is especially important where expatriate populations are large, where it will often suit the ruling family to ensure that key citizens are made to feel secure and their interests protected by the state. There are downsides too, however. Networks of extended families can create large blocks of people supporting each other, leading to factionalism within the political system or within the economy. More obviously, personalized and heavily trust-based informal systems sustain *wasta* and other forms of reciprocity and symbiosis. *Wasta* is not only simply corruption, and can be beneficial, for example as a means of resolving conflict or building trust. However, it is also negative, especially where it provides certain people or groups with targeted access, opportunities and benefits, and so to some extent is, in its impact, little different from corruption. Finally, Gulf societies are also very conservative, not only in terms of social values and religion, but also economically. This is not only a result of the strength of family and tribe, but a source of their power. To the extent that conservatism makes the Gulf's societies and economies resistant to change or unwilling to adapt when necessary, this too is a negative aspect of the strength of primordial loyalties.

ECONOMIC GEOGRAPHY AND THE ENVIRONMENT

The history of the Gulf, outlined in Chapter 2, suggests that geography has had a significant role in shaping the Gulf and thus has helped determine its fate. Its location made it an important and, at certain times and places, wealthy area as its ports hosted traders and pilgrims, and given its historical role in producing anything from spices to frankincense to pearls. Its position has attracted external powers over the centuries, whose actions shaped the nature of current Gulf states and economies. Obviously its geography is the reason for its oil and gas wealth, with all the impacts that this has brought. Geography defines climate, too, and the Gulf's climate and ecology have defined it and shaped its social and economic attributes. The harsh climate, especially the heat of summer, is a source of its nomadic traditions, as well as having made food and water scarce and controlling the size of the population that the area has traditionally supported. Only in areas such as modern-day Iran and Iraq, where there are large river and lake networks, have larger populations been sustainable prior to modern times.

The Gulf can do little about products of fate such as geography, although it can exacerbate or alleviate the impacts through state policy. In the past, Gulf states have paid little attention to the environment and to issues such as water scarcity, and where these have gained attention, the policies pursued have often been imprudent. Saudi Arabia provides a particularly stark example of this, with its ill-founded agricultural and food security policies of past decades. From the 1970s until the early 2000s, in a confusion of food *security* with food *self-sufficiency* and in an ill-considered attempt at economic diversification, they actively encouraged and subsidized an agricultural sector, despite having no comparative advantage in food production and having to draw down underground aquifers for the necessary water. This is only the most extreme example from several, as other states toyed with similar policies in the past. The UAE had a self-sufficiency goal under its former ruler Sheikh Zayed Al Nahyan (r. 1966–2004 as Emir of Abu Dhabi, 1971–2004 as President of the UAE), as did Qatar more briefly.[9]

Not only are such policies now a thing of the past, but as states have redefined concepts such as "food security", and as technology has improved, so too has the capacity and potential to address issues such as water security. These have promised much, but the Gulf is a long way from being self-sufficient in renewable, sustainable water. Considerable hope has been placed in seawater desalination, for example, since rainfall is so low, at less than 250mm per year on average, and the renewable fresh water supply from sources such as underground aquifers is only about 400m^3 per person per annum. Desalination has become increasingly common as a supply source for water: by the early 2010s, the Gulf had almost 60 per cent of the world's desalination plants and in some states, such as Bahrain, Kuwait, Qatar, and the UAE, these were supplying the majority of potable water.[10] However, water is still not being produced at a sustainable rate. The Gulf's water supply from renewable sources such as underground aquifers is currently being depleted at around six times the sustainable rate.[11] At the same time, there is the question of whether desalination is sustainable. It is a highly energy-intensive activity, and by returning highly salty water to the Persian Gulf, risks damaging that ecosystem, which is especially fragile and already very high in salinity. This issue has the potential to be a key determinant of the future of the Gulf political econ-omies, not least of all because water security underlies so many aspects of the economy. It is integral to the sense of human security overall, but is also essential to the maintenance of certain economic sectors, including industry such as smelting, fabricating, and very importantly oil refining, and is also crucial for services such as tourism.

A broader long-term problem related to water, but potentially even more serious in nature yet also poorly addressed thus far, is that of climate change. While the specific impacts of climate change remain uncertain, the Gulf states remain unprepared for most scenarios. All six have very high carbon emissions, among the highest in the world: Qatar's, at 45.5 tonnes per capita per annum in 2014, is the world's highest.[12] It is followed by Kuwait (at 25.2 tonnes), Bahrain (23.4 tonnes), the UAE (23.3 tonnes), Saudi Arabia (19.5 tonnes), and Oman (15.4 tonnes). This compares with an upper income average of 11 tonnes, a US figure of 16.5 tonnes, 9.5 tonnes for Japan and 8.9 tonnes for Germany. These are the results in part of the subregion's wealthy lifestyle, but given how high they are against other developed economies, other factors are involved as well. These include high energy subsidies, which encourage higher consumption; energy-intensive activities such as water desalination, as discussed, and smelting; and a reliance on automobiles and very cheap petroleum. The high pop-ulation growth rates in these states suggest that carbon emissions overall will not fall in the future, absent a policy to substantively address the issue, and yet reaffirms that such levels are not sustainable in the long term.[13]

The risks of climate change are severe for the Gulf states. The waters of the Persian Gulf are projected to rise over the twenty-first century by anything from 0.09 metres to 0.88 metres. Even the former would have a noticeable impact; the latter would be potentially catastrophic for coastal cities and towns that often lie only a few metres above sea level.[14] Global average temperature rises of between 1.8°C and 3.6°C would be even more marked over land, since the temperatures over land are likely to

rise more than over the oceans. This would add to desertification, elimi-
nate the small nomadic herding that still exists in the region, and deplete
underground aquifers even faster than would be the case on current projections.[15] More extreme weather events and more varied precipitation
levels, which are also expected from climate change, would add further
uncertainty in the subregion, including to its economic performance and
potential. All this is before more dramatic problems that might also come
from climate change are considered, such as the risk of regional refugee
movements, or an increased danger of military conflict related to environmental insecurity. All of these problems would have significant impacts
on economic performance and development, albeit to varying extents.
They are also, for the time being, highly unpredictable and their likelihood
difficult to establish, creating uncertainty and also a degree of deniability
among those who prefer not to consider them.

Indeed, the Gulf seems to be paying too scant attention to the risks
of climate change. For a long time, the Gulf Cooperation Council (GCC)
countries, led by Saudi Arabia, opposed carbon emissions reduction nego-
tiations and agreements, fearing that an agreement would impact their
incomes and undermine employment. With their rapidly-growing populations, finding jobs for their people and ensuring their incomes were
seen as a far more urgent priority that addressing climate change. The Gulf
states did not ratify the 1997 Kyoto Protocol until 2005 and 2006,[16] and
even then, were non-Annex 1 parties, meaning that they had no reduction
target and no obligation to reduce emissions. Prior to this, they had firmly
opposed the Protocol. Their argument, followed by many net hydrocarbon exporters, as well as the United States during the George W. Bush
administration (2001–09), was that the Protocol would unfairly harm the
economies of energy exporters and was thus unfair to these states.

The Kyoto Protocol did, however, focus greater attention on the Gulf
states and probably made them take more notice of climate change as
well. During the oil boom of 2004–08, most of the Gulf states developed
environmental and climate change policies of some sort. These "green"
initiatives were more focused on economic diversification goals than

environmental ones, however, and were often experiments in supporting emerging technology and providing research and investment frameworks and opportunities.[17] From the early 2010s onwards, these states began to develop a more active approach to the issue. But it is difficult to assess how serious these policies, as they exist in the late-2010s, actually are. These policies include, for example, renewable energy targets for their economy overall, such as Qatar's goal of meeting 20 per cent of its energy needs from renewables by 2024, and sector-specific goals such as the UAE's target to generate 25 per cent of its power from nuclear energy sources by 2020.[18] They are also pursuing research and testing new initiatives in climate science, such as in carbon capture and storage, as well as pursuing actions to cut emissions, such as by minimizing gas flaring at oil sites.

The problem is that these actions, while laudable, are not sufficient to substantially impact carbon emissions: they are likely to have some effect, certainly, but fall far short of what is needed to reduce carbon emissions to the level of, say, the average developed economy. Moreover, for their economic security they should be considering climate change mitigation strategies, but have only just begun to do so, and again only at a basic level. The difficulty they face is that for many years to come, their economic diversification strategies will require them to maintain their levels of energy exports and income, to pay for the costs of diversification and fund policies to offset some of the likely negative impacts from economic change and reform. The infrastructural and other investment required by their diversification policies will also be carbon-intensive. While the Gulf states have responded hesitantly to climate change, this is more understandable given their reliance on hydrocarbon exports and the economic imperatives that they face. Climate change is an area of considerable risk for their economic futures, but one that will only be felt in the long term.

ECONOMIC CHANGE AND POLITICAL STASIS

The conservatism of the Gulf's states and societies, and the propensity of rentierism to perpetuate the political status quo, means that change is typically gradual. There can be moments where a dramatic shift occurs, when particular events shake the politics of a particular Gulf state or restructure the subregional order. Events with profound long-term impacts have included the 1978–79 Iranian revolution, the 1979 siege at the Grand Mosque in Mecca, the 1990 Iraqi invasion of Kuwait and the subsequent 1990–91 Gulf War, the 2003 Iraq War, the 2011 Arab uprisings, and the 2014–17 phenomenon of the so-called Islamic state (or ISIS) in Iraq and Syria.

The Gulf has changed, and changed markedly, both economically and to a lesser extent politically. These changes are often so gradual, however, especially those in the political realm, that they are often neglected by observers. Some critics simply assume that the Gulf consists of unreconstituted traditional monarchs, with absolute power and medieval attitudes. There is extensive evidence – much of it already laid out here – to the contrary. There is no evidence that any Gulf rulers will genuinely take the risk of losing power through political reform, but a range of more minor changes have taken place, while reforms in the economic and social spheres will likely flow into the political arena as well. The change of recent decades has been gradual, and is likely to be similar in future, occurring within the rentier and state capitalist frameworks of these political economies, and as almost-exclusively top-down. It is a sign of ruling elites' reactions to externalities, and reflects the back-and-forth struggle between states and societies for agency, influence and advantage.

Political change is often equated with the post-Cold War wave of democratization in the 1990s and early 2000s, but is actually a general and permanent feature of politics. The negotiation around power in Kuwait in the 1930s, especially the 1938 experiment with parliamentary and constitutional politics, was an early example; it also highlights Kuwait's tendency, unique in the Gulf, for change to often come through "bottom-up" pressure rather than from above.[19] This dynamic continued after 1938, through independence and the creation of a constituent assembly in 1962, with multiple suspensions and reformations of the legislature after that time. Bahrain was another early case of legislative reform, having had a parliament soon after independence, over 1973–75,[20] and again after 2002.

As at 2018, Bahrain, Kuwait, and Oman were the only states with elected parliaments. Bahrain's 40-member *majlis al-nuwab* ("Representative Assembly", or lower house) are elected by simple majority for four-year terms, with a 40-member *majlis al-shura* ("Consultative Assembly", or upper house) appointed by the King. Kuwait has a *majlis al-'umma* ("National Assembly"), a unicameral legislature of 50 members elected directly in one of five districts, plus up to 15 government-appointed *ex-officio* members. In Oman, there is a directly-elected, 84-member *majlis al-shura* ("Consultative Assembly"), which acts as a lower house, with a *majlis al-dawla* ("Assembly of State") as upper house. The Omani *majlis al-shura* arguably is weaker than the Bahraini and Kuwaiti assemblies, as it serves predominantly as an oversight body, although it can amend draft legislation and submit questions to the government, but lacks some of the power and authority of the other two. Bahrain and Oman ban political parties, meaning that individuals must run as independents, even though they may have an affiliation to a society or other group with some of the characteristics of a party.

The other three Gulf states do not have elected parliaments. The UAE, however, has an advisory body at the federal level, *al-majlis al-watani al-ittihadi* (the "Federal National Assembly"), with half of its 40 members being chosen indirectly through an electoral college. Qatar does not have a legislature at present, but the terms for one were included in its 2003 constitution. Polls have been postponed several times, most recently until 2019 at the earliest. In Saudi Arabia, there is a consultative body, or *majlis al-shura*, with 150 members appointed by the King. It can propose laws to the King or the cabinet, but cannot initiate, enact, or enforce them. Saudi Arabia has, however, introduced other limited political reforms, including elections for municipal councils. The first was held in 2005, with only men able to vote or run (and for only half the positions), but as of the third poll in 2015, two-thirds of seats were open, and women were also permitted to run and vote. While these consultative bodies and local government reforms have limited reach into national-level politics, they are not entirely impotent or unimportant either. By acting as a consultative mechanism between the ruler (and in effect, the cabinet and wider government), they can have at least a modest role in influencing policy-making and, on occasion, in the framing of legislation. They are also institutions that foster interaction and discussion among their members, providing stronger societal links than would otherwise be the case in their absence. To some observers, moreover, they signal a reform impetus, however limited, that could potentially pave the way for more substantial political liberalization.[21]

While there has long been debate about the relationship, if any, between economic and political change, the Gulf seems to present a case of economic transformation and modernization with only very limited political liberalization. The political reform which has occurred has been limited to initiatives such as the expansion of parliaments, introduction of local elections, and other changes. To assume that this will lead to deeper political liberalization, or especially democratization, would be unfounded given the subregion's current political settings. Perhaps most importantly, there is simply no agreement in place for an exchange of greater societal political agency for state legitimacy. States and regimes are reliant upon deeply embedded rentier tactics, which create sufficient durability in the system to deter the main actors from undertaking substantial reform, especially where this could upset existing patterns of privilege. While rentierism *can* bestow legitimacy on a state and its political leadership, it does not need to do so. For their survival, incumbent rulers and elites need only a sufficiently broad societal acquiescence. It is telling that the Gulf leaderships' first responses to the 2011 Arab uprisings were predominantly economic in nature, a recognition of both the economic nature of many of the protestors' grievances, but also a sign that the rentier bargain was open to tinkering and a limited restructuring, but not to wholesale reform or liberalization, much less abandonment. In essence, "the social contract in the GCC has not been fundamentally rewritten".[22]

Where political reforms have occurred, as with the introduction of polls or the expansion of legislatures' influence, this is a sign of late rentierism at work. Specifically, even where rentier states have durable cooptive bargains in place with society, they still must listen to society and be responsive to a certain degree, and appear to be so. Limited reforms that give people a sense of greater agency or which symbolize more open political systems, while not threatening the stability of the state or those at its upper levels, are attractive to regimes. They are not particularly risky to introduce and send a message of reform to society. It is for this reason that these systems cannot be characterized simply as crude autocracies, nor is the argument sustainable that society has no influence with the state. However to assume that such reforms foretell democratization is imprudent. Political reform is likely to continue on its gradual and modest trajectory, and as with economic reform, state-led. The Gulf states are essentially, if at different speeds, pursuing the "liberalized autocracy" strategy that Brumberg outlined.[23] This accounts not only for the limited depth of political reforms, but for the fact that political reforms have been the most scant in the UAE and Qatar, the two states which faced no significant protests during the 2011 Arab uprisings and have exceptionally low levels of popular dissent.

Could this change, especially if the era of low oil prices after 2014 undermines the rentier bargain and forces states into making new or further political concessions to society? This is possible, even though the cooptive and repressive capacity of these states is enormous. Substantial political change is only likely to come in one of two ways. One is from the bottom-up, through revolutionary pressure or other deep, popular unrest, at a scale which threatens the survival of a regime. Bahrain is the only state in the Gulf that has witnessed anything close to this level of societal discontent in recent times, and even there a combination of cooptation and repression still gives the regime substantial durability. The second way in which more substantive change may occur is if a new leader emerges and introduces it. The Gulf states are in an intergenerational transition from older rulers to younger ones, with only Kuwait and Oman having elderly rulers in power, and Saudi Arabia having an older King but a young and very powerful crown prince. It is conceivable that a young leader may choose to undertake political reform to stamp his own mark on the system, or in pursuit of a political legacy, with the assumption that he and the system would survive the transformation. Such reform would be extremely risky, however, and remains a distant prospect for as long as there is elite consensus to preserve the status quo, and provided the rentier capacity of the state remains in place.

LINGERING REFORM IMPERATIVES

Despite the durability of Gulf regimes, and the overall stability of the Gulf's political economies, they suffer from a number of problems, and face risks in the future if these are left unaddressed. This dilemma must necessarily begin with a high-level question: is a predominantly rentier and highly traditional system capable of reform? Or is rentierism so embedded that it establishes entrenched interests that will never permit genuine reform that might cost them power? Early rentier state theorists mostly answered this question in the affirmative, often emphatically so. If this were the case, however, then the economic and social transformations in recent decades, and even the more modest political reforms, would not have been possible. Rather, late rentier frameworks actually provide considerable scope for reform, which may serve the interests of incumbent elites. This is especially true where reform can serve to enhance the state's or regime's image in society, or where it will strengthen social accord or help reduce risks of societal unrest or conflict.

One area of Gulf politics where reform is especially desirable is in sectarian relations, especially in Saudi Arabia and Bahrain, where Sunni–Shia tensions are the most troubled in the subregion. Some attempts have been made to address this problem, but there are also constraints, real or actual, on the state's ability to do so. In Saudi Arabia, the ruling Al Sa'ud family needs the political support of the Wahhabi clerics, who take a negative view of the Shia. In future, as the power of the clerics seems likely to decline, this may change, but for now it retains an ability to check some state policies, especially in the religious realm. In Bahrain, the ruling Al Khalifa dynasty is part of the Sunni minority, ruling over a Shia majority, and so there is a fear that any substantial reform, much less the transfer of any genuine power to the Shia, would be destabilizing and even a threat to the ruling regime. This may well be the case, but there is a risk – arguably a greater one – in letting valid Bahraini Shia grievances fester or in responding too heavy-handedly to Shia dissatisfaction.

In the near- and medium-term future, the most substantial reforms are most likely to come in the economic realm, and to vary in their detail somewhat between the various states. As Hvidt has noted, while all six states have good infrastructure, they differ markedly in the degree of international competition in their economies, the quality of their education systems, the sophistication of their financial markets, and in the extent of innovation shown by their state-owned and private-sector firms.[24] Innovation is an area of particular concern, as despite some improvements over time, the Gulf states remain heavily reliant on imported technology and have not been able to successfully instil a culture of technological innovation into their private sectors or key government institutions.[25] They all perform reasonably well on measures of basic competitiveness, such as the standard of their infrastructure, their economic stability and the quality of their health care systems, but they have been far less successful in lifting "efficiency enhancers" such as higher education quality, financial market sophistication, and their use of and adaptability to technology.[26]

In recent years they have tried to address some of these more complicated elements of competitiveness and economic adaptability. For a time, the GCC was a potential mechanism for such initiatives. The GCC has had a Unified Economic Agreement (UEA) in place since 1981, the year it was formed, covering free trade, technical cooperation, transport, and financial and other cooperation. As its role shifted in the 1990s from a security focus to a far more economic, scientific, and sociocultural emphasis, its members adopted a range of further measures to free up trade across their borders, encourage investment, ease border controls, foster research and development and encourage commercial innovation. Apart from a basic free trade area structure, which was achieved in 1983, most of these reforms have been gradual, even sluggish. The customs union was only agreed in 2001, to be brought in two years later. It is telling that free trade agreements with other economies such as the United States and European Union have typically been more comprehensive and yet proceeded far faster. The GCC has been slightly more successful in initiatives such as fostering investment across member states and collaborating on industrialization policies, although the impacts of these have been limited.

The 2004–08 oil boom provided an incentive for some of the Gulf states to move in their own direction. They remained members of the GCC, but did not give it an emphasis in their foreign economic policies. The proposal for a single GCC currency arguably was a case where the competition and rivalries between various states, as well as the limited scope for full economic integration among them, made them unwilling, at least for the time being, to surrender a key part of their economic sovereignty to a multilateral body like the GCC. The debate over the economic value of a single currency is contentious, and discussed, and since June 2017 the Qatar crisis has placed the future of the GCC itself in peril. That Qatar has weathered the crisis well, maintaining its economic performance, adds to this, especially as the other boycotting states, especially Saudi Arabia, have seemingly gained little from the crisis while also suffering some (albeit minor) economic costs as well. This outcome means that the two sides are cornered: the Qataris have less reason to capitulate now that the economic impacts are more modest than expected, while for Saudi Arabia and its allies, any resolution involving compromise runs the risk of appearing like a Qatari victory. Arguably, therefore, even if the GCC survives, it will take a long time to recover its influence with member states, and is unlikely to prove a useful vehicle for cooperation and collaboration for a long time to come. Instead, Gulf states will likely continue to pursue certain reforms, including in business reforms, technology, and innovation, individually or at a sub-GCC level.

What all the six economies share in common is the strong need for economic diversification. The fluctuations in oil and gas rents carry substantial political risks for rentier systems, and this unpredictable variation in state incomes has been a driver of past reforms. Despite its economic value, the energy sector does not create a large number of jobs, and so there is a need to create jobs in other parts of these economies that are more labour-intensive. This has led to some failed policies, such as the Saudi agricultural schemes already discussed, but also to some successes, including the dramatic rise in certain manufacturing enterprises, tourism and airlines, as well as the expansion of higher education and other service industries. Diversification gained additional impetus when oil prices plummeted in 2014. The Gulf states' average GDP dropped, in that single year alone, by an extraordinarily steep 10 per cent.[27] After 2014, the Gulf states no longer had the same level of cooptive power they had enjoyed during the periods of high prices over 2004–08 and 2010–14. Low oil prices are almost-certainly a key driver of the major reforms being pushed by the Saudi government in its *Vision 2030* strategy, and probably have driven the similar plans formulated in other states. Unlike during the 1973–83 boom, Gulf governments have subsequently demonstrated a far more long-term and development-centred mindset since the early 2000s.

Some of the other areas where reform is important or urgent have already been discussed, such as in subsidies. Gulf governments have already started to address this issue, especially energy subsidies, which in the past have been expensive and yet of little economic use. In the past, it was often assumed that subsidy reform was too politically difficult, that society had come to expect subsidies as part of the rentier bargain. However the allocative bargain was probably not this significant of a hurdle, especially if, as seems to be the case, subsidy reform is done in a measured way and if the poorest segments of society are protected from its negative effects. The removal of subsidies also requires care because the growth and diversification of the private sector has traditionally been assisted by subsidized economic inputs.[28] Since private sector expansion and innovation is central to economic diversification, this will be undermined if subsidy reform is done hastily or clumsily and negatively impacts the creation of new businesses or new investment by existing ones.

Probably the most tricky and political risky area of reform is in labour markets. While there are both economic and political advantages in the reliance on expatriate labour, in the long term it is not a sustainable or desirable policy, especially given the population growth rate in the Gulf and the increasing inability of the state to guarantee good jobs to the bulk of new entrants in the labour market. Yet the Gulf continues to rely on these workers as much as ever. It has proved extremely difficult to encourage citizens to work in the private sector, while for employers, the wages that can be offered to expatriates are far below what citizens would be willing to accept. If states were to change this arrangement, it would be seen by society as breaking the allocative bargain and by business as dramatically shifting the cost of labour and undermining their operations. Most people in these economies do not want to take the types of jobs they would have to accept if real reform was made to the labour market, and there is scant evidence that employers would prefer to hire citizens anyway. Moreover, as one recent report noted, Gulf citizens have become used to the current system in other respects, such as the cheap domestic labour available from it: some 90 per cent of Kuwaiti families, it noted, have at least one domestic servant, and they expect this to continue.[29] Among the various reforms that are needed or are desirable for the Gulf economies, labour market reform is probably the toughest and most politically risky of them all.

The challenges and dilemmas of labour market reform are a reminder that, desirable as reform may be, promising change and actually delivering on these promises are very different things. Low oil prices after 2014 created an urgency for more substantial economic reform, and leaders seem to have recognized the opportunity, with subsidy reductions, new economic diversification measures, the introduction of a sales tax, and new or higher charges for state services all the product of the pressures on state budgets after 2014. Two issues remain, however. One is whether reforms will be followed through on, especially if oil prices rise again in the future. The second and greater challenge is whether deeper but crucial reforms, such as to the labour market, can be made at all in a rentier system.[30] The first issue is predominantly a test of will and discipline, but the second would change the state–society relationship. This may prove too great a step for either ruling elites or citizens, at least where the end of the oil era is such a distant prospect.

LINGERING REGIONAL CONSTRAINTS

The Gulf has been able to construct an international image of relative stability, marking itself out from other parts of the Middle East, which has a far more negative popular image in the rest of the world. Nonetheless, the Gulf is still part of the Middle East, and is shaped and affected by what happens further afield in the region and by the economic, political, and other linkages that it has with the wider region. There are also some international political issues within the Gulf itself that could pose a threat to the security and economic prospects of the Arab Gulf states in the future.

As discussed in Chapter 4, regional conflicts such as the Israeli–Palestinian conflict will occasionally have an impact on the Gulf, but is manageable because of the Gulf's distance from the core of that conflict. It is also a long-term conflict, meaning that regional actors beyond the core antagonists have generally adapted to the risks and uncertainties created by it. It may feed into certain threats closer to home – it is a major grievance that Islamic extremists draw upon for support and to incite their supporters, for example – but again, Gulf rulers have addressed this through a mixture of modest support for the Palestinians, by taking care of their citizens' other, more pressing needs through rentier allocations and other state spending, and by repressing Islamist groups where they pose a real threat to political stability. The Arab–Israeli issue is not irrelevant to Gulf states' politics, but nor is it a core problem for political stability within their borders either.

Within the Gulf, and of more immediate and substantial concern, are the two issues of the future role of Iran and the long-term stability of Iraq. In the case of Iran, there is a deep suspicion in the Arab Gulf states about Tehran's long-term goals and about its nuclear programme. Saudi Arabia, in particular, is engaged in a rivalry with Iran for regional influence, often backed by its closer Arab Gulf allies, most notably the UAE and Bahrain. It has been loath to accept the Iranian nuclear deal, signed between Iran, the P5+1 and the EU, at face value, viewing it as highly risky and worried about its long-term viability. They are also nervous about Iran's military capabilities, especially its large conventional armed forces, and the proficiency of its intelligence services and asymmetrical warfare capability. The Saudis in particular, but with the other GCC states following, have sought a qualitative military capability to offset Iran's numerical advantage. They have also engaged in indirect, proxy conflict in Syria, Yemen and elsewhere, as previously noted.

In the case of Iraq, there is concern among the Gulf states about the Shia dominance of post-2003 politics, including as to whether this is fostering greater Iranian strategic reach and influence into Iraq. Perhaps most of all, they worry that their own Shia populations may be motivated by the rise of Shia power in Iraq and demand more political voice or autonomy. The turmoil in post-2003 Iraq also created a fear in the Gulf states about Islamic extremism in, and stemming from, that country. The rise of ISIS, and especially their quick military conquests in 2014, stoked these fears further.[31] Had the ISIS caliphate been able to survive, it would have transformed Islamic radicalism in the Muslim world and potentially drawn political legitimacy away from the Gulf monarchies. As it was, ISIS still managed to attract foreign fighters, including some from the Gulf states, with the potential that some of them will pose a future terrorism or political risk after returning home. By late 2017 ISIS was defeated on the battlefields of Iraq and Syria, and its experiment in creating an Islamic state destroyed, but there is still the uncertainty as to what sort of extremist models might arise in future, perhaps radicalized by the ISIS precedent or seeking to copy it.

While concerns about Iran and Iraq have some legitimate basis, they are also symptomatic of an underlying security problem in the Gulf: the lack of any effective, comprehensive security architecture covering the subregion as a whole. Even when its prospects looked more positive, the GCC was only ever a body of six of the eight states that have a coastline on the Persian Gulf. Iraq and Iran were both excluded, and deliberately so. The GCC was intended, in effect, as an institution of conservative Sunni monarchies, occupied most of all with ensuring the security and maintenance of the member states' regimes. For the security conditions in the Gulf to genuinely improve, some substantive security architecture is required, including a body that incorporates the entire subregion and probably some other, neighbouring states as well. For the time being, this simply is not plausible: not only is the level of antagonism between Iran and the Arab Gulf states too great, but after the 2017 Qatar crisis, even the future of the GCC itself seems in doubt.

Even if the GCC survives – even if it were to thrive – there remain other security questions for the Gulf states. One already mentioned several times is that of sectarianism, including both how the Gulf's leaderships choose to treat their own Shia minorities, but also how concerned they remain about sectarianism as an international security threat. There is little evidence that a new generation of leaders will view this much differently. For example, while Muhammad bin Salman, Saudi Arabia's crown prince, is often lauded as a reformer, he was also the principle architect and proponent for the Saudi-led intervention in Yemen, which was driven by the Kingdom's rivalry with Iran. Other younger leaders have taken positions on sectarian issues based on their specific security perspectives. Bahrain's King has, by necessity, followed the Saudi lead, along with the UAE, in contributing to the Yemeni intervention. Qatar's young Emir Tamim has been informed by his country's historically closer economic ties to Iran and his father's legacy of seeking a diverse set of foreign relationships, and so has been more open to Iran. The Qatari–Iranian relationship was one of the key concerns that drove Saudi Arabia to confront and blockade Qatar in June 2017. Oman also has a history of trade and engagement with Iran, and there is some worry that Saudi Arabia and others might put it under the same pressure as they have with Qatar.

Even if the issue of sect did not exist, the revival of political Islam in the Middle East has been addressed by the Gulf states in varying ways. This has been all the more important since the 2011 Arab uprisings, which reminded Gulf rulers that underlying oppositional forces existed in most of their societies; that these could potentially become Islamized was an even greater concern, especially given the Sunni radicalism that confronted the Saudi regime in the 1990s and into the 2000s.[32] The response of leaders has varied, however. The Saudis, as in the 2000s and in line with their approach to sectarianism, have been relatively repressive of political Islamists, if also supporting de-radicalization programmes and other alternatives to simple punitive approaches. The UAE has followed similar lines in the 2010s; as one study noted, the UAE's approach has been a security-centred one, in contrast to Qatar, which has sought to engage with Islamist groups such as the Muslim Brotherhood.[33] This may stem from their differing strategies in marking out their regional roles, or it may be a product of their histories, since Qatar never had an indigenous Islamist force in society that seriously challenged the ruling family, while Saudi Arabia, Egypt, and others did – although not the UAE. Islamists remain sufficiently weak in the Gulf states to not pose an existential threat to ruling regimes, at least for the time being. However, they operate discreetly, making it difficult to discern how they might act if they were ever to gain power or be brought into a formal political role. The experience of Islamists coming to power in Egypt and Tunisia after the 2011 uprisings suggests, however, that on economic policy, at least, they may well have some sympathies for business, and certainly would want to ensure economic stability, if only to support their legitimacy, and provided that their welfare concerns are also addressed.

The Arab Gulf states' perspectives on the issues of sect, relations with Iran, and political Islam are all a reminder of the differences, even divisions, among them. While the Gulf as a subregion is generally more stable than many other parts of the Middle East, challenges may still arise to threaten this stability in the future. The 2017 Qatar crisis is a reminder that even the most prosperous and dynamic of the Gulf states can find its circumstances changed, often unpredictably and with far greater consequence and cost than they would have imagined.

7

Conclusion:
prospects for the Gulf economies

The Gulf states have come a long way just in the years since the start of the new millennium, and much further still since Dubai began its experiment in conditional but aggressive state-led globalization in the mid-1980s. In differing ways and with different prospects for success, all six of the Arab Gulf states examined here are seeking to continue this transformation, informed by – though not merely copying – the example set by Dubai. These states entered the twenty-first century as wealthy economies and, despite the reforms that remain to be done, with largely stable political orders and economies. They are not likely to collapse in the near future, barring some dramatic unforeseeable event, despite the predictions of their demise that are sometimes made.[1] In fact, the 2011 Arab uprisings affected the Gulf *less* than it did the republics, turning on its head the assumption that had reigned among observers until that point, that the monarchical systems of the Gulf were passé and that the future belonged to republican forms of government rather than monarchical ones.

This said, there are a range of global shifts taking place that will continue to test the Gulf's leaders, put pressure on its economies, and impact its societies. Moreover, if these economies begin a period of more intense and deep economic reform, this will bring additional forces to bear on the subregion. Indeed, the pace of change across the subregion may well accelerate in the coming years, even though the basic dynamics underlying these political economies – rentierism, state capitalism, top-down strategies of elite consensus-building – will probably govern these systems for as long as hydrocarbons dominate them.

CONTINUING AND EMERGING ENERGY ISSUES

Although the centrality of oil and gas in the political economies of the Gulf is not something that is about to change any time soon, the global energy system is changing rapidly, bringing with it a new set of challenges for hydrocarbon exporters such as those of the Gulf.

As recently as the early 2000s, a fear in the subregion, and in oil importing states even more so, was of "peak oil". This concept was, essentially, that since oil is a non-renewable resource of finite amounts, at some stage global oil output would stall and then begin to permanently decline, either until it was near depletion or, more likely, until it became so expensive that it would no longer be possible to use it in the quantities that have sustained world economic growth and development since the mid-twentieth century. The term "peak oil" captured the image of total production which, it was argued, would form a bell-curve shape when displayed as a chart: production would rise, peak, and then decline. Since the decline in production would be uncontrollable – there would simply be not enough oil available to extract – then unless demand fell at a commensurate rate, the gap between falling supply and continued demand would push the price extremely high. This would create stagflation (simultaneously high inflation and unemployment together), affect the ability to use what are currently common oil and gas products such as fertilizers, pesticides, and of course transport, and lead to conflicts over the small remaining resources. As discussed earlier, a range of scholarly works and documentary films were produced in the early- and mid-2000s with a peak oil argument. While peak oil seems to have been allayed for decades as unconventional energy has become viable, for the Gulf, as both a key producer and heavy consumer of hydrocarbons, its predictions were the stuff of nightmares.

Instead, as the global oil industry changes and technology advances, the Gulf states may find itself in a weaker position than in the past. First, unconventional oil is found more widely than conventional. The Middle East dominates the latter, with the eight states in the Persian Gulf accounting for almost half the world's proven conventional supplies. In contrast, unconventional oil is found in Canada, Venezuela, the United States, and smaller amounts in Western Europe, Australia, Mongolia, North Africa, Brazil, and a range of other places. There is thought to be more unconventional oil in Venezuela than there is conventional oil in Saudi Arabia.[2] More immediately, the United States has begun to extract and process unconventional oil at impressive rates. In 2013, the US was producing an average of 3.22 million bbls/day of tight oil, with this figure expected to reach 9.6 million bbl/day by 2020.[3] Total US oil production previously peaked in 1970 at just under 10 million bbl/day and then fell to (just) under 5 million bbl/day in 2008. By 2015 it has risen again to 9.4 million bbl/day and was over 8.8 million bbl/day in 2016.[4] Tight oil accounted for the majority of this increase, and its share of production is expected to rise further into and over the 2020s.

The most obvious implication of this is that net oil importing states can reduce their reliance on net exporters, such as the Gulf states, if they have reserves of unconventional oil. The United States is the clearest example of renewed rates of production driven by unconventional oil, but other states will join them in due course. The strategic importance of the Gulf for US security, and in the future for the security of other key states, is likely to decline. There is already the question of whether US interest in the Gulf is beginning to wane as its reliance on Gulf energy falls. Second, if unconventional oil rises markedly as share of global production, then more and varied suppliers will mean that the Gulf will lose some of its importance in the global energy market, including having less control of price and therefore less market power. Related to this is the risk that unconventional oil has the potential to increase global supply to a point where prices remain suppressed over the very long term, which would necessitate substantial and sustainable reform of Gulf states' budgets. Finally, the high costs of unconventional oil production will mean that the Gulf will have to compete even more fiercely than at present for a share of global energy investment, or take on new risks by making such investments itself.

How serious are these risks? The evidence that the US interest in the Gulf is in decline seems premature. For the security of global supply, and therefore price stability, the US will retain a strong interest in the Gulf sub-region. It also has other non-energy interests in the Middle East, including in the Gulf, such as counter-terrorism, its relationship with Israel, the potential for arms sales, and to a lesser extent general trade and investment interests. As new powers such as China arise, and old ones such as Russia seek to play a more active role in the Middle East again – or perhaps even reinvigorated by these shifts in global power – the US will remain strongly engaged with the Gulf for the short- and medium-terms. The risks of lower prices and less influence are perhaps the greater ones for the Gulf, although the dynamics of energy prices are complex. This is illustrated by the case of Saudi Arabia, a powerful oil exporting state since the 1960s and a dominant one since US production declined in the 1970s. At certain times it has been a "swing" producer, able to affect the global price of oil by increasing and decreasing its production, but it had in effect lost that power by the time unconventional oil was becoming viable in the early 2000s, and has probably now lost it for the long term.

What will assist conventional oil exporting states such as those of the Gulf is their price adaptability and competitiveness. They are able to extract conventional oil extremely cheaply, at far lower cost than unconventional oil but also cheaply compared to the costs of conventional production in most other places. The Gulf not only has a lot of oil, but for the most part it is good quality and found in shallow, high pressure wells. In early 2016, the total cost of producing a barrel of oil was $8.98 in Saudi Arabia and $10.57 in Iraq.[5] In contrast, it was $19.21 in Russia and $44.33 for the UK to produce a barrel of North Sea oil. It cost $23.35 to produce a barrel of US shale oil. Importantly, also, the amount of capital spending required per barrel is lower in the Gulf than in any other major producing states, meaning there is comparatively less pressure to find investment. On balance, while there is a lot of uncertainty around unconventional oil (and gas), including controversy about its environmental impacts, it will have mixed impacts both globally and on the Gulf.

OPPORTUNITIES AND RISKS IN THE GLOBAL ARENA

The changes in the global energy system are one aspect of a much larger and broader shift that is currently taking place at the global level. Another change is in major power dynamics, which are shifting with the rise of China, the resurgent international role of Russia, and the emergence of new middle powers. These, too, will have an impact on the political economies of the Gulf, although the exact outcomes of this shift and what the international order will look like in another decade or two remains to be seen.

The rise of China has been explored extensively and in depth in a range of works. What is most important here is how its rise will impact the Middle East and especially the Gulf. During the Cold War, the Middle East was a field of US–Soviet rivalry, and China played only a modest role, although this grew in the 1970s after the People's Republic of China (PRC) was admitted to the United Nations and recognized over Taiwan as the legitimate government of China.[6] Egypt and Syria had established diplomatic relations with Beijing in 1956, but other Middle Eastern states did not follow until the 1970s. The Gulf was fairly late in doing so. Apart from Kuwait, which recognized the PRC in 1971, and then Oman, which did so in 1978, the others did not switch their recognition to the PRC until the 1980s: the UAE in 1984, Qatar in 1988, Bahrain in 1989 and Saudi Arabia in 1990. China's links to the Gulf subsequently grew, as the latter became an increasingly important source of energy for China and a destination for Chinese goods exports. This economic relationship then boomed in the 1990s as China began its global rise. While there are political, strategic, cultural, and other elements to the Gulf's relationship with China, economics dominates it. For the time being China has not articulated a grand strategy, or even a comprehensive policy on the Middle East, suggesting that this economic and trade focus will continue to be Beijing's priority.

This means that for the moment the rise of China offers the most to the Gulf states in the economic sphere. As China's rise accelerated, the Chinese–GCC trade relationship boomed into the first decade of the twenty-first century. Trade increased over the decade of 2000–09 at an annual rate of 57.8 per cent and China's exports to the GCC states leaped from $3.68 billion to $31.25 billion, while their imports increased from $6.45 billion to $29.45 billion.[7] By 2016, two-way trade totalled $114 billion, and the GCC, taken as a whole, was China's eighth-largest trading partner.[8] This was supplemented by an expansion in the investment relationship, especially from the Gulf during the oil booms of 2004–08 and 2010–14, and at the same time from China, which had trade surpluses it was looking to invest abroad.[9]

For China, the overarching driver in the relationship is energy security. In the early 2010s, it was obtaining over a third of its oil imports from the Arab Gulf states (20% from Saudi Arabia. 7.2% from Oman, 3.8% from Kuwait, and 3.4% from the UAE), and closer to half from the Gulf as a whole with another 8.1 per cent from Iran and 5.7 per cent from Iraq.[10] Since China became a net oil importer in 1993, it has needed energy security from abroad, the importance of which has risen with its booming economy. This gives it a strong incentive to retain good relations with key source countries such as Saudi Arabia. At the same time, China is seeking to broaden its economic links. The Gulf is part of China's "New Silk Road" initiative (sometimes called "One Belt, One Road"), which was launched in 2013 and which is a broad state-led strategy aimed at strengthening and diversifying China's economic activities and ties across much of the Asian continent and on to Europe. This is likely an early indication of China trying to shift from a purely economic strategy to a more multifaceted one, including one with security and soft power dimensions.[11] For the Gulf, meanwhile, closer ties with China mean a better guarantee of energy exports and inward investment, but also a destination for Gulf investment.

Investment in both directions form part of the Gulf's attempts at economic diversification, and are also important in solidifying broader commercial relationships. The Gulf likely also sees some broad opportunities in "One Belt, One Road",[12] including economic opportunities in third countries, possible Chinese involvement in the major transport and infrastructure initiatives planned by some of the Gulf states, and perhaps the chance to generally build goodwill with Beijing.

While China is not about to match or supplant the United States as a military power, its economic power is now second only to that of the US, and if its economic expansion continues, it is likely to evolve into a strategic and military power in the future. This is something that the Gulf seems to recognize. There are, however, complexities to the China–Gulf relationship. One issue is the concern among the conservative monarchies about the strength of China's ties with Iran. One of the "One Belt, One Road" routes runs to Iran, and Beijing has a strong interest in Iranian energy exports. So far, China has been careful about moving too close to Tehran, predominantly to avoid antagonizing the US, although it also helps with its relations with Saudi Arabia as well. After the Iranian nuclear deal, however, the prospects increased that, in the long term, Chinese trade and investment might help strengthen Iran's economy and, by extension, its military capability and strategic reach. For China, in turn, a matter of worry in the Gulf was the 2017 Qatar crisis. Given the diversity of China's economic interests across the subregion, it trod very lightly as the crisis erupted, trying to avoid antagonizing either side, and repeatedly calling on them to find an end to the issue.[13] It is a reminder of how unexpectedly Gulf politics can change, with attendant risks to states with economic and commercial interests there.

Other changing power dynamics are likely to be important for the Gulf in future, too. The relationship with India is far more modest than that with China, but is still important. The Gulf supplies around 80 per cent of India's oil, and will probably supply an even greater percentage in the future, making it of great strategic and economic interest to India.[14] India also gets the majority of its gas from the Gulf, mostly Qatar, and it is estimated that its imports of gas will rise from 21 million tonnes to 50 million tonnes in the coming few years, as India tries to shift more to gas for its energy needs.[15] In turn, the Gulf and India are linked by the strong expatriate labour relationship. The Gulf is the source of about half of India's foreign labour remittances, sent by its 6–7 million workers living in the Gulf.[16] Longer term, India's economic potential is impressive, albeit not to the same extent as China. However the relationship has progressed only modestly and in certain areas, due to India's focus on its immediate neighbourhood and to the east, the lack of coordination on it among the Gulf states, and an Indian reluctance to become militarily or strategically involved in the Middle East.

Russia, in contrast, is keen to re-engage with the Middle East, including the Gulf. Its military intervention in Syria, beginning in September 2015, was probably designed in part to signal this intention. It also has commercial interests in the Middle East, albeit fewer in the Gulf, with which it is instead, arguably, a rival in the global energy system. The Syrian conflict has caused a significant deterioration in Russian relations with the Arab Gulf monarchies, since in effect the two sides support opposite sides in the Syrian conflict.[17] There is not a lot that naturally draws the two together, and the United States is arguably a more attractive external power to the Gulf than Russia. However Russia also has some advantages in how it is viewed in the Middle East. It is seen as less ideologically driven than the US and more pragmatic, less concerned with forming strategic alliances, and more focused on its domestic front and near-neighbours in its battle with Islamic extremism.[18] This may help ease it into a stronger role in the region. Moreover, if Russia is careful in engaging with the Gulf states, it may be able to increase its role without being seen as necessarily hostile. Trade and especially investment between Russia and the Gulf has increased in recent years, especially in the gas sector. Politically, Moscow has been careful to try to engage the Gulf states on the issue of Syria, and to avoid being seen as trying to usurp Saudi Arabia in the subregion. Russia has a fairly close strategic relationship with Iran, but has been quite successful at avoiding this being seen as a "pro-Shia" position.

Meanwhile, changing power dynamics will impact and influence each of the major actors and therefore, to a considerable extent, will be beyond the ability of the Gulf states to control. US–Chinese relations will shape the behaviour of those two powers in the Gulf, for example. If Washington and Beijing become strategic rivals, this will have an obvious impact as it is likely to prompt China into expanding its strategic reach into the Gulf. The US–Russian dynamic was, by 2017, more concerning, starting to appear like a new Cold War. If that is indeed the outcome, then the more overt strategic rivalry between those two powers will almost invariably play out in the Gulf. Whether it would make Moscow more inclined to strengthen its ties with Iran, or to seek to undercut the US by building links to the Arab Gulf states, is a matter of conjecture, but regardless it would almost certainly lead Russia to engage more deeply in the region. Any future Indian strategic role in the region would probably be more modest, but is still a possibility in the longer term.

On the other hand, global power could instead become fragmented, for example if the US were to decline somewhat, China's rise were to stall, and other states only managed to obtain middle power status. This would have an equally important impact on the Gulf, but a very different one. It might mean, for example, an exacerbation of the Saudi–Iranian rivalry, if those two states were to become even more competitive middle powers in the Middle East. They are already rivals now, so this scenario is more about how severe or aggressive the rivalry might become. However, such a scenario might mean instead that the Gulf states have to balance the interests of multiple, competing external powers with differing or even opposing interests in the Gulf. This may make their strategic outlook more complex and undermine their security, without necessarily delivering them many advantages.

A UNIQUE REGION AT A UNIQUE MOMENT

If the above scenarios paint something of a concerning picture of the future of the Middle East, it is important to return to where this book began, with the observation that the Arab monarchies of the Gulf have experienced a dramatic transformation since the oil age took off in the mid-twentieth century, and especially since the accelerated globalization of the Gulf as of the 1990s. They have gone from a series of small trading towns and heavily-tribalized societies a century ago, to globally-engaged societies with standards of living comparable, in large part, to those of the United States, Europe, or Japan. They have done so despite the setbacks of being situated in a tumultuous part of the world, and even as regional conflicts such as the 1980–88 Iran–Iraq War, the 1990–91 Gulf War, the 2003 Iraq War, and the rise and fall of ISIS all took place in, or were directly connected to, the Gulf. The transformation of the Arab states of the Gulf in the past two or three decades has been quite remarkable, and has occurred to a considerable extent on the subregion's own terms.

The prospects for the region over the medium term – say, over the coming two decades or so – depend largely on three main dynamics. The first is the ability of states, and within them, the ruling elite, to manage the relationship with society effectively. In the past, they have relied on rentier strategies to achieve societal acquiescence, and most have built a substantial pool of support and even legitimacy through a combination of allocative tactics, legitimization narratives, and by delivering relative stability and prosperity to large segments of their societies. This has been supplemented with strong elite consensus in support of ruling families and the political and economic status quo. They will have to respond just as effectively in the future as they have, on balance, in the past few decades. Their ability to do so is strong, given their relative stability and the resources at the command of leaders. Nevertheless, there are pressures on the Gulf's rulers to reform, above all to transform their economies, expand the private sector, and to start building a larger and more diverse taxation base. This would potentially constitute more substantial change than what has come in the past couple of decades. It would also have the potential to significantly disrupt old patterns of privilege and to marginalize or anger segments of society. Even though they are aware of the need for economic reform, leaders will tread carefully, meaning that the prospects for rapid change should not be overstated. Some will face greater urgency with such strategies, however, especially Oman and Bahrain, which will be the first to see their hydrocarbons dwindle to marginal levels.

Much has been made of the new generation of leaders in the Gulf, including King Hamad of Bahrain, Emir Tamim of Qatar, and most recently but prominently, the crown prince of Saudi Arabia, Muhammad bin Salman (or "MbS", as he is often referred to). To a certain extent, these leaders do offer the prospect of bringing about even more substantial change, and they are likely more in touch with the concerns of their compatriots of the same generation. However they also lack experience. This is especially the case with MbS, and may be a reason why he has already built a mixed record of performance.[19] Born in 1985, he was appointed defence minister in 2015 at the age of 29, and then crown prince, in June 2017, at the age of 31. In the domestic sphere, his willingness to pursue significant economic and social reform has been lauded. He is the main driver behind *Vision 2030*, as well as a range of austerity measures necessitated by the low oil prices of the mid-2010s. He was also behind social reforms such as the decision to permit women to hold driver's licenses and reopening cinemas in the Kingdom, both of which came into effect in 2018. More controversially, he was assumed to be behind the November 2017 arrests of prominent senior Saudi figures for corruption, which was widely interpreted as more of a political move against entrenched elites than a real anti-corruption measure. He has perhaps been most controversial, however, in the international arena. He was the architect of the Saudi-led intervention in Yemen, and has maintained it even as international pressure has grown because of the humanitarian impacts. He was also behind the Saudi-led blockade of Qatar in June 2017 and the subsequent Qatar crisis. He has not been able to gain any advantages for Saudi Arabia in the Syrian mess. Most recently, the murder of US-based Saudi opposition figure Jamal Khashoggi at the Kingdom's consulate in Istanbul, in October 2018, has raised questions about the crown prince's involvement which is likely to harm his image abroad and possibly at home as well.

While MbS is a highly ambitious and energetic young leader, there remains an uncertainty around him, as *The New York Times* noted:

> [T]he question many raise – and cannot yet answer – is whether the energetic leader will succeed in charting a new path for the kingdom, or whether his impulsiveness and inexperience will destabilize the Arab world's largest economy at a time of turbulence in the Middle East.[20]

The answer will determine much about the medium-term future of the Gulf more widely, given the dominant size, economic power, and diplomatic clout of Saudi Arabia in the region and among the six states examined here. At the same time, all six of these states are trying to develop their economies, carve a greater space for themselves in the region, and adapt proactively to economic, social and technological change. They are sometimes doing this in different ways, but they all face very similar challenges to MbS – from regional rivals to opposition at home from entrenched elites – and they all have the temptation of similar rewards. The rewards, whether financial or political, are considerable, but so too are the challenges.

Notes

1. INTRODUCING THE GULF ECONOMIES

1. The figures cited here are taken from *BP Statistical Review of World Energy 2017* available at: http://www.bp.com/en/global/corporate/energy-economics/statistical-review-of-world-energy.html (accessed 19 September 2017).

2. A scholarly survey of this issue is Bosworth, "The Nomenclature of the Persian Gulf".

3. The figures here are from Ramazani, *International Straits of the World: The Persian Gulf and the Strait of Hormuz*, 7; and *The CIA World Factbook*, Iraq country profile.

4. Potter, *The Persian Gulf in History*, 10–14; see also Legrenzi, *The GCC and the International Relations of the Gulf*, 50–56.

5. World Trade Organization (WTO), *World Trade Statistical Review 2017*, 102 (Table A4).

6. United Nations Conference on Trade and Development (UNCTAD), *World Investment Report 2017*, 226–9 (Annex Table 2).

7. Sovereign Wealth Fund Institute, "Fund Rankings". Available at: https://www.swfinstitute.org/fund-rankings/ (accessed 15 October 2018).

8. World Bank, *Doing Business 2017*.

2. THE GULF ECONOMIC STORY

1. The discussion here on pre-Islamic Arabia is sourced from Daryaee, "The Persian Gulf in Late Antiquity: The Sasanian Era (200–700 C.E.)"; Potts, "The Archaeology and Early History of the Persian Gulf"; and Peters, *Mecca: A Literary History of the Muslim Holy Land*, 18–45.

2. Hourani, *A History of the Arab Peoples*, 26.
3. Whitcomb, "The Gulf in the Early Islamic Period: The Contribution of Archaeology to Regional History", 75–8.
4. Sheriff, *Dhow Cultures of the Indian Ocean*, 173.
5. Anscombe, *The Ottoman Gulf*, 12–15; and Commins, *The Gulf States*, 37–8.
6. Commins, *The Gulf States*, 51.
7. See Vassiliev, *The History of Saudi Arabia*, 64–209.
8. Commins, *The Gulf States*, 66–8.
9. *Ibid.*, 40–45, 68–72.
10. Davidson, *Abu Dhabi: Oil and Beyond*, 4–7.
11. Commins, *The Gulf States*, 121.
12. al-Tajir, *Bahrain 1920–1945*, 35–46.
13. Crystal, *Oil and Politics in the Gulf*, 47–55.
14. *Ibid.*, 129–32.
15. Davidson, *Abu Dhabi*, 32–7.
16. Vassiliev, *The History of Saudi Arabia*, 210–86.
17. See Al-Rasheed, *A History of Saudi Arabia*, 71–7.
18. *Ibid.*, 69–101; also Vassiliev, *The History of Saudi Arabia*, 287–311.
19. Sampson, *The Seven Sisters*, 84.
20. Yergin, *The Prize*, 503–55, 782, elsewhere *passim*. The "Seven Sisters" were: the British-controlled Anglo-Iranian Oil Company, later British Petroleum; the Anglo-Dutch firm Royal Dutch Shell; and the American firms Gulf Oil, Standard Oil of California (SoCal, later Chevron), Standard Oil of New Jersey (Esso, later Exxon and then ExxonMobil), Standard Oil New York (Socony, later Mobil, then ExxonMobil), and Texaco (later acquired by Chevron).
21. Yergin, *The Prize*, 395.
22. Bronson, *Thicker Than Oil*, 100–101; and Vassiliev, *The History of Saudi Arabia*, 326–7.
23. Yergin, *The Prize*, 410.
24. *Ibid.*
25. Abrahamian, *Iran Between Two Revolutions*, 267–80; Gasiorowski, *U.S. Foreign Policy and the Shah*, 72–84.
26. The 1973 Arab-Israeli War is known by various names, typically the "Yom Kippur" War in Israel, the "Ramadan" War in the Arab world, and the "October" War in some western countries; see O'Balance, *No Victor, No Vanquished*, 1. Separately, for a retrospective on the conflict and the embargo, including substantial discussion of OAPEC, see Mabro, "The Oil Weapon", 56–60.
27. Iraqi dinar (ID) figures are from Committee against Repression and for

Democratic Rights in Iraq (CARDRI), *Saddam's Iraq: Revolution or Reaction?*, 56. The US$ calculations are the author's own: the ID exchange rate was set at par with the British pound throughout this period, with one pound in turn set at 2.8 US dollars.

28. Luciani, "Allocation vs. Production States", 65–84.

29. Gray, "A Theory of 'Late Rentierism' in the Arab States of the Gulf".

30. Bremmer, *The End of the Free Market*.

31. Gray, "A Theory of 'Late Rentierism'", 34–5.

32. Hudson, *Arab Politics*, 18–20; also see Bill & Springborg, *Politics in the Middle East*, 137–76.

33. Hillman, "A Storm in a Teacup": The Iraq-Kuwait Crisis of 1961.

34. Smith, *Britain's Revival and Fall in the Gulf*, 49–77.

35. Davidson, *Abu Dhabi*, 54–61; Smith, *Britain's Revival and Fall in the Gulf*, 78–108; and Heard-Bey, *From Trucial States to United Arab Emirates*, 370–78.

36. The term "eudaemonic legitimacy", referring to a regime gaining legitimacy from delivering welfare and other spending, was originally applied to post-Mao China, but has been used in Middle East studies too; see, for example, Niblock, *Saudi Arabia: Power, Legitimacy and Survival*, 12.

37. El-Gamal & Jaffe, *Oil, Dollars, Debt, and Crises*, 26–7; Yergin, *The Prize*, 567.

38. Yergin, *The Prize*, 625.

39. El-Gamal & Jaffe, *Oil, Dollars, Debt, and Crises*, 33–4.

40. al-Naqeeb, *Society and State in the Gulf and Arab Peninsula*, 82.

41. Kurbursi, *Arab Economic Prospects in the 1980s*, 20, cited in Owen, "The Arab Economies in the 1970s", 6.

42. Hertog, "The Evolution of Rent Recycling During Two Booms in the Gulf Arab States", 57–66.

43. Niblock, with Malik, *The Political Economy of Saudi Arabia*, esp. 57–8.

44. al-Naqeeb, *Society and State in the Gulf and Arab Peninsula*, 84–5.

45. Sadowski, *Scuds or Butter?*, 8–10; Gause, "Arms Supplies and Military Spending in the Gulf", 12–14.

46. See, for example, Jones, "America, Oil, and War in the Middle East", 208–18.

47. El-Gamal & Jaffe, *Oil, Dollars, Debt, and Crises*, 34.

48. *Ibid.*, 34–5; and Commins, *The Gulf States*, 232–8.

49. Azzam, *The Gulf Economies in Transition*, 3.

50. Maloney, *Iran's Political Economy since the Revolution*, 107–20.

51. Johnson, *The Iran-Iraq War*, 12–45; and Razoux, *The Iran-Iraq War*, 45–67.

52. Razoux, *The Iran-Iraq War*, 568–74 (Appendices I and J). Adjusted at US

consumer prices inflation rates, Razoux's exact 1988 figure of $1,097 billion would equal just under $2.27 trillion in 2017 dollars.

53. What follows is drawn in part from Johnson, *The Iran-Iraq War*, 93–6, 98–100, 139–50; and Mabon, *Saudi Arabia and Iran*, 50–52, 55–7.

54. El-Gamal & Jaffe, *Oil, Dollars, Debt, and Crises*, 36–8; Bill & Springborg, *Politics in the Middle East*, 416–7; and al-Naqeeb, *Society and State in the Gulf and Arab Peninsula*, 83–5.

55. Haass, "The Gulf War", 70–77.

56. Ulrichsen, *Insecure Gulf*, 29.

57. Gervais, "The Changing Security Dynamic in the Middle East and its Impact on Smaller Gulf Cooperation Council States' Alliance Choices and Policies", 32–5.

58. Dodge & Higgott, "Globalization and its Discontents", 17.

59. Sadik, "The Economic Implications of Globalization for the GCC Countries", 83–112.

60. Ehteshami, *Globalization and Geopolitics in the Middle East*, 138.

61. Lawson, "The Persian Gulf in the Contemporary International Economy", 13–38; King, *The New Authoritarianism in the Middle East and North Africa*, 88–192 *passim*; and Sassoon, *Anatomy of Authoritarianism in the Arab Republics*, 156–84.

62. Most famous were the random, unannounced checks on public sector workers by Dubai's Sheikh Muhammad in the early 2000s, where officials found to be absent from work without good reason were summarily dismissed. See Davidson, *Dubai: The Vulnerability of Success*, 179.

63. Naser, "The Role of the Gulf Cooperation Council's Sovereign Wealth Funds in the New Era of Oil", 1657–64.

64. Ulrichsen, *The Gulf States in International Political Economy*, 132–3.

65. Gray, "A Theory of 'Late Rentierism'".

66. Gray, *Global Security Watch – Saudi Arabia*, 61–2, 72–4, 126–7.

67. Gause, *The International Relations of the Persian Gulf*, 136–48, 241–3; Niblock, *Saudi Arabia*, 163–70.

68. Yergin, *The Quest*, 160.

69. *Ibid.*, 161–2.

70. El-Gamal & Jaffe, *Oil, Dollars, Debt, and Crises*, 58–9.

71. Among many works on the topic are books such as Roberts, *The End of Oil: On the Edge of a Perilous New World* and Simmons, *Twilight in the Desert: The Coming Saudi Oil Shock and the World Economy*.

72. Compare the two charts on these in Husain, "IMF Survey: Riding the Crest of the Oil Boom", *IMF News*.

73. See Kamrava, "The Political Economy of Rentierism in the Persian Gulf", 56 (Figure 3.5).

74. International Monetary Fund (IMF), "Learning to Live With Cheaper Oil Amid Weaker Demand", see especially Table 6 in the statistical appendix on the website.

75. Hvidt, "The Dubai Model", esp. 401–8.

3. MEASURING THE GULF ECONOMIES

1. Author's calculations, based on UN data for GDP at current US dollar values.

2. Espinoza et al., *The Macroeconomics of the Arab States of the Gulf*, 17.

3. See Cammett et al., *A Political Economy of the Middle East*, 161 (Table 5.1).

4. On Qatar's North Dome see Dargin, "Qatar's Gas Revolution", 306–42, esp. 308–22; and on Iran's South Pars, see Adibi & Fesharaki, "The Iranian Gas Industry", 272–305, esp. 272–4, 278–83.

5. McGlade, "A Review of the Uncertainties in Estimates of Global Oil Resources", 265.

6. On the opacity of oil field information in Saudi Arabia, as one example, see Simmons, *Twilight in the Desert*, 69–98.

7. Unconventional oil (in the form of heavy oil, tight oil, tar sands, etc), and unconventional gas (coal seam gas, tight gas, etc) is even more plentiful than conventional oil and gas, but only since the early 2000s or so has it become affordable, and thus viable, to extract. When both conventional and unconventional reserves are considered, the relative size of the Middle East's reserves declines, given the large unconventional oil reserves elsewhere in the world.

8. Niblock, with Malik, *The Political Economy of Saudi Arabia*, 72–9, 83–8, 116–23, 127–31; and Woertz, *Oil for Food*, 63–86.

9. Niblock, with Malik, *The Political Economy of Saudi Arabia*, 20–21.

10. Abboud, "Oil and Financialization in the Gulf Cooperation Council", 96–103.

11. See the tables in Callen et al., "Economic Diversification in the GCC", 8 (Figure 1).

12. There is a good discussion of some of these, and other, points in Ulrichsen, "Knowledge Based Economies in the GCC", 95–122.

13. Rivlin, *Arab Economies in the Twenty-First Century*, 224–5.

14. The simplest TFP formulas are almost this straightforward, generally given as something like TFP = Y – (K + L + N), where Y is total, or aggregate, output; K is capital; L is labour; and N is natural resources. The Solow Residual, which seeks to measure TFP growth, is given as $g_Y - \alpha * g_K - (1-\alpha) * g_L$, where g_Y is the growth rate of aggregate output; g_K is the growth rate of aggregate capital; g_L is the growth rate of aggregate labour; and alpha the capital share.

15. The points here come predominantly from Espinoza *et al.*, *The Macroeconomics of the Arab States of the Gulf*, 30–31.

16. On the Gulf's basic taxation structures, see Alreshan *et al.*, "Tax Policy Reforms in the GCC Countries", esp. 4–11.

17. Author's calculations.

18. On the Gulf states' budget expenditures, including some of the points noted here, see Espinoza *et al.*, *The Macroeconomics of the Arab States of the Gulf*, 65–85.

19. *Ibid.*, 67.

20. *Ibid.*, 71 (Table 4.1).

21. See Lahn & Stevens, *Burning Oil to Keep Cool*, 2 (Figure 1).

22. Young, "Understanding Vision 2030".

23. Espinoza *et al.*, *The Macroeconomics of the Arab States of the Gulf*, 33–4.

24. Kandil & Morsy, "Determinants of Inflation in GCC", 3–4.

25. AlKholifey & Alreshan, "GCC Monetary Union", esp. 27–8, 30–31.

26. Kim & Hammoudeh, "Impacts of Global and Domestic Shocks on Inflation and Economic Growth for Actual and Potential GCC Member Countries", 299.

27. Espinoza *et al.*, "Regional Financial Integration in the GCC", 354–70.

28. Espinoza *et al.*, *The Macroeconomics of the Arab States of the Gulf*, 155–6.

29. For more details see the discussion in Gardner, "Why Do They Keep Coming?", 41–58.

30. See, for example, Begum, "Gulf States' Slow March Toward Domestic Workers' Rights". The *Human Rights Watch* website has a range of reports on workers' conditions in various GCC countries: https://www.hrw.org/publications (accessed 3 October 2018).

31. Espinoza *et al.*, *The Macroeconomics of the Arab States of the Gulf*, 40–41.

32. Naufal, "Labor Migration and Remittances in the GCC", 309 (Figure 1).

33. *Ibid.*, 313–15.

34. Ahmad, "Beyond Labor", 21–7.

35. Figures taken from the WTO's *World Trade Statistical Review 2016*, 132 (Table A56).

36. IMF, *Qatar: Staff Concluding Statement for the 2018 Article IV Mission*.

37. See UNCTAD, *World Investment Report 2015*, 52–7, esp. 53 (Figures A and B).

38. *Ibid.*, 52–3.

39. Maloney, "The Gulf's Renewed Oil Wealth", 129.

40. UNCTAD, *World Investment Report 2015*, ix–x, 52–3.

41. For example, MSCI treats the UAE, Qatar and Saudi Arabia as emerging

markets, and Bahrain, Kuwait and Oman as frontier markets; see "MSCI ACWI & Frontier Markets Index" at https://www.msci.com/market-classification (accessed 4 January 2018). Most other research firms and risk advisors rate the GCC economies similarly. For background on frontier markets, with a focus on the Middle East, see Andrikopoulos *et al.* (eds), *Handbook of Frontier Markets*.

42. Seznec, "The Sovereign Wealth Funds of the Persian Gulf", 71–3.

4. THE FORM OF THE GULF POLITICAL ECONOMIES

1. The ideas here on patrimonialism and neopatrimonialism are drawn in part from Bank & Richter, "Neopatrimonialism in the Middle East and North Africa"; Bill & Springborg, *Politics in the Middle East*, 152–76; and Erdmann & Engel, "Neopatrimonialism Reconsidered", 95–119.

2. The concept of neopatrimonialism was first formulated by Shmuel Eisenstadt in his work *Traditional Patrimonialism and Modern Neopatrimonialism*, and then further developed by other scholars.

3. Gray, *Global Security Watch – Saudi Arabia*, 31–2.

4. Gray, *Qatar: Politics and the Challenges of Development*, 56–64.

5. Herb, *All in the Family*, 235–8.

6. Kéchechian, *Power and Succession in Arab Monarchies*, 25–6.

7. Although the so-called "Islamic State" or ISIS/ISIL, which controlled parts of Iraq and Syria over 2014–17, claimed to be a caliphate, and members of the Ahmadiyya sect in South Asia believe that they are a revivified extension of the early pre-schism caliphate, neither group achieved broad acceptance of their claims.

8. Kéchechian, *Power and Succession in Arab Monarchies*, 26.

9. Crystal, *Oil and Politics in the Gulf*, 118–21, 129–32, and 147–61 *passim*.

10. This is the main argument in Kamrava, "Royal Factionalism and Political Liberalization in Qatar", 401–20.

11. Herb, *All in the Family*, 47–9.

12. Salehi-Isfahani, "Population and Human Capital in the Persian Gulf", 147–71.

13. Hertog, "Lean and Mean", 17–29; and Hertog, "Defying the Resource Curse", 261–301.

14. Hertog, "Lean and Mean", 26.

15. Gaub, *Guardians of the Arab State*, 155–62. Gaub focuses on Saudi Arabia, but this point is applicable to all six of the Gulf states.

16. Quinlivan, "Coup-proofing", 282.

17. Hertog, *Princes, Brokers, and Bureaucrats*.

18. *Ibid.*, 31.

19. See Brumberg, "The Trap of Liberalized Autocracy", 56–68.

20. Zakaria, "The Rise of Illiberal Democracy", 22–43.

21. For an assessment of these arguments, see Herb, *The Wages of Oil*, 60–106.

22. On the East Asian developmental state see, for example, Pempel, "The Developmental Regime in a Changing World Economy", 137–81.

23. Gray, *Qatar*, 10–11, 63–6, 67–70.

24. Marcel, with Mitchell, *Oil Titans*, 34.

25. *Ibid.*, 78–9.

26. *Ibid.*

27. This example is detailed in Tétreault, *The Kuwait Petroleum Corporation and the Economics of the New World Order*, 200–2.

28. Marcel, *Oil Titans*, 224.

29. Gray, *Qatar*, 93–100; and author's interviews, Doha, Qatar, October 2011.

30. Marcel, *Oil Titans*, 224.

31. Niblock, with Malik, *The Political Economy of Saudi Arabia*, 26–7, 136, 218–20.

32. Hvidt, "The Dubai Model", 410; Thompson, "Dubai: An Exemplar of State Capitalism", 159–69; and Gray, *Qatar*, 68 (Table 3.1).

33. Ulrichsen, *Qatar and the Arab Spring*, 86.

34. Gray, "A Theory of 'Late Rentierism' in the Arab States of the Gulf", 34.

35. Hertog, "State and Private Sector in the GCC after the Arab Uprisings", 175.

36. For details, see Abdalla & Abdelbaki, "Determinants of Economic Growth in GCC Economies", 49 (Figure 1).

37. Luciani, "From Private Sector to National Bourgeoisie", 150–1.

38. Valeri, "Towards the End of the Oligarchic Pact?", 77–98.

39. Azoulay, "The Politics of Shi'i Merchants in Kuwait", 67–99.

40. Hanieh, *Capitalism and Class in the Gulf Arab States*, 103–48, and esp. 145–8.

41. *Ibid.*, 132–45.

42. See Transparency International, *Corruption Perceptions Index 2017*.

43. Luciani, "Allocation vs. Production States", 76.

44. Foley, *The Arab Gulf States*, 4–5; Moore, "Rents and Late Development in the Arab World", *passim*; and Rosser, "The Political Economy of the Resource Curse".

45. Gray, "A Theory of 'Late Rentierism'".

46. See Bill & Springborg, *Politics in the Middle East*: the term is used in the title of Chapter 3 (85–136).

47. *Ibid.*, 85–6.

48. Alsharekh, *The Gulf Family*, 9–20.

49. Hertog, "Rent Distribution, Labour Markets and Development in High Rent Countries", 11–15.

50. Toledo, "The Political Economy of Emiratization in the UAE", 41. While this figure is high, and has likely fallen since the early 2010s, it is for male citizens only; the sum includes transfers intended to go to other family members.

51. See the example of Kuwait in El-Katiri *et al.*, "Anatomy of an Oil-Based Welfare State", 174–7. For a wider discussion, including some excellent statistical data and illustrative charts, see Krane & Hung, "Energy Subsidy Reform in the Persian Gulf".

52. Rugh, "Backgammon or Chess?", 58–62.

53. See the examples in various chapters in Rabi (ed.), *Tribes and States in a Changing Middle East*.

54. Bill & Springborg, *Politics in the Middle East*, 94–6.

55. *Ibid.*, 94–5.

56. Author's interviews, Doha, Qatar, October 2011, and Dubai, UAE, April 2012.

57. On the Bahrain uprising, see Matthieson, *Sectarian Gulf*, esp. 18–32 on sectarianism, and 33–49 on the early 2011 protests; see also Wehrey, *Sectarian Politics in the Gulf*, 73–102.

58. Wehrey, *Sectarian Politics in the Gulf*, 137–56.

59. Jones & Ridout, *A History of Modern Oman*, 248–59.

60. Wehrey, *Sectarian Politics in the Gulf*, 145–6.

61. Gray, *Qatar*, 3, 220, 225.

62. MacFarquhar, "In Saudi Arabia, Royal Funds Buy Peace For Now".

63. Okruhlik, "Rethinking the Politics of Distributive States", 33.

64. As noted in Herb, *All in the Family*, 64.

65. Davidson, *Dubai: The Vulnerability of Success*, 193–206.

66. This was the approach of an early but influential work on the topic, Dodge & Higgott (eds), *Globalization and the Middle East*.

67. Looney, "The Arab World's Uncomfortable Experience with Globalization", 341; and Henry, "A Clash of Globalizations", esp. 62–3.

68. This is the argument in Niblock, "Globalization as Economic Phenomenon", 90–106.

69. Dodge & Higgott, "Globalization and its Discontents", 17.

70. The term is from Appadurai, "Disjuncture and Difference in the Global Cultural Economy", cited in Sakr, *Satellite Realms*, 27.

71. Sakr, *Satellite Realms*, 27.

72. Wilson, "Saudi Arabia's Role in the Global Economy", 165.

73. *Ibid.*, 166–7; Thatcher, "Governing Markets in the Gulf States", 127–45.

74. O'Connell, "The Rise of the Arabian Gulf Carriers", 339–46.
75. Stephenson, "Introduction: Deciphering International Tourism Development in the GCC Region", 5–13.
76. Gray, *Qatar*, 166–70.
77. This is the argument in Khanna, *Connectography*, 259–76. While Khanna has been criticized in some quarters for being overly-rosy in his assessments, his points about Dubai's global status are convincing, and to a lesser degree are applicable to some other Gulf cities as well.
78. This is the central argument in Legrenzi, *The GCC and the International Relations of the Gulf*, 1–9, 150–5.
79. See Gray, *Qatar*, 185–213.
80. Gause, *The International Relations of the Persian Gulf*, 168–79; and Milani, "Iran's Strategies and Objectives in Post-Saddam Iraq", 73–97.
81. Entessar, "A Regional Great Game?", 127–41.
82. Ibish, "What's at Stake for the Gulf Arab States in Syria?".
83. Sharp, "Yemen: Civil War and Regional Intervention", 2.
84. Keynoush, *Saudi Arabia and Iran*, 227–30.
85. Matthieson, *Sectarian Gulf*, 30.
86. For more context, see Almezaini, "The Transformation of UAE Foreign Policy since 2011", 191–203.

5. HUMAN FACTORS IN THE GULF ECONOMIES

1. United Nations Development Programme, *Arab Human Development Report 2002: Creating Opportunities for Future Generations*, 26.
2. Ross, *The Oil Curse*, 13.
3. *Ibid.*, 13, 189–207.
4. Ross, "Does Oil Hinder Democracy?", 334.
5. *Ibid.*, 334.
6. Champion, *The Paradoxical Kingdom*, 200.
7. Peterson, "Life after Oil", 17.
8. *Ibid.*, 17–18.
9. International Crisis Group, "Popular Protests in North Africa and the Middle East (III)", 4–5; Matthieson, *The Other Saudis*, 8–10, 89–90, 101–3.
10. Various attempts have been made to quantitatively measure inequality in Middle Eastern and/or Gulf states; see, as examples, Ali, "Globalization and Inequality in the Arab Region"; Ianchovichina, "How Unequal are Arab Countries?"; and United Nations Development Program, Regional Coordination Mechanism (RCM) Issues Brief for the Arab Sustainable Development Report.

11. Espinoza *et al.*, *The Macroeconomics of the Arab States of the Gulf*, 45–7.

12. Author's interviews, Doha, Qatar, October 2011; Dubai, UAE, April 2012; and Muscat and Salalah, Oman, September 2014.

13. Anon., "The Middle East's Migrant Workers: Forget about Rights".

14. Al-Khoury, "Population Growth and Government Modernisation Efforts", 2.

15. Rivlin, *Arab Economies in the Twenty-First Century*, 219–21.

16. See the projections for populations in 2050, contrasted with the numbers for 2010, in Mirkin, "Population Levels, Trends and Policies in the Arab Region", 31–3 (Tables 1 and 2).

17. Niblock, with Malik, *The Political Economy of Saudi Arabia*, 114 (Table 4.7).

18. See the related discussion in Kinninmont, "Vision 2030 and Saudi Arabia's Social Contract", 3–8, 18.

19. Kinninmont, "Citizenship in the Gulf", 52–3.

20. *Ibid.*, 51–2.

21. Babar, "The 'Enemy Within'", 525–43.

22. This and other points are drawn in part from Gardner, "Why Do They Keep Coming?", 45.

23. There are a number of examples in Okruhlik, "Dependence, Disdain, and Distance", 130–2.

24. For background on the term, see Anon., "What Dutch Disease is, and Why it's Bad". The term "Dutch Disease" was first coined by *The Economist* in 1977.

25. Kamrava & Babar, "Situating Labor Migration in the Persian Gulf", 7–8.

26. What follows is mostly drawn from Cammett *et al.*, *A Political Economy of the Middle East*, 339–42.

27. Jones & Ridout, *A History of Modern Oman*, 225, 261–5.

28. Valeri, *Oman: Politics and Society in the Qaboos State*, esp. 205–13.

29. International Crisis Group, "Bahrain's Sectarian Challenge", 9–10.

30. See the Vision 2030 document for more details: Council of Economic and Development Affairs of Saudi Arabia (2016), *Saudi Vision 2030*, 34–59.

31. El-Katiri, "Saudi Arabia's Labor Market Challenge".

32. Commins, *The Gulf States*, 143–4.

33. Yisraeli, *Politics and Society in Saudi Arabia*, 227–37.

34. Al-Khaldi, "Education Politics in the GCC States", 33–4.

35. *Ibid.*, 11.

36. Abdelkarim, "Oil, Population Change and Social Development in the Gulf", 39–44.

37. Foley, *The Arab Gulf States*, 195–6.

38. Coffman, "Higher Education in the Gulf", 17.

39. Weber, "The Role of Education in Knowledge Economies in Developing Countries", 2591–2.

40. World Bank, *The Road Not Travelled*, xvi.

41. Donn & Al Manthri, *Globalisation and Higher Education in the Arab Gulf States*, 95–6.

42. *Ibid.*, 100.

43. Lawrence, "Are Vocational and Applied Training the Same Thing in a GCC Context?", 2–3.

44. Ernst & Young, *How Will the GCC Close the Skills Gap?*, 16.

45. Foley, *The Arab Gulf States*, 170.

46. al-Khateeb, "The Oil Boom and its Impact on Women and Families in Saudi Arabia", 85.

47. Foley, *The Arab Gulf States*, 171.

48. This is often described as a "ban" on women driving; in fact, it was not a formal or complete ban, but rather a very tight restriction that meant that most women living in an urban location would not be approved for a driving licence. Nonetheless, women still could often gain permission to drive if they lived in more isolated areas of the country or on compounds.

49. Doumato, "Women in Civil and Political Life", 202–3.

50. al-Khateeb, "The Oil Boom and its Impact on Women and Families in Saudi Arabia", 99–105.

51. See the examples cited from interviews in *ibid.*, 89–94.

52. Al-Rasheed, "Caught between Religion and State", 302; and Doumato, "Women in Civil and Political Life", 194.

53. Hendy, "Female Labor Force Participation in the GCC", 1.

54. Willen *et al.*, *Power Women in Arabia*, 3.

55. *Ibid.*, 4.

56. See the details in Anon., *GCC Women – Entrepreneurs in a New Economy*, 10–13.

57. Aguirre *et al.*, "The Future of Women Leaders in the Middle East".

58. Sperling *et al.*, *GCC Women in Leadership – From the First to the Norm*, 18–22. Other sources make similar arguments, plus of course, many of the problems faced by Gulf women are not unique.

59. Anon., "Meeting the Needs of a Growing Youth Population in the Middle East".

60. *Ibid.*

61. Economist Intelligence Unit, *The GCC in 2020*, 9. While now somewhat dated, the report's main findings for the most part are as applicable as they were in 2009.

62. Author's interview, Doha, Qatar, October 2011, cited in Gray, *Qatar*, 231–2.
63. *Ibid.*
64. Sowayan, "Pressures of Youth and Rich-Poor Gap Mean Time Right for Saudis to Widen Search for Solutions", 248–52.
65. Beeman, "Gulf Society: An Anthropological View of the Khalijis", 147–59; Legrenzi, *The GCC and the International Relations of the Gulf*, 50–54.
66. This argument of pan-Gulf class cohesion is made in Hanieh, *Capitalism and Class in the Gulf Arab States*, 23–6.
67. Moore, "Rentier Fiscal Crisis and Regime Stability", 34–56; and Schwarz, "The Political Economy of State-Formation in the Arab Middle East", 599–621.
68. Ali, *Business and Management Environment in Saudi Arabia*, 53.
69. Marcel, with Mitchell, *Oil Titans*, 57.
70. Brynen *et al.*, *Beyond the Arab Spring*, 233.
71. *Ibid.*, 238 (Table 11.2).
72. Al-Jenaibi, "The Twitter Revolution in the Gulf Countries", 65–7.
73. *Ibid.*, 70.
74. McKinsey & Co., *Digital Middle East*, 9, 22.
75. *Ibid.*, 22.
76. Taylor, "The Internet in the Gulf Countries", 2.
77. Ulrichsen, "Knowledge Based Economies in the GCC", 121.
78. Viviez *et al.*, *Getting in on the GCC E-Commerce Game*, 1 (Figure 1).
79. McKinsey & Co., *Digital Middle East*, 22–3.

6. MAKING THE GULF ECONOMIES: UNIQUE FACTORS

1. Kolster *et al.*, "From Resource Curse to Rent Curse in the MENA Region".
2. al-Tarrah, "Family in the Kinship State", 121.
3. Rugh, *The Political Culture of Leadership in the United Arab Emirates*, 28–9.
4. Ali, *Business and Management Environment in Saudi Arabia*, 232–5.
5. *Ibid.*, 234–5.
6. While this comment was about Oman specifically, it is true across the Gulf. Valeri, *Oman: Politics and Society in the Qaboos State*, 102.
7. Niblock, with Malik, *The Political Economy of Saudi Arabia*, 138 (Chart 4.2).
8. This point is made in Davidson, *Dubai: The Vulnerability of Success*, 151–3.
9. Woertz, *Oil for Food*, 19.
10. Saif, "The Future Outlook of Desalination in the Gulf", 3.
11. Kumetat, "Climate Change in the Persian Gulf", 2–3.

12. These carbon emissions figures are from https://data.worldbank.org/indicator/EN.ATM.CO2E.PC (accessed 24 October 2018).

13. Luomi, *The Gulf Monarchies and Climate Change*, 1–3, 9–31.

14. Kumetat, "Climate Change in the Persian Gulf", 2.

15. *Ibid.*, 2–3.

16. Kuwait, Oman, Qatar, Saudi Arabia and the UAE ratified it in 2005; Bahrain in 2006. See Reiche, "Energy Policies of Gulf Cooperation Council (GCC) countries", 2399.

17. Luomi, *The Gulf Monarchies and Climate Change*, 44–6.

18. Mahmoud, "Weathering Climate Change in the Gulf", 8.

19. Tétreault, "Bottom-Up Democratization in Kuwait", 73–98.

20. Peterson, *The Arab Gulf States*, 74–6.

21. This type of argument can be found in, for example, Baaklini *et al.*, *Legislative Politics in the Arab World*, 29–61.

22. Lucas, "The Persian Gulf Monarchies and the Arab Spring", 340.

23. Brumberg, "The Trap of Liberalized Autocracy", 56–68.

24. Hvidt, "Economic and Institutional Reforms in the Arab Gulf Countries", 98.

25. Tseng, "Technological Innovation Capability, Knowledge Sourcing and Collaborative Innovation in Gulf Cooperation Council countries", 212–23.

26. Hvidt, "Economic and Institutional Reforms in the Arab Gulf Countries", 98.

27. Moerenhout, "Energy Pricing Reforms in the Gulf", 1.

28. Hertog, "The Private Sector and Reform in the Gulf Cooperation Council", 24; and Lahn, "Fuel, Food and Utilities Price Reforms in the GCC".

29. Kinninmont, "Future Trends in the Gulf", 18.

30. Ulrichsen, *The Politics of Economic Reform in Arab Gulf States*.

31. Younis, "The Rise of ISIS: Iraq and Persian Gulf Security", 113–26.

32. Gray, *Global Security Watch – Saudi Arabia*, 123–34.

33. Roberts, "Qatar and the UAE", 544–62.

CONCLUSION: PROSPECTS FOR THE GULF ECONOMIES

1. Most recently was Davidson's *After the Sheikhs: The Coming Collapse of the Gulf Monarchies*, which predicted that "pressures will soon lead to the collapse of the Gulf monarchies, or at least most of them in their present form" (2).

2. Salameh, "The Potential of Unconventional Oil Resources", 17–20.

3. Bahgat, "The Emerging Energy Landscape", 67.

4. These figures are from Anon., "U.S. Field Production of Crude Oil".

5. Anon., "Barrel Breakdown".

6. Scobell & Nader, *China in the Middle East*, 3–7.

7. Mo, "Exploring Economic Relations between China and the GCC States", 89.

8. Fulton, "The G.C.C. Countries and China's Belt and Road Initiative (BRI)".

9. Mo, "Exploring Economic Relations between China and the GCC States", 91–3.

10. Scobell & Nader, *China in the Middle East*, 8 (Figure 2.1).

11. Norris, *Chinese Economic Statecraft*, 54–6.

12. Fulton, "The G.C.C. Countries and China's Belt and Road Initiative"; and Scobell & Nader, *China in the Middle East*, 11–13.

13. Edens, "The China Wildcard in the Qatar Crisis".

14. Markakis, "India: A Rising Power in the Persian Gulf?", 99.

15. Dasgupta, "India Asks Qatar to Invest in Power Plants as Conditions for LNG Deals".

16. Markakis, "India", 99.

17. Ramani, "How Russia is Courting the Gulf".

18. See Charap, "Is Russia an Outside Power in the Gulf?", 153–70.

19. Mazzetti & Hubbard, "Rise of Saudi Prince Shatters Decades of Royal Tradition".

20. *Ibid.*

Further reading

A good historical analysis is essential for a deeper understanding of the region. Surprisingly, there are few recent Gulf-wide histories: one recent and widely available one is David Commins, *The Gulf States: A Modern History* (London: I. B. Tauris, 2012). Also recommended is Rosemary Said Zahlan, *The Making of the Modern Gulf States: Kuwait, Bahrain, Qatar, the United Arab Emirates and Oman*, revised edition (Reading: Ithaca Press, 1998). Works on Middle Eastern history more generally, which cover the Gulf, include Albert Hourani, *A History of the Arab Peoples*, updated edition (London: Faber & Faber, 2013) and Eugene Rogan, *The Arabs: A History*, revised and updated edition (London: Penguin, 2018). A good scholarly collection on history is Lawrence G. Potter (ed.), *The Persian Gulf in History* (Basingstoke: Palgrave Macmillan, 2009).

A range of works have been published in recent years that examine the contemporary Gulf in its entirety, or at least multiple states. On the Gulf's economies, a work referenced regularly here is Raphael Espinoza, Ghada Fayad and Ananthakrishnan Prasad, *The Macroeconomics of the Arab States of the Gulf* (Oxford: Oxford University Press, 2013). Useful political economy studies are David Held and Kristian Ulrichsen (eds), *The Transformation of the Gulf: Politics, Economics and the Global Order* (Abingdon: Routledge, 2012); Mehran Kamrava (ed.), *The Political Economy of the Persian Gulf* (London: Hurst, 2012); and Kristian Coates Ulrichsen, *The Gulf States in International Political Economy* (London: Palgrave Macmillan, 2016). Adam Hanieh's class-centered *Capitalism and Class in the Gulf Arab States* (Basingstoke: Palgrave Macmillan, 2011) provides a unique angle.

For an examination of politics, a good reference work is Joseph A. Kéchechian, *Power and Succession in Arab Monarchies: A Reference Guide* (Boulder, CO: Lynne Rienner, 2008); also Michael Herb, *All in the Family: Absolutism, Revolution, and Democracy in the Middle Eastern Monarchies* (Albany, NY: SUNY Press, 1999). A good political study by both theme and country is Mary Ann Tétreault, Gwenn Okruhlik and Andrzej Kapiszewski (eds), *Political Change in the Arab Gulf States: Stuck in Transition* (Boulder, CO: Lynne Rienner, 2011). A more critical work, which predicted a coming crisis in Gulf politics, is Christopher M. Davidson, *After the Sheikhs: The Coming Collapse of the Gulf Monarchies* (London: Hurst, 2012). One of the few detailed works on climate change in the subregion is Mari Luomi, *The Gulf Monarchies and Climate Change: Abu Dhabi and Qatar in an Era of Natural Unsustainability* (London: Hurst, 2012). A range of books have appeared on sectarianism in recent years: notable are Lawrence G. Potter (ed.), *Sectarian Politics in the Persian Gulf* (London: Hurst, 2013) and Frederic M. Wehrey, *Sectarian Politics in the Gulf: From the Iraq War to the Arab Uprisings* (New York: Columbia University Press, 2014).

Some multidisciplinary works with unique political angles and ideas include Sean Foley, *The Arab Gulf States: Beyond Oil and Islam* (Boulder, CO: Lynne Rienner, 2010); John W. Fox, Nada Mourtada-Sabbah and Mohammed al-Mutawa (eds), *Globalization and the Gulf* (London: Routledge, 2006); and Kristian Coates Ulrichsen, *Insecure Gulf: The End of Certainty and the Transition to the Post-Oil Era* (London: Hurst, 2011).

On the international relations of the Gulf, see F. Gregory Gause, III, *The International Relations of the Persian Gulf* (Cambridge: Cambridge University Press, 2010); Matteo Legrenzi, *The GCC and the International Relations of the Gulf: Diplomacy, Security and Economic Coordination in a Changing Middle East* (London: I. B. Tauris, 2011); and Kristian Coates Ulrichsen (ed.), *The Changing Security Dynamics of the Persian Gulf* (London: Hurst, 2017).

There is less on the social dynamics of the Gulf, although Foley's *The Arab Gulf States* covers this well. A good outline of family is provided by Alanoud Alsharekh (ed.), *The Gulf Family: Kinship Policies and Modernity* (London: Saqi, 2007), while the issue of migrant workers is tackled in Mehran Kamrava and Zahra Babar (eds), *Migrant Labor in the Persian Gulf* (New York: Columbia University Press, 2012).

At the country-specific level, the best histories of Saudi Arabia are Alexei Vassiliev, *The History of Saudi Arabia* (New York: New York University Press/Saqi, 2000), and Madawi Al-Rasheed, *A History of Saudi Arabia*, second edition (Cambridge: Cambridge University Press, 2010). Other works contain considerable historical background, such as Toby Matthieson's *The Other Saudis: Shiism, Dissent and Sectarianism* (Cambridge: Cambridge University Press, 2015); Tim Niblock's, *Saudi Arabia: Power, Legitimacy and Survival* (London: Routledge, 2006); and his political economy, with Monica Malik, *The Political Economy of Saudi Arabia* (London: Routledge, 2007).

An excellent recent edited volume on Saudi Arabia is Bernard Haykel, Thomas Hegghammer, and Stéphane Lacroix (eds), *Saudi Arabia in Transition: Insights on Social, Political, Economic and Religious Change* (Cambridge: Cambridge University Press, 2015). The best piece on the development challenges facing the country is Steffen Hertog, *Princes, Brokers, and Bureaucrats: Oil and the State in Saudi Arabia* (Ithaca, NY: Cornell University Press, 2010). Religion is covered to varying degrees by most works on the country, but is a focus of Stéphane Lacroix, *Awakening Islam: The Politics of Religious Dissent in Contemporary Saudi Arabia* (Cambridge, MA: Harvard University Press, 2011), and Thomas Hegghammer, *Jihad in Saudi Arabia: Violence and Pan-Islamism since 1979* (Cambridge: Cambridge University Press, 2010).

The history of the UAE is comprehensively examined in Frauke Heard-Bey, *From Trucial States to United Arab Emirates: A Society in Transition* (Dubai: Motivate, 2004). Christopher M. Davidson has published several books on it, including *The United Arab Emirates: A Study in Survival* (Boulder, CO: Lynne Rienner, 2005); *Dubai: The Vulnerability of Success* (London: Hurst, 2008); and *Abu Dhabi: Oil and Beyond* (London: Hurst, 2009). A more specialized but great work is Andrea B. Rugh, *The Political Culture of Leadership in the United Arab Emirates* (Basingstoke: Palgrave Macmillan, 2007).

Qatar is examined in, among others, Allen J. Fromherz, *Qatar: A Modern History* (London: I. B. Tauris, 2012); Mehran Kamrava, *Qatar: Small State, Big Politics* (Ithaca, NY: Cornell University Press, 2013); David B. Roberts, *Qatar: Securing the Global Ambitions of a City-State* (London: Hurst, 2017); Kristian Coates Ulrichsen, *Qatar and the Arab Spring* (London: Hurst, 2014); and my own *Qatar: Politics and the Challenges of Development* (Boulder, CO: Lynne Rienner, 2013).

Qatar is also covered by Jill Crystal, in her now-classic work, *Oil and Politics in the Gulf: Rulers and Merchants in Kuwait and Qatar*, updated edition (Cambridge: Cambridge University Press, 1995), although Kuwait is also a case study and gets slightly lengthier treatment. Her other work, also excellent, is *Kuwait: The Transformation of an Oil State* (Boulder, CO: Westview Press, 1992), recently reissued by Routledge in 2017. A good and recent social history is offered by Farah Al-Nakib in *Kuwait Transformed: A History of Oil and Urban Life* (Stanford, CA: Stanford University Press, 2016). Also good are the works by Mary Ann Teatreault, *The Kuwait Petroleum Corporation and the Economics of the New World Order* (Westport, CT: Quorum, 1995) and *Stories of Democracy: Politics and Society in Contemporary Kuwait* (New York: Columbia University Press, 2000).

On Oman, two recent, excellent works are Marc Valeri, *Oman: Politics and Society in the Qaboos State*, revised and updated edition (London: Hurst, 2017), and the history by Jeremy Jones and Nicholas Ridout, *A History of Modern Oman* (Cambridge: Cambridge University Press, 2015). There are a number of other historical pieces on Oman, especially on its civil conflict in the 1960s and 1970s, such as J. E. Peterson, *Oman's Insurgencies: The Sultanate's Struggle for Supremacy* (London: Saqi, 2007).

Surprisingly, given the events of 2011, there is not a lot of recent works published on Bahrain. An older work that remains useful is Emile Nakhleh's *Bahrain: Political Development in a Modernizing Society*, reprinted by Lexington Books (Lanham, MD) in 2011. On the 2011 uprising, see Toby Matthiesen's *Sectarian*

Gulf: Bahrain, Saudi Arabia, and the Arab Spring That Wasn't (Stanford, CA: Stanford University Press, 2013).

Although this book excludes Iran and Iraq, some knowledge of them is invaluable in understanding the Gulf. There is now a massive volume of work on Iran, but particularly recommended are Michael Axworthy, *Revolutionary Iran: A History of the Islamic Republic* (London: Allen Lane, 2013), on Iran's recent history, and on its political economy Suzanne Maloney, *Iran's Political Economy since the Revolution* (Cambridge: Cambridge University Press, 2015). Likewise, Iraq has never been far from the news headlines since the 1980s. Worth consulting on its wars are, among many, Pierre Razoux (trans. Nicholas Elliott), *The Iran-Iraq War* (Cambridge, MA: Harvard University Press, 2015) and Jeffrey A. Engel (ed.), *Into the Desert: Reflections on the Gulf War* (New York: Oxford University Press, 2013). There are many good histories, including Charles Tripp, *A History of Iraq*, third edition (Cambridge: Cambridge University Press, 2007). For those particularly interested in Iraq's place in the region, a good if now dated work is Henri J. Barkey, Scott B. Lasensky and Phebe Marr (eds), *Iraq, Its Neighbors, and the United States: Competition, Crisis, and the Reordering of Power* (Washington, DC: United States Institute of Peace, 2011).

References

Aarts, P. & G. Nonneman (eds), *Saudi Arabia in the Balance: Political Economy, Society, Foreign Affairs*. London: Hurst, 2005.

Abboud, S., "Oil and Financialization in the Gulf Cooperation Council" in M. Legrenzi & B. Momani (eds), *Shifting Geo-Economic Power of the Gulf: Oil, Finance and Institutions*, 91–105. Farnham: Ashgate, 2011.

Abdalla, M. & H. Abdelbaki, "Determinants of Economic Growth in GCC Economies", *Asian Journal of Research in Business Economics and Management* 4(11) (2014), 46–62.

Abdelkarim, A., "Oil, Population Change and Social Development in the Gulf: Some Major Trends and Indicators" in A. Abdelkarim (ed.), *Change and Development in the Gulf*, 25–48. Basingstoke: Macmillan, 1999.

Abdelkarim, A. (ed.), *Change and Development in the Gulf*. Basingstoke: Macmillan, 1999.

Abrahamian, E., *Iran Between Two Revolutions*. Princeton, NJ: Princeton University Press, 1982.

Adibi, S. & F. Fesharaki, "The Iranian Gas Industry" in B. Fattouh & J. Stern (eds), *Natural Gas Markets in the Middle East and North Africa*, 272–305. Oxford: Oxford University Press, 2011.

Aguirre, D., M. Cavanaugh & K. Sabbagh, "The Future of Women Leaders in the Middle East", *strategy+business* 63 (2011). Available at: https://www.strategy-business.com/article/11209?gko=dc8bf (accessed 28 February 2018).

Ahmad, A., "Beyond Labor: Foreign Residents in the Persian Gulf States" in M. Kamrava & Z. Babar (eds), *Migrant Labor in the Persian Gulf*, 21–40. New York: Columbia University Press, 2012.

Ali, A., *Business and Management Environment in Saudi Arabia: Challenges and Opportunities for Multinational Corporations*. London: Routledge, 2009.

Ali, A., "Globalization and Inequality in the Arab Region", Arab Planning Institute – Kuwait: Working Paper Series 0307. Kuwait: Arab Planning Institute, Information Center, 2003. Available at: http://www.arab-api.org/images/publication/pdfs/263/263_wps0307.pdf (accessed 24 February 2018).

Al-Jenaibi, B., "The Twitter Revolution in the Gulf Countries", *Journal of Creative Communications* 11(1) (2016), 61–83.

Al-Khaldi, S., "Education Politics in the GCC States", Gulf Research Center Research Paper. Dubai: Gulf Research Center, 2007. Available at: https://www.files.ethz.ch/isn/97639/2007-01_Education_Policies_in_GCC_States_Digital_5830.pdf (accessed 27 February 2018).

al-Khateeb, S., "The Oil Boom and its Impact on Women and Families in Saudi Arabia" in A. Alsharekh (ed.) *The Gulf Family: Kinship Policies and Modernity*, 83–108. London: Saqi, 2007.

Al-Khoury, A., "Population Growth and Government Modernisation Efforts: The Case of GCC Countries", *International Journal of Research in Management & Technology* 2(1) (2012), 1–9.

AlKholifey, A. & A. Alreshan, "GCC Monetary Union", *Irving Fisher Committee on Central Bank Statistics Bulletin*, No. 32. Basel: Bank of International Settlements, 2010. Available at: https://www.bis.org/ifc/publ/ifcb32b.pdf (accessed 2 January 2018).

Almezaini, K., "The Transformation of UAE Foreign Policy since 2011" in K. Ulrichsen (ed.), *The Changing Security Dynamics of the Persian Gulf*, 191–203. London: Hurst, 2017.

Almezaini, K., "Private Sector Actors in the UAE and their Role in the Process of Economic and Political Reform" in S. Hertog, G. Luciani & M. Valeri (eds), *Business Politics in the Middle East*, 43–66. London: Hurst, 2013.

Almezaini, K. & J.-M. Rickli (eds), *The Small Gulf States: Foreign and Security Policies Before and After the Arab Spring*. Abingdon: Routledge, 2017.

al-Naqeeb, K., *Society and State in the Gulf and Arab Peninsula: A Different Perspective*, Routledge Library Edition reprint. Abingdon: Routledge, 2012.

Al-Rasheed, M., "Caught between Religion and State: Women in Saudi Arabia" in B. Haykel, T. Hegghammer & S. Lacroix (eds), *Saudi Arabia in Transition: Insights on Social, Political, Economic and Religious Change*, 292–313. Cambridge: Cambridge University Press, 2015.

Al-Rasheed, M., *A History of Saudi Arabia*, second edition. Cambridge: Cambridge University Press, 2010.

Alreshan, A. *et al.*, "Demystifying Government Revenue in the GCC: Next Steps". Paper prepared for the *Annual Meeting of Ministers of Finance and Central Bank Governors*, Riyadh, Saudi Arabia, 26 October 2016. Washington, DC:

International Monetary Fund, 2016. Available at: https://www.imf.org/external/np/pp/eng/2016/102616.pdf (accessed 29 December 2017).

Alreshan, A. *et al.*, "Tax Policy Reforms in the GCC Countries: Now and How?". Paper prepared for the *Annual Meeting of Ministers of Finance and Central Bank Governors*, Doha, Qatar, 10 November 2015. Washington, DC: International Monetary Fund, 2015. Available at: https://www.imf.org/external/np/pp/eng/2015/111015.pdf (accessed 29 December 2017).

Alsharekh, A., "Introduction" in A. Alsharekh (ed.), *The Gulf Family: Kinship Policies and Modernity*, 9–20. London: Saqi, 2007.

Alsharekh, A. (ed.), *The Gulf Family: Kinship Policies and Modernity*. London: Saqi, 2007.

al-Tajir, M., *Bahrain 1920–1945: Britain, The Shaikh and the Administration*. London: Croom Helm, 1987.

al-Tarrah, A., "Family in the Kinship State" in A. Alsharekh (ed.), *The Gulf Family: Kinship Policies and Modernity*, 119–24. London: Saqi, 2007.

Andrikopoulos, P., G. Gregoriou & V. Kallinterakis (eds), *Handbook of Frontier Markets: Evidence from Middle East North Africa and International Comparative Studies*. London: Academic Press, 2016.

Anon., "U.S. Field Production of Crude Oil", *US Energy Information Administration*, 28 February 2018. Available at: https://www.eia.gov/dnav/pet/hist/LeafHandler.ashx?n=pet&s=mcrfpus2&f=a (accessed 8 March 2018).

Anon., *GCC Women – Entrepreneurs in a New Economy*. Dubai: Al Masah Capital Limited, August 2016. Available at: http://www.almasahcapital.com/uploads/news/news_399.pdf (accessed 28 February 2018).

Anon., "Meeting the needs of a growing youth population in the Middle East", *Oxford Business Group* (2016). Available at: https://oxfordbusinessgroup.com/analysis/dividend-or-liability-meeting-needs-region%E2%80%99s-growing-youth-population-0 (accessed 1 March 2018).

Anon., "Barrel Breakdown", *Wall Street Journal*, 15 April 2015. Available at: http://graphics.wsj.com/oil-barrel-breakdown/ (accessed 8 March 2018).

Anon., "What Dutch disease is, and why it's bad", *The Economist*, 5 November 2014. Available at: https://www.economist.com/blogs/economist-explains/2014/11/economist-explains-2 (accessed 27 February 2018).

Anon., "The Middle East's migrant workers: Forget about rights", *The Economist*, 10 August 2013. Available at: https://www.economist.com/news/middle-east-and-africa/21583291-attempts-improve-lot-migrants-working-middle-east-are-unlikely (accessed 24 February 2018).

Anon., "Historical Energy Production Statistics", *The Shift Project Data Portal*, no date. Available at: http://www.tsp-data-portal.org/Energy-Production-Statistics (accessed 3 October 2017).

Anscombe, F., *The Ottoman Gulf: The Creation of Kuwait, Saudi Arabia, and Qatar*. New York: Columbia University Press, 1997.

Appadurai, A., "Disjuncture and Difference in the Global Cultural Economy" in M. Featherstone (ed.), *Global Culture: Nationalism, Globalization and Modernity*, 295–310. London: Sage, 1990.

Axworthy, M., *Revolutionary Iran: A History of the Islamic Republic*. London: Allen Lane, 2013.

Azoulay, R., "The Politics of Shi'i Merchants in Kuwait" in S. Hertog, G. Luciani & M. Valeri (eds), *Business Politics in the Middle East*, 67–99. London: Hurst, 2013.

Azzam, H., *The Gulf Economies in Transition*. Basingstoke: Macmillan, 1988.

Baaklini, A., G. Denoeux & R. Springborg, *Legislative Politics in the Arab World: The Resurgence of Democratic Institutions*. Boulder, CO: Lynne Rienner, 1999.

Babar, Z., "The 'Enemy Within': Citizenship-Stripping in the Post-Arab Spring GCC", *The Middle East Journal* 71(4) (2017), 525–43.

Bahgat, G., "The Emerging Energy Landscape: Economic and Strategic Implications" in K. Coates Ulrichsen (ed.), *The Changing Security Dynamics of the Persian Gulf*, 61–75. London: Hurst, 2017.

Bank, A. & T. Richter, "Neopatrimonialism in the Middle East and North Africa: Overview, Critique and Alternative Conceptualization", paper presented at the GIGA workshop, "Neopatrimonialism in Various World Regions", Hamburg, 23 August 2010. Available at: https://www.researchgate.net/publication/258325694_Neopatrimonialism_in_the_Middle_East_and_North_Africa_Overview_Critique_and_Alternative_Conceptualization (accessed 23 February 2017).

Beblawi, H., "The Rentier State in the Arab World" in G. Luciani (ed.), *The Arab State*, 85–98. London: Routledge, 1990.

Beeman, W., "Gulf Society: An Anthropological View of the *Khalijis* – Their Evolution and Way of Life" in L. Potter (ed.), *The Persian Gulf in History*, 147–59. Basingstoke: Palgrave Macmillan, 2009.

Begum, R., "Gulf States' Slow March Toward Domestic Workers' Rights", *Human Rights Watch*, 16 June 2017. Available at: https://www.hrw.org/news/2017/06/16/gulf-states-slow-march-toward-domestic-workers-rights (accessed 2 January 2018).

Bill, J. & R. Springborg, *Politics in the Middle East*, third edition. Glenview: Scott, Foresman/Little, Brown, 1990.

Bosworth, C., "The Nomenclature of the Persian Gulf" in A. Cottrell (ed.), *The Persian Gulf States: A General Survey*, xvii–xxxiv. Baltimore, MD: Johns Hopkins University Press, 1980.

Bremmer, I., *The End of the Free Market: Who Wins the War Between States and Corporations?* New York: Portfolio, 2010.

British Petroleum (BP), *BP Statistical Review of World Energy 2017*. London: BP, 2017. Available at: http://www.bp.com/en/global/corporate/energy-economics/statistical-review-of-world-energy.html (accessed 19 September 2017).

Bronson, R., *Thicker Than Oil: America's Uneasy Partnership with Saudi Arabia*. New York: Oxford University Press, 2006.

Brumberg, D., "The Trap of Liberalized Autocracy", *Journal of Democracy* 13(4) (2002), 56–68.

Brynen, R. *et al.*, *Beyond the Arab Spring: Authoritarianism and Democratization in the Arab World*. Boulder, CO: Lynner Rienner, 2012.

Callen, T. *et al.*, "Economic Diversification in the GCC: Past, Present, and Future", IMF Discussion Note SDN/14/12. Washington, DC: International Monetary Fund, 2014. Available at: https://www.imf.org/external/pubs/ft/sdn/2014/sdn1412.pdf (accessed 26 April 2018).

Cammett, M., *A Political Economy of the Middle East*, fourth edition. Boulder, CO: Westview Press, 2015.

Central Intelligence Agency (CIA), *CIA World Factbook*. Washington: CIA, 2017. Available at: https://www.cia.gov/library/publications/the-world-factbook/geos/iz.html (accessed 11 September 2017).

Champion, D., *The Paradoxical Kingdom: Saudi Arabia and the Momentum of Reform*. London: Hurst, 2003.

Charap, S., "Is Russia an Outside Power in the Gulf?", *Survival* 57(1) (2015), 153–70.

Coffman, J., "Higher Education in the Gulf: Privatization and Americanization", *International Higher Education* 33 (2003), 17–19.

Commins, D., *The Gulf States: A Modern History*. London: I. B. Tauris, 2012.

Committee against Repression and for Democratic Rights in Iraq (CARDRI), *Saddam's Iraq: Revolution or Reaction?*, updated edition. London: Zed, 1989.

Council of Economic and Development Affairs, Saudi Arabia, *Saudi Vision 2030*, April 2016. Available at: http://vision2030.gov.sa/en (accessed 27 February 2018).

Craze, J. & M. Huband (eds), *The Kingdom: Saudi Arabia and the Challenge of the 21st Century*. London: Hurst, 2009.

Crystal, J., *Oil and Politics in the Gulf: Rulers and Merchants in Kuwait and Qatar*, updated edition. Cambridge: Cambridge University Press, 1995.

Dargin, J., "Qatar's Gas Revolution" in B. Fattouh & J. Stern (eds), *Natural Gas Markets in the Middle East and North Africa*, 306–42. Oxford: Oxford University Press, 2011.

Daryaee, T., "The Persian Gulf in Late Antiquity: The Sasanian Era (200–700 C.E.)"

in L. Potter (ed.), *The Persian Gulf in History*, 57–70. Basingstoke: Palgrave Macmillan, 2009.

Dasgupta, N., "India asks Qatar to invest in power plants as conditions for LNG deals", *Reuters*, 10 June 2017. Available at: https://in.reuters.com/article/india-qatar/india-asks-qatar-to-invest-in-power-plants-as-condition-for-lng-deals-idINKBN19B0I8 (accessed 9 March 2018).

Davidson, C., *After the Sheikhs: The Coming Collapse of the Gulf Monarchies*. London: Hurst, 2012.

Davidson, C., *Abu Dhabi: Oil and Beyond*. New York: Columbia University Press, 2009.

Davidson, C., *Dubai: The Vulnerability of Success*. London: Hurst, 2008.

Dodge, T. & R. Higgott, "Globalization and its Discontents: The Theory and Practice of Change in the Middle East" in T. Dodge & R. Higgott (eds), *Globalization and the Middle East: Islam, Economy, Society and Politics*, 13–35. London: Royal Institute of International Affairs, 2002.

Dodge, T. & R. Higgott (eds), *Globalization and the Middle East: Islam, Economy, Society and Politics*. London: Royal Institute of International Affairs, 2002.

Donn, G. & Y. Al Manthri, *Globalisation and Higher Education in the Arab Gulf States*. Oxford: Symposium Books, 2010.

Doumato, E., "Women in Civic and Political Life: Reform Under Authoritarian Regimes" in M. Tétreault, G. Okruhlik & A. Kapiszewski (eds), *Political Change in the Arab Gulf States: Stuck in Transition*, 193–223. Boulder, CO: Lynne Rienner, 2011.

Economist Intelligence Unit, *The GCC in 2020: The Gulf and its People*. London: Economist Intelligence Unit, 2009. Available at: http://graphics.eiu.com/upload/eb/gulf2020part2.pdf (accessed 1 March 2018).

Edens, R., "The China Wildcard in the Qatar Crisis", *The Diplomat*, 9 August 2017. Available at: https://thediplomat.com/2017/08/the-china-wildcard-in-the-qatar-crisis/ (accessed 8 March 2018).

Ehteshami, A., *Globalization and Geopolitics in the Middle East: Old Games, New Rules*. Abingdon: Routledge, 2007.

Eisenstadt, S., *Traditional Patrimonialism and Modern Neopatrimonialism*. London: Sage, 1973.

El-Gamal, M. & A. Jaffe, *Oil, Dollars, Debt, and Crises: The Global Curse of Black Gold*. Cambridge: Cambridge University Press, 2010.

Elhefnawy, N., "The Impending Oil Shock", *Survival* 50(2) (2008), 37–66.

El-Katiri, L., "Saudi Arabia's Labor Market Challenge", *Harvard Business Review*, 6 July 2016. Available at: https://hbr.org/2016/07/saudi-arabias-labor-market-challenge (accessed 27 February 2018).

El-Katiri, L., B. Fattouh & P. Segal, "Anatomy of an oil-based welfare state: rent distribution in Kuwait" in D. Held & K. Ulrichsen (eds), *The Transformation of the Gulf: Politics, Economics and the Global Order*, 165–87. London: Routledge, 2012.

Energy Information Administration (EIA), *Country Analysis Brief: Saudi Arabia*. Washington, DC: EIA (last updated 20 October 2017). Available at: http://www.ieee.es/Galerias/fichero/OtrasPublicaciones/Internacional/2017/EIA_Saudi_Arabia_20oct2017.pdf (accessed 17 November 2017).

Entessar, N., "A Regional Great Game? Iran–Saudi Relations in Flux" in K. Ulrichsen (ed.), *The Changing Security Dynamics of the Persian Gulf*, 127–41. London: Hurst, 2017.

Erdmann, G. & U. Engel, "Neopatrimonialism Reconsidered: Critical Review and Elaboration of an Elusive Concept", *Commonwealth & Comparative Politics* 45(1) (2007), 95–119.

Ernst & Young, *How will the GCC close the skills gap?* Dubai: EY Middle East and North Africa Practice, 2015. Available at: http://www.ey.com/Publication/vwLUAssets/EY-gcc-education-report-how-will-the-gcc-close-the-skills-gap/$FILE/GCC%20Education%20report%20FINAL%20AU3093.pdf (accessed 27 February 2018).

Espinoza, R., G. Fayad & A. Prasad, *The Macroeconomics of the Arab States of the Gulf*. Oxford: Oxford University Press, 2013.

Etemad, B. *et al.*, "World Energy Production, 1800–1985" in *Historical Energy Production Statistics*, The Shift Project Data Portal, no date. Available at: http://www.tsp-data-portal.org/Energy-Production-Statistics (accessed 3 October 2017).

Fattouh, B. & J. Stern (eds), *Natural Gas Markets in the Middle East and North Africa*. Oxford: Oxford University Press, 2011.

Foley, S., *The Arab Gulf States: Beyond Oil and Islam*. Boulder, CO: Lynne Rienner, 2010.

Fox, J., N. Mourtada-Sabbah & M. al-Mutawa (eds), *Globalization and the Gulf*. Abingdon: Routledge, 2006.

Fulton, J., "The G.C.C. Countries and China's Belt and Road Initiative (BRI): Curbing Their Enthusiasm?", Middle East Institute, 17 October 2017. Available at: http://www.mei.edu/content/map/gcc-countries-and-chinas-belt-and-road-initiative (accessed 9 March 2018).

Gardner, A., "Why Do They Keep Coming? Labor Migrants in the Gulf States" in M. Kamrava & Z. Babar (eds), *Migrant Labor in the Persian Gulf*, 41–58. New York: Columbia University Press, 2012.

Gasiorowski, M., *U.S. Foreign Policy and the Shah: Building a Client State in Iran*. Ithaca, NY: Cornell University Press, 1991.

Gaub, F., *Guardians of the Arab State: When Militaries Intervene in Politics, from Iraq to Mauritania*. London: Hurst, 2017.

Gause, III, F., *The International Relations of the Persian Gulf*. Cambridge: Cambridge University Press, 2010.

Gause, III, F., "Arms Supplies and Military Spending in the Gulf", *Middle East Report* 204 (1997), 12–14.

Gervais, V., "The changing security dynamic in the Middle East and its impact on smaller Gulf Cooperation Council states' alliance choices and policies" in K. Almezaini & J.-M. Rickli (eds), *The Small Gulf States: Foreign and Security Policies Before and After the Arab Spring*, 31–46. Abingdon: Routledge, 2017.

Gray, M., *Global Security Watch – Saudi Arabia*. Santa Barbara, CA: Praeger, 2014.

Gray, M., *Qatar: Politics and the Challenges of Development*. Boulder, CO: Lynne Rienner, 2013.

Gray, M., "A Theory of 'Late Rentierism' in the Arab States of the Gulf", Center for International and Regional Studies occasional paper No. 7. Doha: Center for International and Regional Studies, Georgetown University School of Foreign Service in Qatar, 2011.

Gulf Research Center, "Gulf Labour Markets, Migrations, and Population Programme". Available at: http://gulfmigration.eu/gcc-total-population-percentage-nationals-foreign-nationals-gcc-countries-national-statistics-2010-2016-numbers/ (accessed 27 October 2017).

Haass, R., "The Gulf War: Its Place in History" in J. Engel (ed.), *Into the Desert: Reflections on the Gulf War*, 57–83. New York: Oxford University Press, 2013.

Hanieh, A., *Capitalism and Class in the Gulf Arab States*. Basingstoke: Palgrave Macmillan, 2011.

Hasan, M. & H. Alogeel, "Understanding the Inflationary Process in the GCC Region: The Case of Saudi Arabia and Kuwait", IMF working paper WP/08/193. Washington, DC: International Monetary Fund, August 2008. Available at: https://www.imf.org/external/pubs/ft/wp/2008/wp08193.pdf (accessed 29 December 2017).

Haykel, B., T. Hegghammer & S. Lacroix (eds), *Saudi Arabia in Transition: Insights on Social, Political, Economic and Religious Change*. Cambridge: Cambridge University Press, 2015.

Heard-Bey, F., *From Trucial States to United Arab Emirates: A Society in Transition*. Dubai: Motivate, 2004.

Held, D. & K. Ulrichsen (eds), *The Transformation of the Gulf: Politics, Economics and the Global Order*. London: Routledge, 2012.

Hendy, R., "Female Labor Force Participation in the GCC", online manuscript, 19 May 2016. Available at: https://www.difi.org.qa/wp-content/uploads/2017/12/paper_2.pdf (accessed 28 February 2018).

Henry, C., "A Clash of Globalizations: Obstacles to Development in the Middle East", *Harvard International Review* (2003), 60–64.

Henry, C. & R. Springborg, *Globalization and the Politics of Development in the Middle East*. Cambridge: Cambridge University Press, 2001.

Herb, M., *The Wages of Oil: Parliaments and Economic Development in Kuwait and the UAE*. Ithaca, NY: Cornell University Press, 2014.

Herb, M. *All in the Family: Absolutism, Revolution, and Democracy in the Middle Eastern Monarchies*. Albany, NY: SUNY Press, 1999.

Hertog, S., "Rent Distribution, Labour Markets and Development in High Rent Countries", LSE Kuwait programme paper no. 40. London: Kuwait programme, London School of Economics and Political Science, July 2016. Available at: http://eprints.lse.ac.uk/67381/1/Hertog_rent_distribution.pdf (accessed 21 September 2017).

Hertog, S., "State and Private Sector in the GCC after the Arab Uprisings", *Journal of Arabian Studies* 3(2) (2014), 174–95.

Hertog, S., "The Private Sector and Reform in the Gulf Cooperation Council", LSE Kuwait programme paper no. 30. London: Kuwait programme, London School of Economics and Political Science, July 2013. Available at: https://eprints.lse.ac.uk/54398/1/Hertog_2013.pdf (accessed 7 March 2018).

Hertog, S., "The Evolution of Rent Recycling During Two Booms in the Gulf Arab States: Business Dynamism and Societal Stagnation" in M. Legrenzi & B. Momani (eds), *Shifting Geo-Economic Power of the Gulf: Oil, Finance and Institutions*, 57–66. Farnham: Ashgate, 2011.

Hertog, S., "Lean and Mean: The New Breed of State-Owned Enterprises in the Gulf Monarchies" in J. Seznec & M. Kirk (eds), *Industrialization in the Gulf: A Socioeconomic Revolution*, 17–29. Abingdon: Routledge, 2011.

Hertog, S., *Princes, Brokers, and Bureaucrats: Oil and the State in Saudi Arabia*. Ithaca, NY: Cornell University Press, 2010.

Hertog, S., "Defying the Resource Curse: Explaining Successful State-Owned Enterprises in Rentier States," *World Politics* 62(2) (2010), 261–301.

Hertog, S., G. Luciani & M. Valeri (eds), *Business Politics in the Middle East*. London: Hurst, 2013.

Hillman, J., "A Storm in a Teacup": The Iraq-Kuwait Crisis of 1961. From Gulf Crisis to Inter-Arab Dispute*. Tel Aviv: Tel Aviv University Press, 2011.

Hourani, A., *A History of the Arab Peoples*. London: Faber & Faber, 1991.

Hourani, A., *Arab Politics: The Search for Legitimacy*. New Haven, CT: Yale University Press, 1977.

Husain, A., "IMF Survey: Riding the Crest of the Oil Boom", *IMF News*. Washington, DC: International Monetary Fund, 30 October 2007. Available at:

https://www.imf.org/en/News/Articles/2015/09/28/04/53/socar1030a (accessed 20 October 2017).

Hvidt, M., "Economic and Institutional Reforms in the Arab Gulf Countries", *The Middle East Journal* 65(1) (2011), 85–102.

Hvidt, M., "The Dubai Model: An Outline of Key Development-Process Elements in Dubai", *International Journal of Middle East Studies* 41 (2009), 397–418.

Ianchovichina, E., "How Unequal are Arab Countries?", Brookings Institution blog, 4 February 2015. Available at: https://www.brookings.edu/blog/future-development/2015/02/04/how-unequal-are-arab-countries-2/ (accessed 24 February 2018).

Ibish, H., "What's at Stake for the Gulf Arab States in Syria?", Arab Gulf States Institute in Washington Issues Paper #6. Washington, DC: Arab Gulf States Institute in Washington, 2016. Available at: http://www.agsiw.org/wp-content/uploads/2016/06/Ibish_GCCSyria_Web.pdf (accessed 22 February 2018).

International Crisis Group, "Popular Protests in North Africa and the Middle East (III): The Bahrain Revolt", *Middle East/North Africa Report* No. 105. Brussels: International Crisis Group, 6 April 2011. Available at: https://d2071andvip0wj.cloudfront.net/105-popular-protests-in-north-africa-and-the-middle-east-iii-the-bahrain-revolt.pdf (accessed 21 February 2018).

International Crisis Group, "Bahrain's Sectarian Challenge", *Middle East Report* No. 40. Brussels: International Crisis Group, 6 May 2005. Available at: https://d2071andvip0wj.cloudfront.net/40-bahrain-s-sectarian-challenge.pdf (accessed 27 February 2018).

International Monetary Fund (IMF), "Learning to Live With Cheaper Oil Amid Weaker Demand", *Regional Economic Outlook Update: Middle East and Central Asia*. Washington, DC: IMF, January 2015. Available at: http://www.imf.org/external/pubs/ft/reo/2015/mcd/eng/mreo0115.htm (accessed 20 October 2018).

International Monetary Fund (IMF), "Qatar: Staff Concluding Statement for the 2018 Article IV Mission". Washington, DC: IMF, 5 March 2018. Available at: https://www.imf.org/en/News/Articles/2018/03/05/ms030518-qatar-staff-concluding-statement-for-the-2018-article-iv-mission (accessed 8 August 2018).

Johnson, R., *The Iran–Iraq War*. Basingstoke: Palgrave Macmillan, 2011.

Jones, J. & N. Ridout, *A History of Modern Oman*. Cambridge: Cambridge University Press, 2015.

Jones, T., "America, Oil, and War in the Middle East", *Journal of American History* 99(1) (2012), 208–18.

Kamrava, M. (ed.), *Beyond the Arab Spring: The Evolving Ruling Bargain in the Middle East*. London: Hurst, 2014.

Kamrava, M., "The Political Economy of Rentierism in the Persian Gulf" in M. Kamrava (ed.), *The Political Economy of the Persian Gulf*, 39–68. London: Hurst, 2012.

Kamrava, M. (ed.), *The Political Economy of the Persian Gulf*. London: Hurst, 2012.

Kamrava, M., "Royal Factionalism and Political Liberalization in Qatar", *The Middle East Journal* 63(3) (2009), 401–20.

Kamrava, M. & Z. Babar, "Situating Labor Migration in the Persian Gulf" in M. Kamrava & Z. Babar (eds), *Migrant Labor in the Persian Gulf*, 1–20. New York: Columbia University Press, 2012.

Kamrava, M. & Z. Babar (eds), *Migrant Labor in the Persian Gulf*. New York: Columbia University Press, 2012.

Kandil, M. & H. Morsy, "Determinants of Inflation in GCC", IMF working paper WP/09/82. Washington, DC: International Monetary Fund, April 2009. Available at: https://www.imf.org/external/pubs/ft/wp/2009/wp0982.pdf (accessed 29 December 2017).

Kéchechian, J., *Power and Succession in Arab Monarchies: A Reference Guide*. Boulder, CO: Lynne Rienner, 2008.

Keynoush, B., *Saudi Arabia and Iran: Friends or Foes?* London: Palgrave Macmillan, 2016.

Khanna, P., *Connectography: Mapping the Future of Global Civilization*. New York: Random House, 2016.

Kim, W. & S. Hammoudeh, "Impacts of Global and Domestic Shocks on Inflation and Economic Growth for Actual and Potential GCC Member Countries", *International Review of Economics and Finance* 27, C (2013), 298–317.

King, S., *The New Authoritarianism in the Middle East and North Africa*. Bloomington, IN: Indiana University Press, 2009.

Kinninmont, J., "Vision 2030 and Saudi Arabia's Social Contract: Austerity and Transformation", Chatham House Middle East and North Africa Programme research paper. London: Chatham House, 2017. Available at: https://www.chathamhouse.org/sites/files/chathamhouse/publications/research/2017-07-20-vision-2030-saudi-kinninmont.pdf (accessed 24 February 2018).

Kinninmont, J., "Future Trends in the Gulf", *Chatham House Report*. London: Royal Institute of International Affairs, 2015. Available at: https://www.chathamhouse.org/sites/files/chathamhouse/field/field_document/20150218FutureTrendsGCCKinninmont.pdf (accessed 7 March 2018).

Kinninmont, J., "Citizenship in the Gulf" in A. Echagüe (ed.), *The Gulf States and the Arab Uprisings*, 47–57. Madrid: FRIDE/Gulf Research Center, 2013.

Kolster, J. *et al.*, "From Resource Curse to Rent Curse in the MENA Region", African Development Bank working paper, North Africa Policy series. Tunis: African

Development Bank, 2015. Available at: https://www.afdb.org/fileadmin/uploads/afdb/Documents/Publications/Working_paper_-_From_Resource_Curse_to_Rent_Curse_in_the_MENA_Region.pdf (accessed 5 March 2018).

Krane, J. & S. Hung, "Energy Subsidy Reform in the Persian Gulf: The End of the Big Oil Giveaway", Baker Institute for Public Policy issue brief 04.28.16. Houston, TX: Baker Institute for Public Policy, Rice University, 28 April 2016. Available at: https://www.bakerinstitute.org/media/files/research_document/0e7a6eb7/BI-Brief-042816-CES_GulfSubsidy.pdf (accessed 22 September 2017).

Kumetat, D., "Climate Change in the Persian Gulf: Regional Security, Sustainability Strategies and Research Needs", paper for the conference, "Climate Change, Social Stress and Violent Conflict", Hamburg, 19–20 November 2009. Available at: http://research3.fit.edu/sealevelriselibrary/documents/doc_mgr/424/Kumetat._2009._CC_in_the_Persian_Gulf.pdf (accessed 17 December 2013).

Kurbursi, A., *Arab Economic Prospects in the 1980s*. Beirut: Institute for Palestine Studies, 1980.

Lahn, G., "Fuel, Food and Utilities Price Reforms in the GCC", Chatham House research paper. London: Royal Institute of International Affairs, 2016.

Lahn, G. & P. Stevens, *Burning Oil to Keep Cool: The Hidden Energy Crisis in Saudi Arabia*. London: Royal Institute of International Affairs, 2011.

Lawrence, A., "Are Vocational and Applied Training the Same Thing in a GCC Context?", *Gulf Affairs*, Spring 2017. Available at: https://www.oxgaps.org/files/gulf_affairs_spring_2017_full_issue.pdf (accessed 27 February 2018).

Lawson, F., "The Persian Gulf in the Contemporary International Economy" in M. Kamrava (ed.), *The Political Economy of the Persian Gulf*, 13–38. London: Hurst, 2012.

Legrenzi, M., *The GCC and the International Relations of the Gulf: Diplomacy, Security and Economic Coordination in a Changing Middle East*. London: I. B. Tauris, 2011.

Legrenzi, M. & B. Momani (eds), *Shifting Geo-Economic Power of the Gulf: Oil, Finance and Institutions*. Farnham: Ashgate, 2011.

Looney, R., "The Arab World's Uncomfortable Experience with Globalization", *Middle East Journal* 61(2) (2007), 341–5.

Lucas, R., "The Persian Gulf Monarchies and the Arab Spring" in M. Kamrava (ed.), *Beyond the Arab Spring: The Evolving Ruling Bargain in the Middle East*, 313–40. London: Hurst, 2014.

Luciani, G., "From Private Sector to National Bourgeoisie: Saudi Arabian Business" in P. Aarts & G. Nonneman (eds), *Saudi Arabia in the Balance: Political Economy, Society, Foreign Affairs*, 144–81. London: Hurst, 2005.

Luciani, G., "Allocation vs. Production States: A Theoretical Framework" in G. Luciani (ed.), *The Arab State*, 65–84. London: Routledge, 1990.

Luciani, G., (ed.), *The Arab State*. London: Routledge, 1990.

Luomi, M., *The Gulf Monarchies and Climate Change: Abu Dhabi and Qatar in an Era of Natural Unsustainability*. London: Hurst, 2012.

Mabon, S., *Saudi Arabia and Iran: Power and Rivalry in the Middle East*. London: I. B. Tauris, 2016.

Mabro, R., "The Oil Weapon: Can It Be Used Today?", *Harvard International Review* 29(3) (2007), 56–60.

MacFarquhar, N., "In Saudi Arabia, Royal Funds Buy Peace For Now", *New York Times*, 8 June 2011. Available at: https://www.nytimes.com/2011/06/09/world/middleeast/09saudi.html (accessed 7 August 2018).

McGlade, C., "A Review of the Uncertainties in Estimates of Global Oil Resources", *Energy* 47(1) (2012), 262–70.

McKinsey & Co., *Digital Middle East: Transforming the Region into a Leading Digital Economy*. Digital McKinsey, October 2016. Available at: https://www.mckinsey.com/~/media/mckinsey/global%20themes/middle%20east%20and%20africa/digital%20middle%20east%20transforming%20the%20region%20into%20a%20leading%20digital%20economy/digital-middle-east-final-updated.ashx (accessed 5 March 2018).

Mahmoud, M., "Weathering Climate Change in the Gulf", Arab Gulf States Institute in Washington (AGSIW) issues paper #12. Washington, DC: AGSIW, 2017. Available at: https://www.agsiw.org/wp-content/uploads/2017/11/Mahmoud_Climate-Change_ONLINE.pdf (accessed 6 March 2018).

Maloney, S., *Iran's Political Economy since the Revolution*. Cambridge: Cambridge University Press, 2015.

Maloney, S., "The Gulf's Renewed Oil Wealth: Getting it Right This Time?", *Survival* 50(6) (2008), 129–50.

Marcel, V. with J. Mitchell, *Oil Titans: National Oil Companies in the Middle East*. London: Royal Institute of International Affairs, 2006.

Markakis, D., "India: A Rising Power in the Persian Gulf?" in K. Ulrichsen (ed.), *The Changing Security Dynamics of the Persian Gulf*, 99–112. London: Hurst, 2017.

Matthieson, T., *The Other Saudis: Shiism, Dissent and Sectarianism*. Cambridge: Cambridge University Press, 2015.

Matthieson, T., *Sectarian Gulf: Bahrain, Saudi Arabia, and the Arab Spring that Wasn't*. Stanford, CA: Stanford University Press, 2013.

Mazzetti, M. & B. Hubbard, "Rise of Saudi Prince Shatters Decades of Royal Tradition", *New York Times*, 15 October 2016. Available at: https://www.nytimes.com/2016/10/16/world/rise-of-saudi-prince-shatters-decades-of-royal-tradition.html (accessed 9 March 2018).

Milani, M., "Iran's Strategies and Objectives in Post-Saddam Iraq" in H. Barkey, S. Lasensky & P. Marr (eds), *Iraq, Its Neighbors, and the United States: Competition, Crisis, and the Reordering of Power*, 73–97. Washington, DC: United States Institute of Peace, 2011.

Mirkin, B., "Population Levels, Trends and Policies in the Arab Region: Challenges and Opportunities", Arab Human Development Report research paper series. New York: United Nations Development Programme, 2010. Available at: http://www.undp.org/content/dam/rbas/report/Population%20Levels,Trends. pdf (accessed 24 February 2018).

Mo, C., "Exploring Economic Relations between China and the GCC States", *Journal of Middle Eastern and Islamic Studies (in Asia)* 5(4) (2011), 88–105.

Moerenhout, T., "Energy Pricing Reforms in the Gulf: A trend but not (yet) a norm", *Global Subsidies Initiative Report*. Winnipeg: International Institute for Sustainable Development, 2018. Available at: https://www.iisd.org/sites/ default/files/publications/energy-pricing-gulf-trend-but-not-norm.pdf (accessed 7 March 2018).

Moore, P., "Rents and Late Development in the Arab World", paper for the annual meeting of the American Political Science Association, September 2004. Available at: http://citation.allacademic.com/meta/p_mla_apa_research_ citation/0/6/1/0/9/p61099_index.html (accessed 28 October 2018).

Moore, P., "Rentier Fiscal Crisis and Regime Stability: Business-State Relations in the Gulf", *Studies in Comparative International Development* 37(1) (2002), 34–56.

Naser, H., "The Role of the Gulf Cooperation Council's Sovereign Wealth Funds in the New Era of Oil", *International Journal of Economics and Financial Issues* 6(4) (2016), 1657–64.

Naufal, G., "Labor Migration and Remittances in the GCC", *Labor History* 52(3) (2011), 307–22.

Niblock, T., *Saudi Arabia: Power, Legitimacy and Survival*. London: Routledge, 2006.

Niblock, T., "Globalization as Economic Phenomenon: A Critical Interpretation" in J. Fox, N. Mourtada-Sabbah & M. al-Mutawa (eds), *Globalization and the Gulf*, 90–106. London: Routledge, 2006.

Niblock, T. with M. Malik, *The Political Economy of Saudi Arabia*. London: Routledge, 2007.

Norris, W., *Chinese Economic Statecraft: Commercial Actors, Grand Strategy, and State Control*. Ithaca, NY: Cornell University Press, 2016.

Nugée, J. & P. Subacchi (eds), *The Gulf Region: A New Hub of Global Financial Power*. London: Royal Institute of International Affairs, 2008.

O'Balance, E., *No Victor, No Vanquished: The Arab–Israeli War, 1973*. Novato, CA: Presidio, 1978.

O'Connell, J., "The Rise of the Arabian Gulf Carriers: An Insight into the Business Model of Emirates Airline", *Journal of Air Transport Management* 17(6) (2011), 339–46.

Okruhlik, G., "Rethinking the Politics of Distributive States: Lessons from the Arab Uprisings" in K. Selvik & B. Utvik (eds), *Oil States in the New Middle East: Uprisings and Stability*, 18–38. Abingdon: Routledge, 2016.

Okruhlik, G., "Dependence, Disdain, and Distance: State, Labor, and Citizenship in the Arab Gulf States" in J.-F. Seznec & M. Kirk (eds), *Industrialization in the Gulf: A Socioeconomic Revolution*, 125–42. Abingdon: Routledge, 2011.

Owen, R., "The Arab Economies in the 1970s", *MERIP Reports*, 100/101 (Oct–Dec 1981), 3–13.

Oxford Business Group, *The Report: Saudi Arabia 2016*. London, Oxford Business Group, 2016.

Pempel, T., "The Developmental Regime in a Changing World Economy," in M. Woo-Cumings (ed.), *The Developmental State*, 137–81. Ithaca, NY: Cornell University Press, 1999.

Peters, F., *Mecca: A Literary History of the Muslim Holy Land*. Princeton, NJ: Princeton University Press, 1994.

Peterson, J., "Life after Oil: Economic Alternatives for the Arab Gulf States", *Mediterranean Quarterly* 20(3) (2009), 1–18.

Peterson, J., *The Arab Gulf States: Steps Toward Political Participation*. New York: Praeger/Center for Strategic and International Studies, 1986.

Potter, L., "Introduction" in L. Potter (ed.), *The Persian Gulf in History*, 1–24. Basingstoke: Palgrave Macmillan, 2009.

Potter, L. (ed.), *The Persian Gulf in History*. Basingstoke: Palgrave Macmillan, 2009.

Potts, D., "The Archaeology and Early History of the Persian Gulf" in L. Potter (ed.), *The Persian Gulf in History*, 27–56. Basingstoke: Palgrave Macmillan, 2009.

Quinlivan, J., "Coup-proofing: Its Practice and Consequences in the Middle East", *International Security* 24(2) (1999), 131–65.

Rabi, U. (ed.), *Tribes and States in a Changing Middle East*. New York: Oxford University Press, 2016.

Ramani, S., "How Russia is Courting the Gulf", *The National Interest*, 1 August 2016. Available at: http://nationalinterest.org/feature/how-russia-courting-the-gulf-17207 (accessed 9 March 2018).

Ramazani, R., *International Straits of the World: The Persian Gulf and the Strait of Hormuz*. Alphen aan den Rijn: Sijthoff & Noordhoff, 1979.

Razoux, P., *The Iran–Iraq War*. Cambridge, MA: Harvard University Press, 2015.

Reiche, D., "Energy Policies of Gulf Cooperation Council (GCC) Countries:

Possibilities and Limitations of Ecological Modernization in Rentier States", *Energy Policy* 38(5) (2010), 2395–403.

Rivlin, P., *Arab Economies in the Twenty-First Century*. Cambridge: Cambridge University Press, 2009.

Roberts, D., "Qatar and the UAE: Exploring Divergent Responses to the Arab Spring", *The Middle East Journal* 71(4) (2017), 544–62.

Roberts, P., *The End of Oil: On the Edge of a Perilous New World*. New York: Houghton Mifflin, 2004.

Ross, M., *The Oil Curse: How Petroleum Wealth Shapes the Development of Nations*. Princeton, NJ: Princeton University Press, 2012.

Ross, M., "Does Oil Hinder Democracy?", *World Politics* 53(3) (2001), 325–61.

Rosser, A., "The Political Economy of the Resource Curse: A Literature Survey", Institute of Development Studies working paper 268. Brighton, University of Sussex, 2006. Available at: http://www2.ids.ac.uk/gdr/cfs/pdfs/wp268.pdf (accessed 6 July 2010).

Rugh, A., "Backgammon or Chess? The State of Tribalism and Tribal Leadership in the United Arab Emirates" in U. Rabi (ed.), *Tribes and States in a Changing Middle East*, 57–77. New York: Oxford University Press, 2016.

Rugh, A., *The Political Culture of Leadership in the United Arab Emirates*. Basingstoke: Palgrave Macmillan, 2007.

Sadik, A., "The Economic Implications of Globalization for the GCC Countries" in T. Dodge & R. Higgott (eds), *Globalization and the Middle East: Islam, Economy, Society and Politics*, 83–112. London: Royal Institute of International Affairs, 2002.

Sadowski, Y., *Scuds or Butter? The Political Economy of Arms Control in the Middle East*. Washington, DC: Brookings Institution, 1993.

Saif, O., "The Future Outlook of Desalination in the Gulf: Challenges and Opportunities Faced by Qatar and the UAE", United Nations University. Available at: http://inweh.unu.edu/wp-content/uploads/2015/05/The-Future-Outlook-of-Desalination-in-the-Gulf1.pdf (accessed 6 March 2018).

Sakr, N., *Satellite Realms: Transnational Television, Globalization and the Middle East*. London: I. B. Tauris, 2001.

Salameh, M., "The Potential of Unconventional Oil Resources: Between Expediency and Reality", International Association for Energy Economics 2012, 17–20.

Salehi-Isfahani, D., "Population and Human Capital in the Persian Gulf" in M. Kamrava (ed.), *The Political Economy of the Persian Gulf*, 147–71. London: Hurst, 2012.

Sampson, A., *The Seven Sisters: The Great Oil Companies and the World They Made*. London: Hodder & Stoughton, 1975.

Sassoon, J., *Anatomy of Authoritarianism in the Arab Republics*. Cambridge: Cambridge University Press, 2016.

Schwarz, R., "The Political Economy of State-Formation in the Arab Middle East: Rentier States, Economic Reform, and Democratization", *Review of International Political Economy* 15(4) (2008), 599–621.

Scobell, A. & A. Nader, *China in the Middle East: The Wary Dragon*. Santa Monica, CA: RAND Corporation, 2016. Available at: https://www.rand.org/content/dam/rand/pubs/research_reports/RR1200/RR1229/RAND_RR1229.pdf (accessed 9 March 2018).

Selvik, K. & B. Utvik (eds), *Oil States in the New Middle East: Uprisings and Stability*. Abingdon: Routledge, 2016.

Seznec, J.-F., "The Sovereign Wealth Funds of the Persian Gulf" in M. Kamrava (ed.), *The Political Economy of the Persian Gulf*, 69–93. London: Hurst, 2012.

Seznec, J.-F. & M. Kirk (eds), *Industrialization in the Gulf: A Socioeconomic Revolution*. Abingdon: Routledge, 2011.

Sharp, J., "Yemen: Civil War and Regional Intervention", Congressional Research Service report 7–5700. Washington, DC: Congressional Research Service, 8 February 2018. Available at: https://fas.org/sgp/crs/mideast/R43960.pdf (accessed 22 February 2018).

Sheriff, A., *Dhow Cultures of the Indian Ocean: Cosmopolitanism, Commerce and Islam*. London: Hurst, 2010.

Simmons, M., *Twilight in the Desert: The Coming Saudi Oil Shock and the World Economy*. Hoboken, NJ: Wiley, 2005.

Smith, S., *Britain's Revival and Fall in the Gulf: Kuwait, Bahrain, Qatar, and the Trucial States, 1950–1971*. Abingdon: Routledge, 2013.

Sovereign Wealth Fund Institute, "Fund Rankings". Available at: https://www.swfinstitute.org/fund-rankings/ (accessed 21 September 2017).

Sowayan, S., "Pressures of youth and rich-poor gap mean time right for Saudis to widen search for solutions", 6 March 2007, reprinted in J. Craze & M. Huband (eds), *The Kingdom: Saudi Arabia and the Challenge of the 21st Century*, 248–52. London: Hurst, 2009.

Sperling, J., *et al.*, *GCC Women in Leadership: From the First to the Norm*. McKinsey & Co., 2014. Available at: https://es.uefa.com/MultimediaFiles/Download/uefaorg/CaptainsofChange/02/20/42/36/2204236_DOWNLOAD.pdf (accessed 28 February 2018).

Stephenson, M., "Introduction: Deciphering International Tourism Development in the GCC Region" in M. Stephenson & A. Al-Hamarneh (eds), *International Tourism Development and the Gulf Cooperation Council States: Challenges and Opportunities* 1–25. Abingdon: Routledge, 2017.

Stephenson, M. & A. Al-Hamarneh (eds), *International Tourism Development and the Gulf Cooperation Council States: Challenges and Opportunities*. Abingdon: Routledge, 2017.

Taylor, E., "The Internet in the Gulf Countries: How Issues of Internet Access and Cybercrime Impact the Region", Chatham House discussion paper. London: Royal Institute of International Affairs, 2016. Available at: https://www.chathamhouse.org/sites/files/chathamhouse/events/2016-01-12-internet-in-the-gulf-countries-meeting-summary.pdf (accessed 5 March 2018).

Tétreault, M., "Bottom-Up Democratization in Kuwait" in M. Tétreault, G. Okruhlik & A. Kapiszewski (eds), *Political Change in the Arab Gulf States: Stuck in Transition*, 73–98. Boulder, CO: Lynne Rienner, 2011.

Tétreault, M., *The Kuwait Petroleum Corporation and the Economics of the New World Order*. Westport, CT: Quorum, 1995.

Tétreault, M., G. Okruhlik & A. Kapiszewski (eds), *Political Change in the Arab Gulf States: Stuck in Transition*. Boulder, CO: Lynne Rienner, 2011.

Thatcher, M., "Governing Markets in the Gulf States" in D. Held & K. Ulrichsen (eds), *The Transformation of the Gulf: Politics, Economics and the Global Order*, 127–45. London: Routledge, 2012.

Thompson, P., "Dubai: An Exemplar of State Capitalism", *Turkish Policy Quarterly* 15(2) (2016), 159–69.

Toledo, H., "The Political Economy of Emiratization in the UAE", *Journal of Economic Studies* 40(1) (2013), 39–53.

Transparency International, *Corruption Perceptions Index 2017*. Available at: https://www.transparency.org/news/feature/corruption_perceptions_index_2017?gclid=EAIaIQobChMIjP2Tybbw3AIVSGoqCh3TNgliEAAYASAAEgK5svD_BwE (accessed 15 August 2018).

Tseng, C.-Y., "Technological Innovation Capability, Knowledge Sourcing and Collaborative Innovation in Gulf Cooperation Council Countries", *Innovation: Organization & Management* 16(2) (2014), 212–23.

Ulrichsen, K. (ed.), *The Changing Security Dynamics of the Persian Gulf*. London: Hurst, 2017.

Ulrichsen, K., *The Politics of Economic Reform in Arab Gulf States*. Houston, TX: James A. Baker III Institute for Public Policy, Rice University, 2016. Available at: https://www.bakerinstitute.org/media/files/files/717a5914/CME-GulfEconReform-060116.pdf (accessed 27 September 2018).

Ulrichsen, K., *The Gulf States in International Political Economy*. Basingstoke: Palgrave Macmillan, 2016.

Ulrichsen, K., *Qatar and the Arab Spring*. London: Hurst, 2014.

Ulrichsen, K., "Knowledge Based Economies in the GCC" in M. Kamrava (ed.), *The Political Economy of the Persian Gulf*, 95–122. London: Hurst, 2012.

Ulrichsen, K., *Insecure Gulf: The End of Certainty and the Transition to the Post-Oil Era*. London: Hurst, 2011.

United Nations Conference on Trade and Development (UNCTAD), *World Investment Report 2017*. Geneva: United Nations, 2017. Available at: http://unctad. org/en/PublicationsLibrary/wir2017_en.pdf (accessed 21 September 2018).

United Nations Conference on Trade and Development (UNCTAD), *World Investment Report 2015*. Geneva: United Nations, 2015. Available at: http://unctad. org/en/PublicationsLibrary/wir2015_en.pdf (accessed 4 January 2018).

United Nations Development Programme (UNDP), "Regional Coordination Mechanism (RCM) Issues Brief for the Arab Sustainable Development Report". New York: United Nations Development Programme, 2015. Available at: http://css.escwa.org.lb/SDPD/3572/Goal10.pdf (accessed 24 February 2018).

United Nations Development Programme (UNDP), *Arab Human Development Report 2002: Creating Opportunities for Future Generations*. New York: United Nations Development Programme, 2002. Available at: http://hdr.undp.org/ sites/default/files/rbas_ahdr2002_en.pdf (accessed 26 September 2018).

Valeri, M., "Towards the End of the Oligarcic Pact? Business and Politics in Abu Dhabi, Bahrain, and Oman" in K. Ulrichsen (ed.), *The Changing Security Dynamics of the Persian Gulf*, 77–98. London: Hurst, 2017.

Valeri, M., *Oman: Politics and Society in the Qaboos State*. London: Hurst, 2009.

Vassiliev, A., *The History of Saudi Arabia*. New York: New York University Press/ Saqi, 2000.

Viviez, L. *et al.*, *Getting in on the GCC E-Commerce Game*. A. T. Kearney, 2016. Available at: http://www.middle-east.atkearney.com/documents/787838/8908433/ Getting+in+on+the+GCC+E-Commerce+Game.pdf (accessed 5 March 2018).

Weber, A., "The Role of Education in Knowledge Economies in Developing Countries", *Procedia – Social and Behavioral Sciences* 15 (2011), 2589–94.

Wehrey, F., *Sectarian Politics in the Gulf: From the Iraq War to the Arab Uprisings*. New York: Columbia University Press, 2014.

Whitcomb, D., "The Gulf in the Early Islamic Period: The Contribution of Archaeology to Regional History" in L. Potter (ed.), *The Persian Gulf in History*, 71–87. Basingstoke: Palgrave Macmillan, 2009.

Willen, B. *et al.*, *Power Women in Arabia: Shaping the Path for Regional Gender Equity*. A. T. Kearney, 2016. Available at: https://www.atkearney.com/ documents/10192/7948242/Power+Women+in+Arabia+-+Shaping+the+ Path+for+Regional+Gender+Equality+(1).pdf/febfbf5e-7506-4ee9-bea6- 5f7fc9cb7f29 (accessed 28 February 2018).

Wilson, R., "Saudi Arabia's Role in the Global Economy" in J. Fox, N. Mourtada-Sabbah & M. al-Mutawa (eds), *Globalization and the Gulf*, 165–79. Abingdon: Routledge, 2006.

Woertz, E., *Oil for Food: The Global Food Crisis and the Middle East*. Oxford: Oxford University Press, 2013.

World Bank, *Doing Business 2017*. Washington, DC: World Bank, 2016. Available at: http://www.doingbusiness.org/~/media/WBG/DoingBusiness/Documents/Annual-Reports/English/DB17-Report.pdf (accessed 21 September 2018).

World Bank, *The Road Not Traveled: Education Reform in the Middle East and North Africa*. Washington, DC: World Bank, 2008.

World Bank, "CO_2 emissions: metric tons per capita". Available at: https://data.worldbank.org/indicator/EN.ATM.CO2E.PC (accessed 6 March 2018).

World Bank, "World Economic Outlook Database", April 2017. Available at: http://www.imf.org/external/pubs/ft/weo/2017/01/weodata/index.aspx (accessed 19 September 2018).

World Trade Organization, *World Trade Statistical Review 2017*. Geneva: World Trade Organization, 2017. Available at: https://www.wto.org/english/res_e/statis_e/wts2017_e/wts2017_e.pdf (accessed 21 September 2018).

World Trade Organization, *World Trade Statistical Review 2016*. Geneva: World Trade Organization, 2016. Available at: https://www.wto.org/english/res_e/statis_e/wts2016_e/wts2016_e.pdf (accessed 4 January 2018).

Yergin, D., *The Quest: Energy, Security, and the Remaking of the Modern World*. London: Penguin, 2011.

Yergin, D., *The Prize: The Epic Quest for Oil, Money and Power*. London: Simon & Schuster, 1991.

Yisraeli, S., *Politics and Society in Saudi Arabia: The Crucial Years of Development, 1960–1982*. New York: Columbia University Press, 2012.

Young, K., "Understanding Vision 2030: Anticipating Economic Change in Saudi Arabia", Arab Gulf States Institute in Washington "Market Watch" blog, 28 April 2016. Available at: http://www.agsiw.org/understanding-vision-2030-anticipating-economic-change-in-saudi-arabia/ (accessed 29 December 2017).

Younis, N., "The Rise of ISIS: Iraq and Persian Gulf Security" in K. Ulrichsen (ed.), *The Changing Security Dynamics of the Persian Gulf*, 113–26. London: Hurst, 2017.

Zahlan, R., *The Making of the Modern Gulf States: Kuwait, Bahrain, Qatar, the United Arab Emirates and Oman*, revised edition. Reading: Ithaca Press, 1998.

Zakaria, F., "The Rise of Illiberal Democracy", *Foreign Affairs* 76(6) (1997), 22–43.

Index

Numbers in **bold** refer to tables; those in *italic* refer to figures.